"It is perhaps once in a generation that a book is published that changes the way we think about a major area of public policy. This is one such book. It is both readable and scholarly; theoretical and practical. It is the only academic book I have ever read that I would describe as a page turner. It will be on the 'must read' list of crime scholars for years to come."

Gloria Laycock Professor of Crime Science University College London Jill Dando Institute

"David Kennedy demonstrates an encyclopedic command of the deterrence literature. More important is his balanced and insightful analysis of the promise and limits of deterrence for preventing crime. This book is a must read for students of deterrence and practitioners who can affect the way the punitive powers of the police, courts, and corrections are used to prevent crime."

Daniel S. Nagin Teresa and H. John Heinz III University Professor of Public Policy and Statistics, Carnegie Mellon University

"By the thoughtful application of focused deterrence strategies our community has become a safer place. Our neighborhoods have been freed from the terror of violence associated with overt drug markets. The teamwork that took place between the police and our citizens to make this happen has actually been healing to the relationship between the police and our African-American citizens in particular. We should never again have to admit that we cannot work together successfully due to the baggage of misunderstanding. The ability to produce sustained reductions in violent crime in our most troubled neighborhoods has been achieved. We now enjoy the ability to effectively combat violent crime in a manner that does not produce unintended harm to our relationships within the very community that needs our help so desperately. This book chronicles the path, from the theories to particular application, to achieving long awaited success in this arena.

My sincere gratitude goes to David Kennedy for showing us the way."

Jim Fealy Chief of Police High Point, NC

"Practitioners, policy makers, and scholars should make room for *Deterrence and Crime Prevention* on their special bookshelf reserved for often-used guides to their thinking and practice. This fresh look at deterrence is theoretically sound and empirically based. Most importantly, it heavily relies on Mr. Kennedy's 'on the ground' pathbreaking work in violence prevention and drug market control. My prepublication copy is dogeared already."

George L. Kelling Professor, School of Criminal Justice, Rutgers University; Senior Fellow, Manhattan Institute

"The book succeeds brilliantly at two levels: it reformulates deterrence theory for criminologists and, for law enforcement, it shows how focused partnerships with communities and other agencies can reduce even very serious crime."

Ronald V. Clarke University Professor School of Criminal Justice
Rutgers University

"Academic books tend to be written for other academics – this is an exception. It rightly challenges many of our assumptions about the fundamentals on which policing is based. It goes on to suggest some powerful ways in which we can rethink our approaches to the most intractable problems facing policing today – drugs, gangs, guns and violence. I thoroughly commend it to colleagues across the world."

Paul Stephenson Deputy Commissioner of the London
Metropolitan Police

"David Kennedy's wise book is a must-read for all policy-makers, practitioners and researchers working in criminal justice. It contains the most imaginative, informed and wide-ranging discussion of deterrence as a means of crime control that is yet to appear. The argument is highly accessible and reflects not only Kennedy's fine scholarship but also his wide experience in working with the police and their partners to develop and implement effective crime control strategies."

Nick Tilley Visiting Professor at the Jill Dando Institute of Crime
Science, University College London

"After years on the periphery of crime policy, 'deterrence' can now take center stage. David Kennedy's new book, inspired by his path-breaking work to reduce gang violence in Boston and close drug markets in High Point, North Carolina, illuminates the breadth and power of deterrence as a crime prevention tool. His discussion of the benefits of direct communication with likely reoffenders, the effectiveness of informal sanctions (such as family disapproval), and the ways in which enforcement can unintentionally undermine deterrence should interest any practitioner who seeks to prevent crime, and not simply react to it. Kennedy's work has the potential to reframe our discussion, and practice, of crime control policy."

Paul Seave Director, Governor's Office of Gang and Youth Violence
Policy, Sacramento, California

"This breakthrough book introduces a fresh and hopeful voice to our rancorous debates over crime policy. Blending insightful contributions to deterrence theory with lessons from a decade of street-level innovation, David Kennedy convincingly points the way toward a visionary, yet pragmatic, new direction for the nation. The book prompts an inescapable and stunning conclusion: if we follow Kennedy's lead, we can simultaneously reduce violence, abate drug markets, slow the growth of incarceration, and promote a much-needed racial reconciliation between the police and minority communities. Let's hope policymakers heed Kennedy's advice."

Jeremy Travis President, John Jay College of Criminal Justice

"This is the best book we have had on the subject of deterrence since Zimring and Hawkins. It represents a great advance over that classic text in that it incorporates a huge amount of the new empirical evidence about deterrent effects, and brings in many more nuanced concepts of deterrence. Beyond the idea of deterrence, however, this book raises important questions, and offers some intriguing evidence about new ways we can conceptualize and respond to crime problems throughout the country."

Mark Moore Hauser Professor of Nonprofit Organizations
Center Faculty Chair, Hauser Center for Nonprofit Organizations,
Harvard Kennedy School of Government, Harvard University

"Deterrence – or the threat of sanctions for violation of rules – is a complex concept but an inherent part of any crime-control strategy. David Kennedy has thought long and hard about the complexities and has worked directly with law enforcement and communities in developing innovative deterrent strategies and tactics. In this wide-ranging exploration of the many facets of deterrence, Kennedy draws heavily on his involvement with real-world crime prevention to develop new frameworks to make sure that deterrent threats are framed to do the job."

Alfred Blumstein Heinz School, Carnegie Mellon University

Deterrence and Crime Prevention

Deterrence is at the heart of the preventive aspiration of criminal justice. Deterrence, whether through preventive patrol by police officers or through stiff prison sentences for violent offenders, is the principal mechanism through which the central feature of criminal justice, the exercise of state authority, works—it is hoped—to diminish offending and to enhance public safety. And however well we think deterrence works, it clearly often does not work nearly as well as we would like—and often at very great cost.

Drawing on a wide range of scholarly literatures and real-world experiences, Kennedy argues that we should reframe the ways in which we think about and produce deterrence. He argues that:

- many of the ways in which we seek to deter crime in fact facilitate offending;
- simple steps such as providing clear information to offenders could transform deterrence;
- communities may be far more effective than legal authorities in deterring crime;
- apparently minor sanctions can deter more effectively than draconian ones;
- groups, rather than individual offenders, should often be the focus of deterrence;
- existing legal tools can be used in unusual but greatly more effective ways;
- even serious offenders can be reached through deliberate moral engagement;
- authorities, communities, and offenders—no matter how divided—share and can occupy hidden common ground.

The result is a sophisticated but ultimately commonsense and profoundly hopeful case that we can and should use new deterrence strategies to address some of our most important crime problems. Drawing on and expanding on the lessons of groundbreaking real-world work such as Boston's Operation Ceasefire—credited with the "Boston Miracle" of the 1990s—*Deterrence and Crime Prevention: Reconsidering the Prospect of Sanction* is required reading for scholars, law-enforcement practitioners, and all with an interest in public safety and the health of communities.

David M. Kennedy is the Director of the Center for Crime Prevention and Control at John Jay College of Criminal Justice in New York City.

Routledge Studies in Crime and Economics

Edited by Peter Reuter, University of Maryland, USA and
Ernesto U. Savona, University of Trento, Italy

Deterrence and Crime Prevention

Reconsidering the prospect of sanction

David M. Kennedy

Routledge
Taylor & Francis Group

LONDON AND NEW YORK

First published 2009
by Routledge
2 Park Square, Milton Park, Abingdon, Oxon OX14 4RN

Simultaneously published in the USA and Canada
by Routledge
270 Madison Avenue, New York, NY 10016

Routledge is an imprint of the Taylor & Francis Group, an informa business

Typeset in Times New Roman by
Taylor & Francis Books
Printed and bound in Great Britain by
TJ International Ltd, Padstow, Cornwall

British Library Cataloguing in Publication Data
A catalogue record for this book is available from the British Library

Library of Congress Cataloging in Publication Data
Kennedy, David M., 1958-
    Deterrence and crime prevention : reconsidering the prospect of
sanction / David M. Kennedy.
    p. cm.
    Includes bibliographical references and index.
1. Crime prevention. 2. Punishment in crime deterrence. 3. Sanctions,
Administrative. I. Title.
    HV7431.K448 2008
    364.601–dc22
                        2008008369

ISBN 978-0-415-77415-4 (hbk)
ISBN 978-0-203-89202-2 (ebk)

For Alison
I only wish it worked with the cats

Contents

Illustrations

Acknowledgments

This book is an intellectual project with unusually deep and wide roots. My foremost thanks go to Anne Piehl and Anthony Braga, my extraordinary university partners in the Boston Gun Project. None of this would have happened without them: We glimpsed the new possibilities together, worked out their first application together, and were astonished together at what seemed to be their power in the world. Both of them have continued their own work in this area. I only hope that mine meets with their approval.

Our practitioner partners in Boston showed us the real-world work that opened the door to a new way of thinking about deterrence. Paul Joyce, Gary French, Fred Wagget, Robert Fratalia, Timothy Feeley, Ted Heinrich, Hugh Curran, Tracy Litthcut, James MacGillivray, Teny Gross, William Stewart, and Richard Skinner—among others—were not only exceptionally serious and creative but exceptionally open to showing and sharing what they did. Once again, thank you.

At the Kennedy School of Government at Harvard University, Mark Moore and Frank Hartmann were unstinting supporters of this work in general and this book in particular. A long and fruitful conversation with Malcolm Sparrow, who has explored many of these themes in other settings, was a pleasure and a great help. A Kennedy School project on youth violence and the idea of criminal "epidemics," led by Mark Moore and sponsored by the Alfred P. Sloan Foundation, contributed immeasurably to my thinking on what I here call "contingent nonlinear dynamics."

Innumerable practitioners have made enormous contributions to my understanding of how crime-control work is in fact done, to its real dynamics in the community, and how both of those might change. I thank especially Ted Heinrich, Teny Gross, Mary Lou Leary, Susan Herman, Susan Ginsburg, Tyrone Parker, Rob Lang, Kristin Rosselli, and Elizabeth Glazer. In High Point, North Carolina, where the work, and our thinking about the work, has reached a new level, I bow to James Fealy, Marty Sumner, Jim Summey, and Larry Casterline: very special people doing the right things for the right reasons.

Innumerable scholars have offered encouragement and guidance and have done their best to protect me from myself. I thank especially Mark Kleiman,

Philip Cook, Daniel Nagin, Edward McGarrell, John Klofas, Jens Ludwig, John Eck, Gloria Laycock, Nick Tilley, Robert Garot, and Brandon Koii. Several anonymous reviewers for the first National Institute of Justice (NIJ) draft of this work were of great help.

A work like this is a sobering reminder of the extent to which scholarship is a communal, cumulative enterprise. Every scholar owes special thanks to those stalwarts who, from time to time—in addition to their own original work—embrace a field, put it in perspective, and identify key issues and opportunities. In the modern era of deterrence scholarship, those honors are held by Franklin Zimring and Gordon Hawkins, Philip Cook, and Daniel Nagin. I benefited enormously from their yeoman labors.

Brian Welch provided heroic research assistance. Thank you, Brian.

Jeremy Travis, as Director of NIJ, took a risk on the field research that sparked this thinking, nurtured it when it showed promise, and supported the initial research that became this book. As President of John Jay College of Criminal Justice he has made it possible for me to continue both. He is a better colleague and friend than I have any right to.

The exhibits in Chapter 9 were provided by Dr. Eleazer D. Hunt of the High Point Police Department and are gratefully acknowledged.

Finally, and most deeply, I thank Lois Mock of the National Institute of Justice. Lois saw promise in the crude and odd ideas that led to the Boston Gun Project, created the conditions within NIJ that let Anne Piehl and myself apply for support for that research, shepherded us when we received that support, tirelessly championed the intellectual and operational framework that emerged from and followed on the Boston work, and oversaw the NIJ research that led to this book—all with her signature combination of relentlessness and tolerance. My debt to her is profound.

1　Introduction

Deterrence is at the heart of the criminal-justice enterprise. Criminal sanctions are intended fill a number of functions—to punish, to fulfill justice, to express the public's standards and priorities, to incapacitate—but they are centrally designed to control: to shape, through the prospect of unpleasantness of various kinds, the behavior of offenders and potential offenders. Deterrence is particularly at the heart of the *preventive* aspiration of criminal justice. It is not the only such route; various facilitative and rehabilitative measures, such as job training through probation and drug treatment in prison, also hold out this hope. But deterrence, whether through preventive patrol by police officers or mandatory federal prison sentences for firearms offenders, is the principal mechanism through which the central feature of criminal justice, the exercise of state authority, works—it is hoped—to diminish offending and enhance public safety.

The framework for deterrence is simple and familiar. Offenders and potential offenders, like other people, seek reward and seek to avoid loss. If particular acts carry penalties, then those acts will become less attractive. The stiffer, quicker and more reliable the penalty, the less attractive the act will be. This is, openly and frankly, the business of the socially sanctioned threat. There is a threatener; there is a proscribed act; there is a threat associated with that act; there is an audience for that threat. Get it right and the act is not carried out, or, at least, is carried out less often.

A great deal of scholarly attention has been devoted to the theory and practice of deterrence. It has focused on offenders and the central question of their rationality, on their perceptions of the risks they face and whether those risks influence their behavior. It has focused on particular sanctions and their efficacy. It has focused on the actual behavior of criminal-justice authorities, and on how that behavior is interpreted by offenders. The resulting literature is rich and diverse.

This book seeks to build on and expand that literature. It has its intellectual origins, in part, in concrete field experience—actual attempts to prevent and control crime. It is not an account of, or an evaluation of, those efforts: This is a work of theory, or at any rate aspires to be, and theory cannot rest entirely on any example or narrow set of examples. If we judge that the death penalty deters homicide, that does not mean that all attempts to produce deterrence work, or that the general ideas through which we understand and pursue deterrence are correct. If we judge that it does not, neither does that prove that deterrence does not operate in other cases, or that the general ideas through which we consider deterrence are wrong, or that the death penalty handled differently might deter. The work that provoked the explorations in this book is not a sufficient basis on which to ground those explorations; the explorations, in turn, go well beyond the work. So this is not a book about that work. At the same time, it may be useful to sketch that work and the initial questions it raised, at least in my mind, for deterrence theory, questions I hope this book will help address.

The work emerged from an attempt to address juvenile gun violence, which at the time was epidemic in the USA, through problem-oriented policing.[1] My colleagues at the Kennedy School of Government at Harvard University, Anne Piehl and Anthony Braga, and I set up in 1995 with a group of extraordinary practitioners in Boston: officers from the Boston Police Department's Youth Violence Strike Force, or gang unit; probation officers from Dorchester District Court; prosecutors from the district attorney and US Attorney's offices; fugitive apprehension officers from the Massachusetts Department of Youth Services; special agents from the Boston office of the Bureau of Alcohol, Tobacco, and Firearms; gang outreach workers attached to the city's Streetworker Program. They taught us that the gun-violence problem was almost entirely one of friction within and between small drug crews: "gangs," as our Boston partners called them.

I, at least, resisted what they knew. I was focused on much broader issues: gun availability and use, community-wide violence dynamics, that sort of thing. But they were entirely correct. Some sixty-one crews with something like 1,300 members were killing each other along quite clearly identifiable lines of rivalry and alliance. Most of the violence was personal—respect, boy/girl, Hatfield-and-McCoy vendetta—rather than about the drug business. Participants in the street action were extraordinarily active offenders; three-quarters of both homicide victims and perpetrators had criminal records and averaged nearly ten prior arrests apiece across a wide range of crimes: drug-dealing, drug use, disorder offenses, weapons, and more. Fully a quarter of known homicide offenders were on active probation status at the time they killed. And the issue we had entered focusing upon was mistaken: Juvenile gun violence was a relatively small part of the real problem, which involved young minority men up to, roughly, age twenty-five.

Our practitioner partners also showed us a commonsense but extremely unusual approach that they had used very successfully a number of times to stop the violence of particular drug crews at particular times: They lowered the boom on *all* crimes *every* member of the group was committing, while simultaneously telling them that the crackdown would stop when the shooting did and offering them social services of various kinds. Together we built that approach into something designed to stop the violence of all Boston's drug crews.

What became known as Operation Ceasefire was also commonsense but unusual. Our probation partners ordered members of Boston's drug crews who happened to be on probation into a series of face-to-face meetings we called "forums." There, they were told that business was being handled in a new way in Boston: There was, in effect, a new sheriff in town. If anyone in their crew killed someone, law enforcement would go after the entire crew for any crimes they were committing: drug sales, drug use, gun carrying, outstanding warrants, probation and parole violations, unregistered cars, anything. They were to leave the meeting, go back to their crew, and deliver the clear message that there would henceforth be collective accountability for the violence. The intent was to create peer pressure in the group to refrain from violence: exactly the opposite of what we knew was now going on.

Offenders in the forums were also told that if they wanted off the street, they could get help: from the streetworkers, social-service agencies, probation and parole officers, churches, nonprofit organizations. We would do our best to get them jobs, job training, counseling, mentoring, remedial education, and anything else they needed. And they heard from members of their own community—ministers, parents of murdered children, neighborhood residents—that the violence was wrong, that the community could no longer stand it, and that they had to stop.

The first forum in what came to be called Operation Ceasefire was held in mid-May 1996; it explained a crackdown that had just been wrapped up against a drug crew, and promised more if necessary. The second was held in early September 1996 and explained a scorched-earth operation conducted by the Boston Police Department and the federal Drug Enforcement Administration against a king-of-the-hill crack crew called the Intervale Posse. Its entire core membership, nearly two dozen people, had been arrested and faced huge federal prison terms.

Nobody predicted, or could have, what happened. Violence in Boston tanked. We were keeping data on homicides involving what we called "youth violence" amongst those aged twenty-four and under. Going back to January 1991, there had never in been a month in which nobody was killed. In November of 1996, nobody was, a glad tiding that was subsequently often repeated.[2] Lieutenant Gary French, commanding the Youth Violence Strike Force, was used to getting paged around homicides and shootings; he took his beeper to get checked because he thought it was broken. When we later conducted a full statistical analysis, it showed that youth violence in Boston fell by two-thirds in the two years after Ceasefire, and homicide amongst all ages, citywide, by about half.[3] Before Ceasefire, Boston was averaging around 100 homicides a year. By 1999 it was down to thirty-one.

There has been a vigorous debate in the academic literature regarding whether these results are real. The logic behind the Ceasefire approach does not permit the random assignment experimental designs that would allow a decisive verdict; the approach is designed to operate wherever there is violence citywide, to influence the entire network of violent groups simultaneously, and to amplify the effect of the intervention beyond those individuals and groups touched by it directly. Individual offenders, groups of offenders, and neighborhoods therefore cannot be set aside and used as experimental controls. Our own evaluation found the sort of impact noted and no equivalent declines in thirty-nine similar US jurisdictions.[4] Another evaluation looked for the statistical "break point" in Boston's homicides and located it in June 1996, the point at which Ceasefire was implemented.[5] An evaluation by Rosenfeld *et al.* found some evidence of impact but, due to statistical power difficulties associated with Boston's relatively low homicide rate, essentially rendered the Scots verdict: "not proven."[6] The National Research Council found evidence for Ceasefire's impact "compelling"[7] but not probative, and called for randomized trials, apparently meaning random assignment of cities at the national level[8] (proving, at least, that the Council has a sense of humor).

Two other serious evaluations of the basic Boston approach as applied in other cities found remarkably similar results to the original Ceasefire intervention. McGarrell *et al.*, working in Indianapolis, found the same sort of connection between homicide and violent groups, used the same sort of intervention strategy, and found a citywide homicide reduction impact of slightly more than a third, with larger impacts in the neighborhoods and groups most affected by violence; they found no such reductions in group of regional cities they looked at for comparison.[9] As in Boston, the impact was nearly immediate upon the commencement of the face-to-face meetings. In Chicago, Tracy Meares and her colleagues implemented a variation of the strategy in a set of extremely violent neighborhoods, allowing them to use a more sophisticated quasi-experimental design with other neighborhoods as controls. The best evaluation available to date, it found a 37 percent reduction in homicide, again with very rapid impact when the strategy was implemented.[10]

There is also a large and growing body of cities and other jurisdictions in which the strategy has been implemented with apparent impact. Minneapolis removed a street gang called the Bogus Boyz in the first week of June 1997 and began face-to-face meetings with gang members. In the summer of 1996 there were forty-two homicides in Minneapolis; in the summer of 1997, there were eight.[11] "Operation Peacekeeper" in Stockton, California, addressing Hispanic gangs, was implemented late in 1997. Gang-related homicides fell from eighteen in 1997 to one in 1998 and stayed down for the next several years.[12] Dalton, documenting a US Department of Justice program modeled on the Boston project—the Strategic Approaches to Community Safety Initiative (SACSI)—reports on impact in High Point and Winston-Salem, North Carolina, and Portland, Oregon:

> In High Point, North Carolina, street violence was virtually eliminated and homicides dropped from 15 to 2 in 1999 [...] Winston-Salem's statistics indicated a steep decline in the use of firearms in violent crimes in

targeted areas. In Portland, where the focus was youth gun and gang violence, the data indicated a 74-percent reduction in drive-by shootings from 1995 to 2000. Homicide victims age 24 or under dropped by 82 percent during this same time period. At the time of this writing, none of the SACSI target population had been involved in homicides.[13]

An intervention led by Anthony Braga in Lowell, Massachusetts following the Ceasefire logic adapted to a slightly different street environment appeared to completely eliminate shootings by juvenile Asian gang members.[14] Even poorly implemented strategies seemed to show some impact in Baltimore[15] and Los Angeles.[16]

The approach has also gotten a certain amount of traction in policy circles. Following on SACSI, the Justice Department has made the strategy a central element in its national Project Safe Neighborhoods gun-violence prevention program.[17] Projects based on the same basic logic have apparently shown promise in several communities in Brazil.[18] There have been recent commitments to implement the strategy in London in the UK[19] and Adelaide in Australia.[20]

This is the background from which some fascinating questions about deterrence emerged. We saw the Boston strategy, from the beginning, as a deterrence strategy.[21] We were threatening gangs with consequences, and apparently they were listening. That was simple enough, or so it seemed. In fact it was not so simple. What was going on was in many ways removed from, and even contrary to, usual deterrence theory and practice.

We were, for one thing, bending over backward to try to ensure that law enforcement was *not* used. Rather than, for example, maximizing the use of federal prosecutions against those carrying illegal guns, as Richmond's Project Exile (which we will discuss later) did, we were putting offenders on notice ahead of time that they were under scrutiny, what penalties they might face, and hoping very much to avoid prosecuting them. And it seemed to be working. One element in Operation Ceasefire was explaining, in words and through a handout, what had happened to Freddie Cardoza, a stand-out Boston gang member the US Attorney had prosecuted under a little-used federal firearm statute. Because of his extensive felony record, when Cardoza was caught with a single round of ammunition by Boston Police officers, he was open to—and received—a fifteen-year sentence in federal prison. One of the chief concerns of the US Attorney's office was whether other, similar offenders understood that law; police officers that were part of our team knew that they did not. As part of the face-to-face meetings, therefore, we briefed gang members on the law and handed out a one-page flyer explaining the case.[22] Our partners immediately reported gang members reacting—coming to their probation officers, for example (some dragged in by their girlfriends)—to see if they fit the federal criteria, which many of them did.

That move—using *information* rather than *enforcement*—was central to Ceasefire, and it was employed in many ways. After the initial crackdown, we warned the gangs about what law enforcement would do in future, hoping that they would comply. Between forums, we would often reach out personally—through the streetworkers, or through probation or police officers—to particular gangs that seemed on the verge of violence, to tell them that they were being watched and should calm down, which they invariably did. In addition to the forums, we went to secure juvenile facilities, jails, and public schools to get the message out. Ordinary law enforcement, of course, makes a virtue of arrest and prosecution: Nobody thinks that the way to control crime is to tell the criminals exactly what your plans are.

Ceasefire was extremely *selective.* We would have loved to eliminate gangs, or all gang crime, or all drug crime, or all crime in Boston's dangerous neighborhoods. We could not do that, and knew that our team would crumble if it tried. We settled for addressing homicide and serious violence, and then only that associated with violent groups—a move very much in keeping with the problem-oriented policing framework that we were working in, but very much foreign to traditional enforcement approaches.[23]

In working on those crimes, investigating them and prosecuting them was essentially irrelevant. There were no homicide or shooting investigators attached to the Ceasefire team, and almost no contact with them. When we had a homicide, and we knew who did it or what group was behind it—and we nearly always did, regardless of whether the homicide resulted in an arrest or prosecution—we went after other offenses: drug sales, drug possession, parole and probation violations, anything available. We could punish offenders without ever making an arrest, by parking officers in their area and making it impossible to sell drugs or to have fun. Ordinary enforcement approaches do not encompass punishing offenders for killing by making them poor.

We were not even necessarily, or in fact usually, punishing the shooters: We were punishing the *group they were part of.* The logic here was clear enough: The group, when it understood the new rules, would pressure its members to put their guns down. It is a logic foreign to normal practice, however. When we contemplate deterring homicide, we think about the death penalty, or life without parole. We do not think of putting killers' friends on strict home probation checks. Even the focus on the group was unusual. Boston's "gangs" had no existence in law: They were not, usually, cohesive and corporate enough to allow a Racketeer Influenced and Corrupt Organizations Act prosecution, like real organized crime, or to merit an exotic conspiracy case. But they knew who they were, we knew who they were, and focusing ordinary law-enforcement tools on them worked perfectly well.

Such tools were, in practice, far from the most draconian ones available. There were hardly any cases like those against Freddie Cardoza and the Intervale Posse. Most Ceasefire enforcement action used ordinary state law; some of the most powerful steps turned out to be very minor indeed, according to ordinary thinking. As part of the first Ceasefire gang crackdown, Massachusetts Superior Court Judge Sydney Hanlon ended up with a young gang member before her for illegal possession of a firearm, facing the prospect of considerable prison time. He remained unmoved until she placed him under a pretrial evening curfew, at which point he became extremely upset—because he would not be able to go see his girlfriend. She can come see you, Judge Hanlon told him. No, he replied, his mother would not permit such a thing...[24] We do not usually think of curfews—or mothers—as more onerous than years in prison.

Ceasefire used what can only be considered moral engagement with gang members. In the forums, community people told them that they were causing enormous damage in the community, that there was no justification for the killing, that the community needed them alive and out of prison. They were often visibly moved. Ceasefire engaged with their common sense. In one memorable meeting, Reverend Eugene Rivers, a street-savvy and outspoken black minister, challenged them to be, if nothing else, smarter criminals. The mafia doesn't shoot up the streets for no good reason, he said. The noise brings heat. Get with it. Gang members laughed, but they listened. We do not usually contemplate moral and intellectual discourse with hardened offenders.

Ceasefire offered gang members help: jobs, job-training, education, other social services. Some took them, and the streetworkers were clear that if more jobs, especially, had been available, more would have taken them. The entire Ceasefire partnership supported those avenues. One does not generally see law enforcement telling violent offenders how to get work and avoid arrest.

Above all, perhaps, when we deploy deterrence strategies against, especially, the most hardened or impulsive offenders, we do not expect them to *work*. Ceasefire was aimed squarely at homicide, and beyond that at homicide committed by extreme, gang-involved offenders immersed in the drug trade in the worst neighborhoods of a major urban area. They clearly used drugs and alcohol at very high levels; many were visibly impaired even in the forums. This is an offense, and a set of offenders, usually considered immune to deterrence, or indeed to any criminal-justice intervention. "There is no way you're going to stop homicides," says Philadelphia Police Commissioner Sylvester Johnson.[25] "What are you going to do, send cops to every house?" asks Northeastern University professor Peter K. Manning. "We know that historically, homicide is the least suppressible crime by police action...It is, generally speaking, a private crime, resulting from people who know one another and have relationships that end up in death struggles at home or in semipublic places."[26]

If Ceasefire worked at all, then, it goes against the grain. And if it worked at all, it must be concluded that it worked *too well,* on a number of fronts. The results were vastly out of proportion to what is supposed to have produced them. Homicide plummeted almost immediately after the intervention began. Not very many people had been arrested, and those arrested had not even been prosecuted, much less convicted and sentenced; not very many people had gotten the help they were being offered; not very many people had even been talked to. This appears to have been a feature of the National Research Council's reluctance to believe that Ceasefire was effective. "An activity undertaken at a specific place and time," the committee wrote, "presumably does not generate an instant response in violence."[27] Perhaps not. Or, perhaps, there is something going on here that is producing very distinctive results in very unusual ways.

It is these observations, and these questions, that led to this book, which will attempt to explore these, and some related, issues in the context of traditional deterrence theory and to assess some of their implications for an expanded deterrence theory. It will argue that the existing scholarly framework holds the seeds for an expanded framework, with interesting intellectual and practical implications. It will suggest new ways to think about the offenders who are the target of deterrence, new ways to think about the sanctions on which deterrence relies, new ways to think about the acts deterrence seeks to prevent, new ways to think about the threats through which deterrence operates, new ways to think about framing and communicating those threats, new ways to think about the relationship between authorities and offenders, and new, arguably more powerful and strategic, settings in which deterrence might seek to operate. All of these steps, it will be seen, are nascent in existing thinking about deterrence. As we bring them to the surface and explore their implications, however, both deterrence theory and practice may take important new directions.

1 Does deterrence work?

We begin with the most basic question: Does deterrence work? Strong statements are often made in the negative. "Deterrence is a principal with much immediate appeal," wrote England's Home Office in 1990,

> but much crime is committed on impulse [...] and it is committed by offenders who live from moment to moment [...] It is unrealistic to construct sentencing arrangements on the assumption that most offenders will weigh up the possibilities in advance and base their conduct on rational calculation.[1]

In fact, the world is soaked in deterrence, something that easily escapes notice because of its utter ordinariness. The class of people who persistently put their hands on hot stoves, cross the street without looking, and steal cars in front of police officers is very small. The class of New York City neighborhoods in which drivers routinely ignore alternate-side parking regulations (and, in parallel, fail to respond adroitly to the occasional lifting of those regulations) is precisely nil, a finding confirmed by the author's extensive participant-observer research.

The expectation of official action clearly does not deter all offending, but it equally clearly deters a lot of offending, and when it is altered or removed, people's behavior changes. There is an abundance of examples of such influence and adaptation, much of it fascinating. Many prosecutors, for instance, have office policies setting nonstatutory minima for drug prosecutions, with arrests for less than a set quantity generally being dismissed or charged as possession rather than trafficking. The experience of police in those jurisdictions is that drug offenders soon learn those minima and scrupulously stay under them, carrying, for example, exactly twenty-seven pieces of crack rather than the informal and arbitrary but well-understood twenty-eight.[2] Ethnographic research into illicit gun markets in Chicago showed that gangs restrict their members from carrying and using guns, one reason being that police attention following gun violence interferes with money-making crime such as drug-dealing.[4] Motorcycle gang members in the Midwest were subject, as convicted felons, to substantial federal penalties for carrying guns;

they took, instead, to carrying nineteenth-century percussion firearms exempted under an obscure "curios and relics" provision in the governing criminal statute.[5]

Ordinary experience validates the common sense of deterrence—at least with some people, with respect to some offenses, some of the time—and the idea that existing criminal-justice activities are in fact creating deterrence. When police departments go on strikes, bad things tend to happen.[6] A great deal of research, much of which this book will draw on, ends up pointing to much the same conclusion. "My assessment," writes Philip Cook, one of our most thoughtful and thorough students on the subject, "is that the criminal justice system, ineffective though it may seem in many areas, has an overall crime deterrent effect of great magnitude."[7]

The equally obvious frequent failure of deterrence is not probative that the general idea is mistaken or that sanction structures aimed at deterrence are having no impact. Part of the problem here is the frequent commission of the prison warden's fallacy: that the prisons are filled with men manifestly not deterred by legal threats is not evidence that other men were not deterred. Strong claims that deterrence is ineffective are often in fact arguments that the limits of deterrence have been reached and that additional enforcement and penalties will not produce additional deterrent impact. That may be correct, but it is not evidence that deterrence as such does not work. It does raise the considerably more interesting question of whether deterrence can be extended beyond those limits, and if so how: a question that will consume most of this book.

Assessments of particular policy interventions also support the operation of deterrence: in, again, given contexts. There are very few controlled experiments in deterrence, but quasi-experiments and more ordinary evaluations frequently show impact. In a set of controlled trials, mandatory arrest for domestic violence reduced recidivism in a number of cities;[8] in another controlled trial, increased police presence in high-crime areas reduced crime in those areas.[9] A controlled trial that applied largely deterrent tactics reduced crime in drug-trafficking hot spots.[10] Intensive police patrol reduced robberies in New York City subways.[11] The prospect of greatly enhanced drunk-driving enforcement in the United Kingdom reduced both drunk driving and related accidents.[12] Steps to increase the apprehension of airline hijackers in the early 1970s all but ended hijacking, not because of actual apprehensions but because the likelihood of being detected rose to such a prohibitive level that people stopped trying.[13] A mandatory one-year sentence for the illegal possession of a firearm reduced gun-carrying and gun crime in Massachusetts.[14] Mandatory sentences for gun offenses reduced violent crime in a pool of six cities.[15] A study of arrest ratios in 171 cities found that increased enforcement deterred street crime.[16] Crackdowns on street dealing dried up drug markets in Lynn, Massachusetts.[17] The announcement that a vigorous and established powder cocaine market in Houston would be, on a date certain, the focus of an interagency law enforcement crackdown dried up the market before the crackdown could actually be implemented.[18] Intensive directed patrol aimed at identified offenders reduced homicide and gun crime in Indianapolis, Indiana.[19] The record thus shows that deterrence is not just operating, it can be deliberately created in at least some settings and against at least some forms of offending.

A long tradition of "perceptual deterrence" social-science research has gone at the deterrence question in a different way.[20] This research sought to unpack—using individual-level cross-sectional survey and scenario studies, and panel survey studies—how and why people reacted to what they thought, or were told, would happen if they offended; why they did, or did not, care about that; and how it shaped their subsequent behavior. This research, too, is generally supportive of the idea that deterrence is operating. While varied, the cross-sectional and scenario studies tended to find that higher perceived risks of sanction were associated with lack of offending or of likelihood to offend. Waldo and Chiricos, for example, found that college students who thought that they would be arrested and convicted for marijuana use and theft were less likely to say that they would commit those offenses.[21] In general, the certainty and, to a lesser extent, the swiftness of sanction mattered more than the severity of sanction, to the extent that many researchers concluded that severity was all but or in fact irrelevant.

A core theme in deterrence research has to do with what ultimately came to be called the "experiential effect": the observation that, as time passes, many people come to lower their estimates of the risks of offending. The debate began in interpreting survey research showing that low risk estimates were associated with higher levels of offending. The initial conclusion was that low estimates of risk led to offending, with associated ideas of criminogenic personality types resistant to deterrence.[22] Subsequent thinking shifted to the idea that, instead, offenders were simply more informed and realistic: that "most people (young and old) have over pessimistic estimates of their ability to get away with breaking the law [...] but that when they participate in illegal acts they soon discover that they can commit them with relative impunity."[23] According to this idea, as offenders commit crimes and escape sanction, or see others do so, they adjust their risk estimates downward. This is not a problem with the *idea* of deterrence, or with some sort or sorts of undeterrable personality, but with the objective characteristics of the sanction regime supposed to *generate* deterrence. Experience breaches the "shell of illusion" that one can't get away with offending.[24]

This set of issues led to perceptual deterrence research using panel studies that allowed assessment of how attitudes toward risk evolved over time on the basis of concrete experience with offending and sanction, and to other research designed to get at these issues. This research generally supported both the idea that deterrence was operating and that its effects could be vitiated when people thought that their objective risks were low.[25] Much of the research supporting this conclusion was conducted outside populations of serious offenders and assessed attitudes by subjects such as college students to low-level offenses, but the basic proposition—people learn from experience that they face rather low risks and act accordingly—may plausibly be generalized. The rare studies of these dynamics with more or less serious offenders bore them out in that population. Horney and Marshall surveyed incarcerated felons and found that those with more experience of offending had lower risk estimates, and that the actual rate of prior arrests moved those perceptions: For most crimes in the survey, those offenders who had been arrested relatively often, compared to the number of crimes they had committed, felt more at risk.[26] Lochner, analyzing data in large national surveys, found much the same dynamic amongst youth offenders.[27] This turned out to be one of the main reasons that some perceptual research turned up an absence of deterrence effects: Subjects knew perfectly well that risks were low and maintained that knowledge even after being sanctioned. Though they also often updated their risk assessments, they remained low enough to justify further offending. As we shall see, this can be true even for extremely serious crimes.

So, deterrence effects are there to be found. The strong case—"deterrence does not work"—is clearly false. Deterrence effects are also, often, found to be absent. The weaker case—that deterrence does not work very well or does not work where we would particularly like it to, or is not worth the various costs of producing it—is still a live option. Even those who believe in deterrence can be realistically dubious about its actual impact and the prospect for enhancing that impact. "Thus the problem faced by those responsible for the everyday enforcement of law in democratic societies is that deterrent effects are apparently modest [and] certainty of punishment is low under many circumstances," wrote the Committee to Review Research on Police Policy and Practices of the National Academy of Sciences. "As a consequence, deterrence strategies alone are unlikely to be a sufficient basis for an effective system of social regulation."[28]

As on the positive side, the most telling evidence is ordinary and everyday: In the face of a great deal of punishment, offending continues. The death penalty manifestly fails to deter a good many murderers. Recidivism is very high amongst offenders who have had prior arrests and convictions and who thus have good reason to fear sanctions: A 2002 Bureau of Justice Statistics study showed that 67.5 percent of those released from US prisons in 1994 were rearrested for a new crime within three years.[29] Striking increases in sanctions, as for drug crimes in the mid-1980s, failed to curb widespread drug epidemics. Explicit official promises of particular sanctions for particular crimes, as with stiff federal mandatory sentences for gun carrying, fail to reduce gun homicide.[30] Research with actual criminals frequently reveals that the mechanisms designed to produce deterrence are not operating remotely as intended. Doob and Webster report on a study based on interviews with sixty experienced, and presently incarcerated, burglars and armed robbers. "The respondents were blunt in reporting that neither they nor other thieves whom they knew considered legal consequences when planning crimes. Thoughts about getting caught were put out of their minds."[31] This is devastating to the deterrence project: If offenders not only do not fear consequences but willfully refuse to even consider them, we simply cannot reach them.

All this cannot be taken to mean that deterrence is not operating, in principle or in fact. Offending might be even higher than it is in the absence of these sanctions; higher sanctions might yet work. But it is at least evidence that existing deterrence regimes, some involving policies on which we rely heavily, including some involving very stiff sanctions, are not working as intended. This, again, accords with the common sense. We are reluctant to think that consequences do not matter, but it is plain that for many people whose behavior concerns us deeply, the consequences they in fact face do not matter much, or enough, or at all.

Recent research from Cincinnati, Ohio provides a case in point. A project aimed at understanding and addressing homicide and violent crime identified some sixty-nine violent groups—drug crews and the like—comprising something less than 1,000 individuals. Nearly 750 of those individuals were identified by name and found in police records. Those individuals, most of them fairly young, *averaged* more than fourteen prior misdemeanor charges, more than ten misdemeanor convictions, more than seven felony charges, three felony convictions, nearly thirteen charges as juveniles, and nearly nine convictions as juveniles: which is to say, all told, they averaged nearly thirty-five charges and nearly twenty-two convictions apiece. Nearly 57 percent had ten or more misdemeanor charges; nearly a third had ten or more felony charges. This is the very model of failed deterrence. And here, as often, when deterrence fails it matters a great deal: These groups of offenders were associated with nearly three-quarters of the homicides in Cincinnati.[32]

Here too, evaluations of real-world policies support the failure of deterrence. The seminal Kansas City Preventive Patrol Experiment varied vehicular police patrol in Kansas City and found no difference in crime, fear, or public perception between a standard level of patrol, twice that level, and no patrol at all.[33] This is often taken to imply that patrol is not effective, and even that policing is not effective; it means neither, but it can be taken to imply that patrol more or less *as it is in fact usually practiced* is not effective. An evaluation of police foot patrol in Newark found reductions in residents' fear but no reduction in serious crime.[34] Studies of mandatory sentences for gun crime in Detroit and three Florida cities found no effects.[35] Large increases in arrest rates and sanctions for drug crimes showed no impact in New York City.[36] California's energetically applied three-strikes law had no deterrent impact on serious crime.[37] And even many deterrence effects of apparently successful policy interventions seem to decay: The initial impact goes away over time, with offending returning to, or near to, previous levels.[38]

Likewise, the perceptual deterrence literature also includes a substantial body of research indicating deterrence is *not* operating.[39] In one marvelously counterintuitive study, Piquero and Pogarsky found that college students who had avoided being stopped by police while driving drunk, and who knew others who had also gotten away with it, were more likely to drive drunk in the future: So too, however, were students who *had* gotten stopped by police.[40]

Why? Why do some deterrence regimes work, and others not? More particularly, why do they work with respect to some offenders and some offenses at some times, but not others? This is not something we know very much about, either absolutely or with respect to particular crime issues and policies. "The evaluation of these issues," writes Philip Cook, "hinges in part on our assessment of the *marginal* deterrent effects of changes in the certainty and severity of punishment, a more problematic issue than assessing the overall deterrent effect of current threat levels."[41] It may be that deterrence is real, and even that existing sanction regimes generate considerable deterrence. That tells us nothing, however, about what it would take to create any given *additional increment* of deterrence, or whether we have been getting good returns on existing sanctions.

This is certainly a nonlinear process: the first 50 percent of deterrence is going to be more easily won than the next 40 percent, and the next 10 percent will be yet more challenging. Where are we on this curve? Might we already be in the region of little or no marginal return on investment in sanctions: That is, have sanctions been increased to small effect, with equally small or still smaller returns to be expected from additional increases? Are there different ways to obtain deterrence? And how do the answers to these questions differ for different offenses and offenders? These are unanswered questions. At the same time, deterrence research has illuminated a number of these matters in more particular areas, and, with them, pointed toward a set of crucial issues that allow considerable scope for further theoretical and practical development.

2   How, and do, criminals think?

The classical deterrence framework and the meaning of rationality

Common sense and rationality

We begin this exploration with a critical question: Are offenders rational? Much of the power of the deterrence framework, and certainly much of its appeal in policy conversations, stems from the common sense that lies at its core. Harm is something to be avoided, gain something to be sought. We train puppies, raise children, run organizations, and conduct international relations by these precepts. This is, at its heart, what deterrence is about. It is, at this level of exposition, very difficult to argue against. "It is a matter of common observation," write Franklin Zimring and Gordon Hawkins, "that men seek to avoid unpleasant consequences, and that the threat of unpleasant consequences tends to be deterrent."[1]

This sort of common sense is formalized as "rational choice" theory by economists. The rational person of deterrence theory is the "economic man": a "profit maximizer, that is, a calculator of profit from estimates of gain and cost resulting from the proscribed act."[2] In essence, economists applied to deterrence theory that had been developed to characterize choices made around legitimate work: Choosing "work" as an armed robber was framed as parallel to choosing work as a laborer, with the additional element of legal risk.

"Consider," as Piliavin *et al.* wrote,

> the following formal statement of an actor's utility under conditions of risk:
>
> $$E(U) = (1\text{-}p) \, U(y) + p \, U(y\text{-}F),$$
>
> where E(U) is the actor's expected utility from a contemplated activity, P is the likelihood of being punished for the activity, Y is the anticipated returns (material or psychic) from the activity, and F is the anticipated penalty resulting if the actor is punished for the activity.
>
> According to the statement, if for a given person, the expected utility of an illegal (legal) act is greater than the expected utility of other alternatives, the person will engage in the illegal (legal) act.[3]

This is not how we treat crime and criminals in ordinary discourse. This may be more a matter of language and presentation, however, than of substance, for this and similar frameworks do in fact capture the way—or, more accurately, one way—we think about criminals. People have a choice between crime and work (or, as is often the case, to mix the two). They will not choose to commit crimes unless they feel it to be in their interest. What governs that choice? Various kinds of profits and losses. Money can be "earned" through both crime and through work. So can thrills, standing, and other "psychic" rewards: It is exhilarating, at least to some people, to pull off a street robbery. There are costs as well: The robber can get caught, lose the stolen money, and go to prison. There are future consequences of present actions: Getting caught doing that robbery can make it impossible to get a job later as a police officer or commodities broker. The deterrence implications are clear: The higher the chance of getting caught, and the higher the associated costs, the less likely that the crime will be committed.

Clear and parsimonious as this and similar frameworks are, it and they have one large and glaring drawback: Nobody actually thinks like this. Our armed robber will not pause each day or, probably, any day to consider the prospect of law school. He is unlikely to make, on the brink of each crime, fine-grained calculations about the expected value of the robbery or the likelihood of apprehension and punishment, still less about the long-term consequences of an arrest or a prison record. It is, in fact, not at all clear that criminals are even "rational" in the sense used in, and required by, deterrence theory. As one armed robber told Wright and Decker,

> I do [think about the possibility of apprehension], but I try not to. I put forth an effort to try not to think about that. When I was younger, I would tend to think about the consequences. [But] as you get older, anything that you continue to do, [thinking about the risk is] too much of a distraction. You can't concentrate on doing anything if you are thinking, "What's going to happen if it doesn't go right?"[4]

Or this account by a young car thief:

> I've got other friends, they're like, I would really say they're addicted to it because they had a lot, a lot of money you know. They didn't need the money. More the excitement. [...] They would steal like ten cars a night. They would drive down, ride the bus back, pop another car, drive back, pop another car, drive back [...] It's like a natural high for me. It's just great. I think the excitement is most[ly] the reason people steal cars.[5]

This is not rational behavior, at least as the term is commonly used: This is what we commonly, and with reason, call "crazy." And a failure of rationality, or the abandonment of rationality by a whole class of criminal actors, is a fine explanation for the failures of deterrence. This is certainly what

Wright and Decker came to believe through their ethnographic work with armed robbers. "Recent criminological theorizing has been dominated by rational choice explanations that overemphasize the extent to which offending is an independent, freely chosen action," they write. "The reality for many offenders is that crime commission has become so routinized that it emerges almost naturally in the course of their daily lives, often occurring without substantial planning or deliberation."[6]

If offenders are not rational—or if some offenders are not rational, often enough to matter—deterrence is in big trouble (though crime control as such might not be; the routines of offenders and nonoffenders alike may prevent a great deal of what otherwise would be "rational" crime—as we shall see, the costs associated with many crimes are so low that rational calculation might well suggest committing more of them). Some have indeed thought so. Some have believed in a "class of nondeterrable persons"[7] ruled overwhelmingly by impulse. Sutherland and Cressey wrote of the

> widely held belief [...] that criminal behavior is due to some pathological characteristic or trait of the personality which exists prior to the criminal behavior and is the cause of it [...] Some scholars have found the explanation of crime in mental defectiveness, others in psychopathic personality, and others in a composite group of emotional disturbances.[8]

Others have posited nondeterrable crimes such as homicide, "most frequently a crime of passion where rational calculations may be overruled,"[9] particular cases of extreme emotion preventing—perhaps temporarily—rationality. Alcohol, drugs, and addiction may create states in which rationality is prevented. Psychologists have argued that "when a person commits a crime, he does not think of the consequences. The offender commits a crime because criminality is his particular outlet, just as the seriously mentally ill person's outlet is a psychosis."[10]

Such a clear formulation has the same virtue as the strong version of rational choice: It reminds us that this too is not, normally, the way we believe things work. We rarely encounter situations in which literally no control is exercised or expected. Burglars avoid occupied homes, robbers seek out dark alleys, wife beaters control themselves in supermarkets and close the door when they get home. Drunks drive more carefully when they see a patrol car in the rear-view mirror. Schizophrenic street people keep their bottles in brown paper bags. Even psychopaths avoid killing in the direct view of police officers. Discovery, attention, and consequences, we usually think, matter. But we recognize that they matter only as much as they in fact matter. And if forced to make a choice between perfect rationality and some competing explanation, it is not at all clear that perfect rationality comes closest to describing reality. Choices are made constantly; whether they are made *sensibly* is quite another question.

A classic scholarly exchange on these points occurred in 1978 between Herbert Jacob, on one side, and Don W. Brown and Stephen L. McDougal on the other. Jacob, in a brief note responding to a paper on deterrence by Brown and McDougal, summed up the problems real people and their real behavior raise for deterrence theory:

> A utility approach—like so much deterrence theorizing—assumes rationality in the decision to commit a crime. Two problems exist with that assumption. (a) It implies that people who contemplate committing a crime have a realistic perception of the probabilities of being sanctioned and of the severity of the sanction, and that this perception is a constant rather than variable. The little evidence that we have on perceptions of legal sanctions by the general public indicates that these perceptions are incorrect and variable. Many people do not understand the workings of the criminal justice system; their understanding varies with contact and education among other things. (b) It implies that people who commit crimes act after rational calculation rather than on impulse. We have much reason to believe that many crimes are committed on impulse, either under the influence of alcohol or simply as the result of opportunity and need intersecting. Perhaps more violent crime than property crime is impulsively committed, but we really do not know the proportion of each resulting from rational calculation of the odds (or utilities) and from impulse.[11]

He went on to noted that "pain and cost thresholds vary among individuals [...] for some a night in jail is abhorrent, for others it is a lark"; that many people in objectively identical conditions seem to weigh them—if in fact they weigh them—very differently, some offending and some not; and that therefore we "not only need information about the objective conditions in which people find themselves but we also need information about how they perceive their conditions and how they perceive the opportunities and costs of illicit activities."[12]

Jacob's was a subtle and profound—if rather jumbled and telescoped—criticism operating on a number of levels. It is worth organizing and expanding.

In order for deterrence to operate, his argument went, a number of conditions had to obtain. First, offenders will have had to calculate the costs and benefits of their crimes, and to have chosen to commit them on that basis. There is reason to believe that is not the case: That "impulse"—which he took to encompass both the literally irrational or arational (drunkenness and, by implication, probably mental illness and incapacity) and the simple lack of due consideration rising to the level of "rational calculation of the odds (or utilities)"—often dictates offending. Not only crimes of passion but also crimes of ordinary profit may go ungoverned by the meaningful weighing of costs and benefits. To the extent that such is the case, deterrence will not operate.

Then things get worse. Even to the extent that rational calculation is at work, for such calculation to be accurate requires that potential offenders know what they're up against: the likelihood that they will be punished and the weight of that punishment. Many people do not know these things. There was, at the time Jacob wrote, very little research on this point, but Jacob cited a study of the public and prison inmates in California that revealed widespread ignorance in both camps of penal sanctions: The prisoners knew more but were still more often wrong than right. Thus, even if calculation is at work, the calculations will be wrong. And to make things worse still, the meaning to any given person of those sanctions can be quite variable: What one person sees as severe, another will not. This perhaps explains why different people in similar circumstances will behave quite differently in the face of the same legal consequences: They may know the truth about those consequences, or they may not, and they may feel the same way about those consequences (or, at least, those they believe to obtain), or, again, they may not. In the end, when law fails to prevent offending, we are left not knowing whether this was because the offender was irrational, ignorant, mistaken, or simply unimpressed by the sanction at hand, or, still more confusingly, some combination of these.

Rationality in practice

Determined to save the rationalist framework on which deterrence rests, Brown and McDougal responded. At the core of their argument was the position, in essence, that rationality need not be rational.

> Jacob says that a utility approach assumes rationality in the individual decision to commit a crime. Many users of utility analysis have made this assumption, and numerous scholars connect the rationality assumption with any utility approach. [Our] formulation, however, explicitly rejects the assumption that individuals are rational in any objective sense. Instead, it treats utility as self-defined, based on one's subjective perceptions and evaluations (whether realistic or not) in the outcomes of various actions.[13]

They quoted Stover and Brown in arguing that:

> It is important to recognize that utility theory, as we are using it, does not imply that human beings are always rational in the sense of being willing or able to calculate those actions which in fact would maximize net gratification. It merely says that within the limits of their inclinations and ability to make such calculations they will act so as to pursue whatever is at the moment in their own mind defined as most important.[14]

This, too, is worth unpacking.

It answers the critique. Impulse now becomes acceptable. If the offender's "inclination and ability" to consider rewards and penalties in a given situation are nil or next to nil, so be it, as long as impulse moves them toward something they want, in the moment, however fleeting, that they want it. This could include, according to the formulation, wanting something manifestly costly, such as—to take an extreme example—suicide, so long as that was what the actor desired. Bizarre motivations, persistent or momentary, are, in principle, no different than more ordinary ones. Ignorance and incompetence also become acceptable: Offenders can err about the consequences of being caught, the likelihood of being caught, the payoff from being successful, or all three, as a result of poor information, poor calculation, or both. It does not matter that they are undertaking a desperate gamble, only that they have chosen to do so in the belief that it is worth it. Faulty assessments of risk and reward do not matter; what matters is what offenders *believe*. Whether those beliefs are well founded, accurate, or reasonable is neither here nor there.

The cost of this formulation, however, is that the notion of "rationality" becomes a technical one, a term of art, estranged from its ordinary meaning. Rationality, in its common usage, carries the freight of reasonableness and proportion—of good sense. We do not normally consider it rational to, for instance, steal cars all night long for sport in full and deliberate public view, when the concrete payoff is nil, the risk of accident, injury, and apprehension is high, and the life consequences of arrest and conviction are profound. To do such things for the sake of a momentary thrill is, in ordinary terms, the very antithesis of rationality: what we call, again in ordinary language, "crazy." In this new technical sense, however, to behave thus can be either rational or not. If the reward of the excitement is seen as worth the risk—however pathological the need for excitement, however momentary the excitement itself, however mistaken the assessment of risk, and however compromised the balancing of risk and reward—then the standard of "rationality" is satisfied.

Such formulations come perilously close, if not actually to the point, of Boulding's observation that "decision theory states that everybody does what he thinks best at the time, which is hard to deny."[15] It bears asking, to turn this around, what might by this standard count as *irrational*. The answer is not clear. One possibility is that of deep psychological currents—various forms of mental illness or cognitive deficits—driving behavior in ways that are outside the knowledge and control of the actor. Even psychotics, however, exercise choice, and they choose in alignment with their subjective sense of their best interest. The world they live in is real to them, and they act accordingly. Another possibility is that of addiction or other gross compulsion—the desperate heroin addict committing foolish and ill-considered crimes. Again, however, we can well imagine that in the moment, given the objective reality of the addiction and its pressures, such crimes make subjective sense. "Inclination" in such situations is strong, and "ability" is

minimal, but if under that pressure and within those limits the addict chooses the act, it appears that "rationality" has been satisfied. This is such a
broad notion of rationality that perhaps only those situations in which there
is action without any choice at all—if such exists, and can properly be called
"action"—or in which there is calculation of what an actor wishes to do, and
then the deliberate choice of something else. This latter could be of the
mundane variety, as in the common preface of eating dessert with "I really
shouldn't do this," or the more serious idea that there is a criminal type who
"feels the need of punishment and therefore welcomes the severity of the law;
quite often he actively seeks punishment."[16] Even these may collapse into
this special meaning of rational, for they do in fact in some way represent
what the actors really want. If one chooses, as an impulsive and perhaps
drunken adolescent, to steal a car and show it off to friends on a warm
summer night, while systematically underestimating the chances of getting
caught, gaining a felony conviction, and thus being doomed to a life of
menial employment, this still counts as rational. The matter was raised,
weighed, and decided, in however misinformed and telescopic a fashion.

Such thinking does not preclude the operation of deterrence. "Even in
highly emotional situations, we retain some ability to reason, albeit presumably not so well as normally," wrote Gordon Tullock. "It would take
much greater provocation to lead a man to kill his wife if he knew that, as in
England in the 1930s, committing murder meant a two-out-of-three chance
of meeting the public executioner within about two months than if—as is
currently true in South Africa—there were only about a one-in-100 chance of
being executed after about a year's delay."[17] Or, as Jens Ludwig puts it, "the
fact that most eggs are bought on impulse by drunks at 2:00 A.M. in no way
implies that raising the price of eggs 20 percent will not result in fewer eggs
being sold."[18] It may indeed be true that many offenders are not entirely
rational, but it may still be true, as Philip Cook has pointed out, that what
rationality remains can be somewhat effective.[19]

Models of subjective rationality

The question then becomes one of how to understand and characterize such
"rationality in practice." The central theme was set by John Carroll, who
drew on psychological models of decision making and "limited rationality"
to frame the offender as "a thoughtful decision maker who chooses among
alternative courses of action, both criminal and noncriminal" but using "a
variety of strategies in which simple comparisons and partial examinations
of alternatives are made."[20] This offender is not a precise "economic person"
but a looser "'psychological person,' who makes a few simple and concrete
examinations of his or her opportunities and makes guesses that can be far
short of optimal."[21] In practice, these models suggested, people adopted
"simple, additive, and even unidimensional strategies...some people are
drawn by money, some avoid certain types of risk, and so forth."[22]

In turn, these simpler strategies might allow for simple decision rules, what Philip Cook called "rules of thumb" or "standing decisions": basic personal tenets that obviate the need for continual assessments of particular situations and options.[23] Thus, armed robbers have standing rules against returning to school and earning a law degree and for assaulting well-dressed drunks late at night on dark streets with no one else in sight. Clarke and Cornish, in a similar analysis, frame an overall, persistent "involvement decision," in which a potential offender contemplates and chooses criminality, and a subsequent, finer-grained "event decision," in which the offender chooses to commit a particular crime in particular circumstances.[24] Cook raised the intriguing possibility that utility calculations might operate not only on particular choices to offend or not to offend but on such standing or persistent decisions: that, for example, deterrence might shift a potential offender from such a standing decision allowing armed robbery in particular circumstances to one forbidding it, or generally forbidding it.[25] Such rules might be right or wrong in particular circumstances; a standing rule to run for the exit when fire breaks out, eminently sensible on its face, can spell disaster in company, when exits clog. But, as the example suggests, one cannot reason backward from poor results to outright irrationality: One needs to know what went into the calculation, and how it was considered, in order to judge its sense or lack of sense. One can be, according to this thinking, quite rational and at the same time quite wrong. The willful refusal of Wright and Decker's armed robber to consider the consequences of getting caught thus becomes intelligible: Having made a quite possibly carefully considered decision to pursue a career in armed robbery, persistent worrying about consequences is reasonably rejected as an impediment to peak performance.

This kind of analysis, interestingly, has become evident in labor economics, the source for much economic thinking about deterrence. Some of the same issues are quite evident there: When, for example, most young men in a poor rural mining community choose to go into the mines, while most young men in a wealthy suburban white-collar community choose college and professional work, something other than two sets of clear, objective, individual calculations is likely to be at work. Labor economists have reconciled these issues in very similar ways. As Jencks and Mayer write:

> Strong individualists—especially economists—often assume that neighbors have no direct affect on an individual's behavior. They believe that people base their decisions on their own circumstances and long-term interests, not on their neighbors' ideas about what is sensible, desirable, or acceptable. Most anthropologists and sociologists, as well as many psychologists, reject this view, arguing that individual decisions consist largely of choosing among a menu of culturally defined alternatives and that an individual's menu depends in part on the alternatives his friends and neighbors are considering. This "sociological" view does not deny

that most people are rational utility maximizers. It merely denies that they are *imaginative* utility maximizers.[26]

The centrality of subjectivity

What does all this mean for thinking about deterrence? More than anything else, it draws attention to the *radical subjectivity* that is at the heart of the deterrence process. This is a core, irreducible element in deterrence; it is well established theoretically; it gets virtually no attention in practice; it is a central theme in what follows in this book. What matters in deterrence is *what matters to offenders and potential offenders*. It is benefits and costs as they understand them and define them, and their thinking in weighing those benefits and costs, that are dispositive. If deterrence is not working, it may be because the objective environment offenders face is out of alignment: Crime is too attractive and penalties insufficiently unattractive. It could be, though, that offenders simply do not understand what is in fact a profoundly unattractive environment and are thus not swayed by it. It could be that in trying to create an effective deterrence environment we are not paying proper attention to what offenders find attractive and unattractive. And it could be that we are not clear ourselves about how offenders are taking in and making use of the information that is guiding their actions.

This suggests a different route to understanding, and perhaps improving, deterrence. In our usual discussions, when we see a failure of deterrence, we would turn to the detailed workings of the criminal-justice system: the rates at which crime is committed; the rates at which crime is reported; the effectiveness of the police at clearing offenses and making arrests; the likelihood that such arrests will be prosecuted; the likelihood that such prosecutions will bring sanctions; the severity of those sanctions; the overall pace of the entire process, etc. These are objective matters, and they are the ones to which academic, policy, and public attention is almost invariably drawn. Instead, here, following on the logic thus far, we will move to a different set of issues—ones that govern the *subjective* response of offenders and potential offenders to whatever the *objective* facts may be.

3 Some implications of the subjectivity of deterrence

Knowledge

Fundamental to an effective deterrence regime is that offenders and potential offenders *know what they face:* that they are aware of prospective consequences. A sanction, or a risk of sanction, that is unknown cannot, by definition, deter. This begins as a simple and obvious, and therefore arguably trivial, logical point. It is, however, not trivial at all.

In much thinking about deterrence, such knowledge is, implicitly or explicitly, assumed, as a matter of what economists call "unbiased expectations." Ehrlich writes:

> Although information pertaining to criminal sanctions or probabilities of their imposition is incomplete, in the same way that information pertaining to government taxes, probabilities of employment in specific industries, or the supply of money is not fully available, and [sic] assumptions of unbiased (or "rational") expectations concerning the actual magnitudes of these variables is justifiable on the ground that any systematic gaps between perceptions and reality would generate incentives to revise the former in the direction of the latter. The incentives would be particularly strong when the consequences of misperception would be quite costly to the actor, as may be the case in connection with most felonies.[1]

That is to say, a criminal might not know that he faced heightened sanction for selling drugs near a public school, just as a high-school student might not know that the industry that had given his father a living-wage job was in serious decline. But both, on this view, would soon come to understand—or at least come to understand soon enough to allow us to model deterrence as if clear understandings prevailed.

Public policy nearly always operates under the same implicit assumptions. Offenders and potential offenders are presumed to know the enforcement risks they face. It is presumed that new sanction regimes—for example, a three-strikes law, new statutes on waiving juvenile violent offenders to adult courts, or state legislation mandating arrest for domestic assault—are clear to offenders and potential offenders, or at any rate soon will be. These presumptions may be true. They are clearly, however, often *not* true.

Early research established the reality of the problem, showing that public knowledge of both the extent of criminal penalties and changes to those penalties was low.[2] Very little has been done since to illuminate these issues; we know almost nothing about what Nagin calls "the formation of sanction risk perception."[3] Given the absolute centrality of the matter to the workings of deterrence, our ignorance on the matter is glaring. Nagin identifies a series of core questions:

> How do would-be offenders combine prior experience with the criminal justice system and new information on penalties? How long does it typically take for persons to become aware of new sentencing regimes? How do they become aware of changes in penalties, and what information sources do they use in updating their impressions? How do novices form impressions of sanction risks?[4]

A rare piece of research suggests rather dire answers. In a 2005 study, Kleck *et al.* used survey research to compare a range of public perceptions on crime and punishment to actual levels of arrest, punishment, and other dimensions such as speed of case processing in fifty-four large urban counties in the USA. The results were striking: The public, including offenders, had virtually no insight into actual penalties and enforcement risks in their locales. "Evidently, urban criminals' perceptions of punishment risks prevailing in their areas have virtually no systematic correspondence with reality," the authors said.[5] Real levels of penalties, rates of arrest for particular offenses, and rates of prison sentences for those arrests had virtually no bearing on public perceptions on those dimensions. "Either these perceptions are being formed largely at random, or they are produced by factors, perhaps very individualistic and idiosyncratic, that we did not measure," the authors concluded.[6] Their conclusion was straightforward: Variations in sanction level and criminal-justice practice could not be producing deterrence, because those whom such variations were designed to influence had no idea what they were.

Even those professionally involved in applying the criminal law frequently have trouble predicting, and even understanding, the sanctions it contemplates. The California Senate Judiciary Committee wrote of the California criminal code that:

> Existing law contains over 30 possible sentencing triads for felony offenses. The sentencing formulas are complex, inconsistent and confusing. A judge is often required to complete a worksheet which can be more complicated than an IRS form in order to calculate the proper sentence. When mathematical errors or other mistakes are made, the case is often reversed on appeal.[7]

The committee report quoted an appellate judge who wrote that:

> As a sentencing judge wends his way through the labyrinthine proce-
> dures of Section 1170 of the Penal Code, he must wonder, as he utters
> some of its more esoteric incantations, if, perchance, the Legislature had
> not exhumed some long, departed Byzantine scholar to create its see-
> mingly endless and convoluted complexities. Indeed, in some ways it
> resembles the best offerings of those who author bureaucratic memor-
> anda, income tax forms, insurance policies or instructions for the
> assembly of packaged toys.[8]

The resulting confusion and ignorance can in practice reach staggering
levels. In one study of serious firearms offenders, even felons who had been
prosecuted, sentenced, and were interviewed while incarcerated dramatically
underestimated the magnitude of their *current* sentence.[9] We will explore
further below the matter of how such a thing could be, and will find that it is
actually not hard to understand; here, it is enough to establish it as a logical,
and at least sometimes realized, possibility. Makkai and Braithwaite, in their
research on compliance in Australian nursing homes, reported that in their
fieldwork "there were encounters with managers who did not have the
slightest idea of what sanctions might be imposed for noncompliance, let
alone the likelihood that any of these things might happen."[10]

This can be the case, as shown, even where the law is stable. Where new
sanction regimes are concerned, there will be, at the very least, a lag, possibly a significant lag, between the shift and the understanding of that shift.
This can be true even in the case of clear, explicit, and relatively well-publicized statutory shifts, such as the passage of the federal three-strikes law.
The first offender convicted under that law, Tommy Farmer, told the *New
York Times* that "'I ain't never heard anything about the law until they
applied it on me. I never thought anything like this would happen to me,
man.'" He was not, he said, alone. "'It is going to make a few guys think,
but some other guys don't even watch TV or care; they don't know nothing
about the law.'"[11]

It is bound to be true when the law or its application changes without
attendant publicity. Baltimore offenders with previous convictions for violent
crimes were bewildered to find themselves being sent back to prison on probation violations after beating criminal cases for new arrests. The logic of
what was happening to them was straightforward. Probationers frequently
face long sentences for their current offense if a judge finds that they have
violated the terms of their supervision: Their probation can be revoked and
they can be sent to prison for the balance of their existing sentence. The
standard of proof for determining such violations is "a preponderance of the
evidence"—the same standard routinely applied in civil cases—rather than
the criminal court's "beyond a reasonable doubt." So, a defendant can be
found innocent on a relatively minor misdemeanor charge and find that the

same evidence is enough to support a probation violation: and put them away for the sentence that had been suspended in the prior criminal case for which they were serving probation. The rules of evidence in probation hearings are also far looser, allowing evidence that would not make it into criminal court. But because prosecutors used the strategy relatively rarely, defendants and even their defense attorneys were frequently shocked not only that it was being applied, but that it was even possible.[12] And—by definition—those shocked by it could not have been deterred.

Communicating information

This broad ignorance exists in part because legal authorities make next to no effort to inform offenders and potential offenders about penalties and risks. This is a central matter. In Zimring and Hawkin's classic phrase, "the deterrence threat may perhaps best be viewed as a form of advertising."[13] To say it once again, a risk that is not known cannot deter. Yet, "advertising" as such—the deliberate process of communicating information to influence behavior—is rarely employed as part of routine enforcement activities and is particularly rarely employed for more serious crimes. Where the deliberate communication of threats is employed, it tends to be for low-end offenses such as parking violations (a rare near-equivalent for a serious sanction is the use of signs to delineate high-penalty drug trafficking zones near schools). As Philip Cook dryly observes, "Madison Avenue has not yet entered the crime-control business."[14] Media campaigns that do focus on criminal acts, such as drug use and drunk driving, are hardly unknown, but they tend to be silent with regard to penalties: We hear that your brain on drugs looks like a fried egg and that friends don't let friends drive drunk, not that using drugs can land you in prison and that driving under the influence can lose you your license.

What campaigns there are also tend to be broadcast to large populations, most of which are at little or no risk of offending. Their record is not promising. Almost certainly the largest ever was the US Government's $1.2 billion National Youth Anti-Drug Media Campaign. An evaluation of its impact found that both the youth and the parents at which it was aimed were familiar with and had favorable impressions of the campaign; neither changed their behavior, however, and there were no reductions in drug use. In perverse outcomes not at all unheard of with such interventions, the campaign may have led some youth to believe that others' drug use was normative and to small increases in marijuana use is some groups of young people.[15] In the UK, the Home Office examined the impact of a campaign aimed at youth vandalism and two others aimed at car theft, and found none.[16] A campaign in the Netherlands aimed at burglary and street crime used newspaper editorials, radio spots, and opportunities for citizens to interact with police but found "no effect on knowledge of burglary and violence, the image of local crime, risk assessment, fear of crime, outcome expectation, self-efficacy expectation, preventive behaviour, and the attitude towards crime reporting."[17]

There are, of course, other forms of communication: Cook notes media coverage of crime and enforcement activities, the signals sent by the visible presence of enforcement personnel, and the impact and transmission of personal experience.[18] Here too, we know very little about the workings of these modes or the impact of whatever communication is occurring; here too, whatever *is* occurring is doing so largely informally. Whatever information is being imparted may or may not be accurate and may or may not be operating to support deterrence.

There are examples that show quite clearly the importance, or potential importance, of communication. Experiments have shown that "feedback signs" indicating speeding reduce drivers' speeds significantly.[19] There are a number of instances of deliberately communicated threats around drunk drivers having significant impact; indeed, says Sherman, "if anything, they seem to be more sensitive to the threat of communication than to the actual differences in police sanctioning."[20] Ross and his colleagues report on six enforcement actions: two in New Zealand, three in England, and one in France.[21] All were crackdowns employing heavy breathalyzer testing and police enforcement. In the New Zealand crackdowns, tests were greatly increased after heavy publicity; drunk driving went down dramatically even *before* the actual enforcement began. In the French and one of the English crackdowns heavy publicity promised enforcement that was not actually delivered; drunk driving still went down. In the remaining two English crackdowns, both in Cheshire, an initial publicity-free crackdown had no impact, while a publicized one shortly afterward did. Johnson and Bowers examined twenty-one English burglary-prevention projects and found that publicity about the projects was the key element in their success: Burglary reductions were greatest during periods of heightened publicity, and those projects with deliberate publicity campaigns (rather than more inadvertent and indirect means of publicizing the projects, such as household surveys) showed the greatest impact.[22]

Letters threatening legal action sent to sixty-two persons stealing cable television with illegal descramblers led two-thirds of them to remove the devices.[23] Heavy and often inaccurate publicity surrounding the introduction of Massachusetts' Bartley-Fox law, which imposed a one-year mandatory penalty for illegal possession of a firearm, led to increased compliance and indeed to unnecessary "compliance," as firearms owners responded to media portrayals of the law rather than to the law itself.[24] Zimring and Hawkins report on a study of university parking enforcement in which an existing regime of prohibitions and fines—for which the fines had not been collected—was supplemented by an announcement of enhanced fines for repeat violators and the automatic deduction of penalties from university paychecks.[25] Large decreases were observed amongst the worst prior violators, a change Zimring and Hawkins attribute to chronic offenders being put on "notice that *their* parking behavior was *really forbidden*."[26] Jeremy Travis, former Deputy Commissioner for Legal Affairs in the New York City Police Department, relates a similar story: City landlords who had ignored warnings that they were violating legal requirements requiring them to attend to drug trafficking by tenants flocked to comply after being sent a letter reporting that one of their peers had had his building seized under federal asset-forfeiture laws.[27] Finally, as noted, Ceasefire-type interventions have used communication with chronic offenders to establish deterrence regimes.

A special case of such communication produces what Smith *et al.* call "anticipatory benefits": effects from crime prevention initiatives that show results *before* the initiative is actually implemented.[28] They explain the phenomenon primarily in terms of what they call "publicity/disinformation effects": information, sometimes inaccurate, that "police and other agencies are taking action of specific kinds in circumscribed places."[29] Such a pattern is not at all unusual. In a review of fifty-two initiatives, Smith *et al.* found twenty-two that showed such effects. "Insofar as crime prevention reduction tactics work at all, they work through changes in perception," they write.[30] Changing perception, and thus behavior, through information can have the same, or even greater, impact than changing it through more concrete actions.

So, deliberate communication—and, by extension, the absence thereof—can matter a great deal. Absence, though, is the norm, nearly to the point of universality. It would be possible to tell those facing federal three-strikes laws that they faced such a prosecution the next time they were arrested: We know, after all, who they are, since such a possibility is predicated on their criminal records, which could simply be examined to create a list. It would be possible for Baltimore to explain to those probationers whose prior violence made them of interest to prosecutors how probation could and would be used to put them away. It would be possible to tell church hierarchies that investigators were actively seeking allegations of sexual abuse of children and would pursue both criminal and civil charges against both individual perpetrators and the hierarchies themselves. We virtually never do anything of the kind.

Experience and the "experiential effect"

Most offenders, therefore, most of the time, receive information about risk through experience, direct and indirect—their own and that of people they know or hear about. So too do most nonoffenders, such as crime victims and their family, friends, and neighbors. And here, the grounding for the formation of beliefs is more or less immediate and concrete. And, crucially, what matters is not what the law says, or permits, or what authorities say they will do. What matters is what is actually seen, known, and believed to occur.

This often operates to the detriment of deterrence. "If active criminals find that they are rarely arrested, unlikely to be convicted if arrested, and unlikely to be sentenced to prison terms if convicted, then they may acquire a justified sense of invulnerability," writes Cook.[31] Cook argues further that such sensibilities may be very unevenly distributed, due to the vagaries of information gleaned from one's own personal experience and exposure to the experience of others. Even given a stable probability of sanction, committing a crime and getting caught and sanctioned can raise risk estimates for one-self and one's associates, while committing the same crime and getting away with it can lower them for oneself and one's associates. Neither estimate may match the actual probability: The high estimates may be too high, even far too high, and the low estimates may be too low, even far too low. "[U]nlike stock market prices," note Fisher and Nagin, "daily quotations of sanction levels are not available."[32]

This appears to be what often happens with the sorts of announced crackdowns discussed above. The announcement, perhaps backed by heightened enforcement activity, raises perceptions of risk. Behavior changes, for a time. But that effect decays, albeit sometimes slowly.[33] Whether this is because the content of the message is lost, or because the level of the enforcement does not live up to the promise, or because an initial surge in enforcement attenuates—or some combination of all of these—is not always clear. But shifts in perceptions of risk—shifts that can happen quite rapidly—appear to be at the heart of the process.

The structure of risk perceptions

A related question has to do with the *specificity* of risk perceptions. Formal utility theory presumes that offenders weigh risks for particular crimes, risks that of course vary by offense. Sanction structures vary for drug possession, versus drug-dealing, versus the illegal possession of a firearm, versus aggravated assault, versus homicide. Similarly, the attitudes and actions of criminal-justice authorities tend to vary by offense: Drug possession tends to be taken less seriously than drug-trafficking, assault with a firearm more seriously than simple assault, an armed robbery in a usually safe part of town more seriously than an armed robbery in a usually dangerous part of town. All these formal and informal shadings are taken to matter to offenders weighing the risks and benefits of particular crimes.

It may be so. This is not the only possibility, however. Another is that offenders have rather broad and aggregate perceptions rather than specific ones. These could stratify in a number of different ways. One would be *sanction level*: Some crimes could be seen as having high penalties, others low (however those levels are defined by offenders). Another would be *crime type*: Some crimes could be seen as more or less safe, others as more or less risky. Another would be *place*: Some places—neighborhoods, or areas within neighborhoods—could be seen as high-risk places, others as low-risk places. Another would be *time*: There may be times in which it is seen as safe, or safer, to offend—night, police shift change, during a period of relative police quiescence—and others when it is not, as when a high-profile crime creates a period of increased enforcement attention (as Decker and Kohfeld suggest, offenders may note that "the heat is on"—or off—and act accordingly.[34]) Another would be *victim*: It may be seen as safe to rob a young drug dealer, or an out-of-town john, but unsafe to rob a businessman. Whether these things are true and how they work matter quite a lot. If offenders see sanctions in a fairly simple way—"high" and "low," for example—then adding to already "high" sanctions may not matter: the difference between a ten-year sentence and a life sentence will not carry meaning (and, by extension, the higher end of "low" sentences may be made even lower without losing deterrence, or perhaps be made slightly higher to produce enhanced deterrence). If crime types are seen as "risky" and "safe," then variations in sanction level may not matter as long as the original labeling holds. If certain areas are seen as safe in which to offend, then variations in sanctions for particular crimes may not matter in those areas. If certain victims are seen as safe to victimize, the same may hold true. Unless category shifts take place, differences at the margin in risk will not affect offender behavior. And if category shifts take place, they too may be quite general, as, for instance, all offenses attached to "high" penalties become less attractive, or all offenses in what is newly seen as a neighborhood in which it is inadvisable to offend decline.

We know very little about how these operate, and even less about the relationship between particular policy choices and offenders' perceptions of risk.[35] One way to schematize this process is to see it as the product of three factors: *formal sanction regimes*, or law and legal penalties; *enforcement practice*, or what authorities actually do; and *offender interpretation*, or what meaning offenders attach to what they experience directly or vicariously Formal sanction regimes and actual practice can of course be quite different; federal law, for example, has a three-strikes law to which many offenders are in principle exposed, but the law is rarely applied. Between 1994, when the law was passed, and 1996 only nine such federal sentences were imposed nationally. At the same time, Wisconsin, with a similar law, used it only once; Tennessee, New Mexico, and Colorado did not use theirs at all.[36] Both can be considered matters of policy, the first usually more explicit and formal than the latter. The first generally matters more in political and policy debates. The second, it is reasonable to think, generally matters more to offenders.

Formal and informal sanctions

Deterrence is most elementally about sanctions: Nearly all public and policy thinking about deterrence focuses on sanctions, and especially on the seriousness of sanctions. In the public conversation, when deterrence is seen to be failing, the arguments go in two directions: It would make sense to enhance sanctions, since the current level is inadequate, or to reduce them, since the current level is wasteful. What is generally seen to matter is *severity*: Probation means less than a short prison sentence, which in turn means less than a long prison sentence, which in turn means less than the death penalty.

Deterrence theorists have taken a more nuanced view. Here, deterrence is seen as a complicated matter involving sanctions, their severity, their pace, their reliability, their impact on other matters of concern to offenders, the nature of the offense itself, the standing of authorities, and a host of related matters. These include especially, in keeping with the centrality of subjectivity to deterrence, the perceptions of offenders around these matters.

Sanctions can include, in principle, anything that exacts a cost. So framed, the sanctions relevant to deterrence very clearly include, but are not limited to, those of formal criminal dispositions. "In discussing the threat of punishment," say Zimring and Hawkins, "we have to consider not only what is explicit in the threat but also many other elements which are only implicit but may nevertheless exercise a deterrent influence as great as, or greater than, the penalty provided by law."[37] They identify five main "consequences of apprehension for criminal behavior":[38] (1) economic deprivation in the form of fines or seized property; (2) loss of privilege, such as the right to vote and standing to drive; (3) institutional confinement; (4) physical pain and death; and (6) social stigmatization.[39] These can be very potent: A police officer convicted of first-time domestic assault is unlikely to spend a day in prison, but under current federal law will lose his right to carry a firearm—a potentially career-ending restriction. Less dramatic, but also potentially quite meaningful, are such things as the impact of a felony conviction on future employment prospects: A young drug offender, for example, may view a drug conviction and its attendant sentence to probation as trivial, but the effective life-long restriction to low-wage work such a conviction carries can have enormous earnings impact.

Intangible concerns matter as well. People care about what other people think. Social-bonding theory suggests that those with strong ties to others, and with "investments" in those ties, will be less likely to risk those ties and those investments by offending. Hirschi, in a seminal formulation, framed such bonds in terms of a utilitarian *commitment* to conformity and the material rewards it has and might bring; an emotional *attachment* to others and their good opinions; *involvement* in conventional activities, which leaves less time and energy for unconventional ones; and *belief*: felt support for the moral content of the tenets of conventionality.[40] Deterrence theorists have recognized that sanctions for offending are likely to matter more for those with strong social bonds and who thus have more to lose if sanctions threaten those bonds. Those with weak social bonds may both have less to lose and more criminogenic circumstances, such as free time away from school and work and peer networks that promote some sorts of deviance.[41] In each case, the relevant dimension may be less the sanction as such than how the sanction, and the social rule it represents, is viewed by the potential offender and, especially, those whose views matter to him.

Deterrence theorists have built bridges between such frameworks and rational-actor utility models. Nagin and Paternoster collapse the idea of commitments and attachments into the notion of "social capital," "a form of investment that, like their financial analogue, involves the accumulation of a capital stock that yields a future return," and which can then be treated theoretically much like other forms of capital.[42] The more social capital one has, the more reluctant one should be to risk criminal sanction. Issues of personal belief they frame as "moral regret," encompassing the costs of violating or triggering "moral inhibitions," "moral attachments," "conscience," and "shame."[43] This suggests that offenses that are viewed as wrong in and of themselves—*mala in se*—may be more effectively deterred than those less serious offenses that merely happen to be against the law, or *mala prohibita*.[44]

There are some interesting theoretical shadings here. One key area involves what should be considered part of the deterrence process and what should remain outside it. If an offense is put out of bounds because of the personal views of potential offenders and their peers—if it is internal and social control alone that matters, and not fear of arrest and sanction—is that deterrence? "Moral condemnation of these crimes assures conformity in most cases, and this process is correctly termed an extralegal sanction outside of deterrence," write Williams and Hawkins.[45] Others, such as Nagin and Paternoster above, have included these moral and normative aspects as part of deterrence itself.[46] In general, deterrence theorists have tended toward inclusion. "[T]he task for the student of deterrence," write Meier and Johnson, "is to explain the relationship between behavior, on the one hand, and both legal and extralegal sanctions on the other."[47] These dynamics are central to outcomes—to whether offending is prevented or allowed, or even promoted—and in practice the factors that drive them—personal moral views, collective moral views, what is legally sanctioned, and how those sanctions are structured and implemented—are mutually influential.

This is an enormously complicated picture. The simple, commonsense core deterrence framework—sanctions are unpleasant and people will tend to avoid them—is still operating. But how this will play out in practice is not simple at all (though it may in fact still remain rather close to the common sense). Will a given sanction deter a given crime? The likelihood that it will may go up in good economic times, when offenders have better legitimate options and more to lose, and down in bad ones, when they have fewer legitimate options and less to lose. It may go up when general social attitudes lean against the offense in question, and down when they are more neutral or even favorable. It may go up when social structures have instilled in individual offenders beliefs inimical to offending, or to particular offenses, and down when they have not. It may go up when offenders are close to people who care about them and what they do, and who oppose offending; and down when they do not. It may go up when sanctioning authorities are viewed as worthy of respect, and down when they are not. And so on.

This is very much as we in fact think about such things, more so, perhaps, than the idea that people make careful profit-and-loss calculations about the return on offending. Crime should go down when legitimate work is easy to get and lucrative; when general social attitudes frown on offending; when family, schools, churches and the like emphasize the importance of good behavior; when offenders are close to others who disapprove of criminality; when particular offenses are seen as beyond the pale; when the police, courts, and the like are in good repute. These insights are not limited to deterrence theory. But their prominence in deterrence theory reminds us that even in deterrence much more than law and legal sanction, and the level of legal sanction, is at work.

The impact of formal sanctions

We also know relatively little about the narrower question of what sort of formal sanctions deter what sort of offenses and what sort of offenders. There is a commonsense logic to this that guides our thinking. The low end of the scale is official presence without action: police patrol. Next higher is arrest, which may or may not lead to prosecution and sanction. Next is actual punishment, with probation the least serious; jail and prison terms next, with longer sentences seen as more severe; and capital punishment the most extreme. Operating alongside this traditional ordering are what are usually thought of as less central sanctions: fines, asset forfeiture, various forms of work and community service, and the like.

Actual experiments, though conceivable, are all but unheard of: We do not apply randomized research designs to sentencing. Even where experiments are employed, they usually do not test the deterrent power of the sanction *as such,* but the deterrent power of a particular *level of treatment.* Kelling's famous preventive patrol experiment, while it is often characterized as showing that patrol does not "work," in fact does not show anything of the kind; at most, it shows that *typical levels* of patrol do not work. Other research employing higher levels of patrol have shown different results. Nor do experiments usually sort through the various complicated issues involving offender perceptions. Even where patrol was entirely withdrawn in Kelling's experiment, did offenders *know* that it had been withdrawn? Or, to put it another way, what might have been the effect of announcing in those areas that there was, newly, no patrol presence? Our knowledge here—where anything is known at all—is considerably more partial than we would like.

We know surprisingly little about the power of jail and prison to deter, and little positive about the relative impact of longer sentences Cook makes a crucial logical point here, which has to do with the "discounting" economists presume people to apply to distal rewards and punishments. The clear implication is that increases in sentence length may matter a great deal when the starting point is low, but may matter much less when the starting point is already high. Using a simple model, Cook points out that a typical offender might view a two-year sentence as 87 percent more severe than a one-year sentence: but a twenty-year one as only 25 percent more severe than a ten-year one.[48] Even what appear to be stark increases in sentence severity can be profoundly attenuated by this process. In a review of studies of California's 1982 Proposition 8, which mandated that those newly convicted of certain crimes receive a five-year sentence enhancement for each prior conviction of a number of predicate felonies, Cook noted that that average sentence enhancement under the law for those with the relevant priors was less than a year on top of the existing average six-year sentence (not all those eligible under the law were in fact so prosecuted, a routine matter to which we will return). "A rational robber with an annual subjective discount rate of 20 percent would discount that enhancement to the equivalent of just three months in prison—a seemingly small price increase, especially given the small probability of arrest and conviction," Cook writes.[49]

There has been a small but fascinating body of survey work done with actual offenders that clearly bears out this kind of diminishing return. McClelland and Alpert found that recent arrestees rated a five-year prison sentence as only twice as severe as a one-year sentence, and a twenty-year sentence as only 1.6 times as severe as a ten-year sentence.[50] Apospori and Alpert found that arrestees rated ten years in prison as 4.26 times more severe than one year, and twenty years as 6.16 times more severe than one year; twenty years was judged to be only 1.4 times as severe as ten years.[51]

These patterns, if they hold generally, could go a long way toward explaining why increasing sentences does not seem to have the deterrent power it would seem it ought to have. Doob and Webster reviewed the scholarly literature on the deterrent power of enhanced severity in sentencing and found, in their view, sufficient accumulated evidence to justify a verdict of the null hypothesis: no impact. Despite extensive research, in their view, "no consistent body of literature has developed over the last twenty-five to thirty years indicating that harsh sanctions deter."[52] Even for changes in sentencing as stark and as well-publicized as California's three-strikes law—which could shift the penalty for a predicate offense from relatively low to life in prison, and which received massive publicity—careful studies found no shift in predicate offenses relative to nonpredicate offenses,[53] or any enhanced effect in counties that pursued the new sentences vigorously versus those that did not.[54] States that imposed strict new regimes common in public-policy responses to crime, such as "truth in sentencing" laws and mandatory minimum sentences, saw no greater crime reductions than those that did not.[55] This finding—that stiffer sentences do not produce enhanced results—is the dominant theme in the research. Tonry and Farrington note that in the USA, the 1967 President's Commission on Law Enforcement and the Administration of Justice, the 1978 National Academy of Sciences Panel on Research on Deterrence and Incapacitative Effects, and the 1993 National Academy of Sciences Panel on the Understanding and Control of Violent Behavior all came to similar conclusions, as have equivalent review panels in England, Canada, and Finland.[56] "Although the statistical and methodological sophistication of efforts to examine the effectiveness of sanctions has increased over time," they write, "the conclusions have changed little."[57]

The highest-profile such question of all—the deterrent impact of the death sentence—remains, at best, uncertain. After a long spell of general scholarly consensus that there was, at least, no credible evidence of such an effect, a series of recent studies seemed to find it once again. Cloninger and Marchesini, for example, examined a period of greatly reduced executions vs. a period of greater than normal executions in Texas and found a substantial reduction in homicides in the latter period.[58] Mocan and Gittings, using national data, found that each execution prevented five to six homicides.[59] As in earlier periods, however, such studies have been followed by others finding disqualifying statistical problems, leaving—once again—a verdict of, at best, "not proven."[60] (Such technical criticisms are, in the author's mind, supported by the utter lack of face validity of other findings in the literature finding deterrence from the death penalty. Mocan and Gittings, for example, in their research, find that *pardons* of convicted offenders facing the death penalty are associated with *increases* of homicide by a factor of 1 to 1.5.[61] Given what we know about those at risk of capital offenses, the circumstances that produce those offenses, and the workings of deterrence, the idea that such offenders would be aware of and respond to capital pardons and commutations strains credulity beyond the breaking point.)

Such findings defy common sense and invite political and policy rejection. How can sometimes huge increases in the severity of sentences have no impact on offending? Even criminals, we often think, are not so stupid or self-destructive. But such findings may not defy the logic of how deterrence must in fact operate in the world. Doob and Webster write that, for increases in sentencing to enhance deterrence, "the potential offender—who knows about the change in punishment and perceives that there is a reasonable likelihood of apprehension—must calculate that it is 'worth' offending for the lower level of punishment but not worth offending for the increased punishment."[62] It is true that sentence increases sometimes increase penalties dramatically. The earlier, lower level, however, is often quite severe to begin with. It is fair to view, for example, any penalty that involves prison as a very serious sanction. It may simply be—and this too is common sense—that those who stand ready today to take a chance, often on impulse, often while impaired, on what they view as a very small likelihood of an already very serious sanction will stand ready tomorrow to take the same chance on what they still view as a very small likelihood of a somewhat more serious sanction. This is, importantly, not to say that offenders are irrational and that deterrence is not operating. It may be to say that our existing sentence levels are operating about as well as they can, and that stiffening them will not buy us much.

Complicating these aggregate studies of sanctions and their impact is the simple, but crucial, point that particular sanctions can mean quite different things to different people. Punishment is in the eye of the beholder. "[P]eople's values differ," note Grasmick and Bryjack. "What is felt as extremely costly (or rewarding) by one individual may be considered insignificant by another."[63] There is patchy, but tantalizing, evidence that this is important in practice. Grasmick and Bryjack cite work by Buikhuisen in which a group convicted of drunken driving split evenly when asked whether a two-week jail term or a six-month license revocation constituted a harsher sentence; Buikhuisen concluded that a penalty deemed serious by some "may be perceived as only a minor inconvenience by others"[64]—or, on this evidence, vice versa. Wright and Decker, in their ethnographic work with armed robbers, interviewed one who felt that, "Basically jail fun for real. Most people look at jail [as a bad place]. I look at jail as another place to lay my head at. I might be safer in jail than on the streets."[65] Many jurisdictions currently report that incarcerated offenders are choosing to serve out their sentences rather than take options to be released to community supervision—a sign that prison is seen as *preferable* to these other regimes.[66]

Survey work, again, supports the idea that our assumptions about what counts as severe may be well adrift. Two-thirds of Texas prison inmates surveyed by Crouch preferred one year of prison to ten years of probation; half preferred one year of prison to five years of probation; fully a third preferred a year of prison to three years of probation. Older offenders, unmarried offenders, and those with more experience with prison—exactly those we would expect to find probation trivial—were in fact *more likely* to reject it in favor of incarceration.[67] Texas inmates surveyed by Spelman viewed, for example, a year of electronic monitoring as about equivalent to a year in jail; three-quarters viewed some form of community supervision as more severe than a low-end jail term.[68] Kentucky probationers and parolees surveyed by May *et al.* saw county jail and boot camp as about twice as punitive as prison, and day fine (a monetary fine tied to the offender's daily income) as almost exactly equivalent.[69]

In another setting, Weisburd, Waring, and Chayet found no impact from short prison terms on reoffending amongst white-collar offenders. They found this of particular interest because the offenders they examined were not impulsive street offenders and seemed to "make decisions about crime with a significant degree of rationality."[70] Prison was ineffective, they theorized, because they were dealing with two disparate groups within their sample. One was in general quite stable and conventional; for it, the process of discovery, arrest, prosecution, and perhaps probation was sufficiently punitive and created sufficient stigma that prison added little additional sanction. The other group was more committed to criminality; for it, a short prison term was not sufficient sanction to inhibit offending in future.[71]

It is thus reasonable to believe that the meaning to offenders of sanctions can vary considerably by offender, and that perceived rankings of severity are simply not in alignment with conventional notions of seriousness. And it is those perceptions that matter to deterrence: which may be part of the reason it is difficult to find impact from even gross escalation of conventional sentencing.

The impact of informal sanctions

More is known about the impact of informal sanctions. And, in contrast to the murkiness attached to formal punishment, there is a strong convergence of evidence in favor of the power of informal sanctions. The evidence is drawn largely from the perceptual deterrence literature, which uses survey, panel, or scenario studies to gather individual-level data.

Grasmick and Bursik, examining the impact of "significant others" and "conscience" and characterizing costs, respectively, as "embarrassment" and "shame," found shame to be a powerful deterrent to tax offending, drunk driving, and petty theft; for the first two offenses, shame was a stronger deterrent than the threat of legal sanction.[72] Paternoster *et al.*, looking at a range of petty offenses amongst college and high-school students, found similar results for "moral commitment" and "social disapproval."[73] Paternoster and Simpson, looking at decisions to commit corporate crime, found deterrent effects from informal sanctions and loss of self-respect and, to a lesser degree, from formal sanctions. The power of moral beliefs was also substantial, with the authors concluding that "an independent, and very potent, source of inhibition of corporate crime is therefore noninstrumental or deontological."[74] Makkai and Braithwaite found similar results for moral beliefs in a study of nursing-home noncompliance in Australia.[75] Minor found such beliefs to be mediated by "belief in the legitimacy of the law."[76] Richards and Tittle, looking at gender-specific deterrence dynamics, found "stakes in conformity" and "visibility"—which enhanced perceived sanction risk—to be especially powerful for women.[77] Tittle found "fear of losing respect among people one knows personally" to be the major deterrent factor; formal sanctions mattered, but no more than "the probability of simple discovery by someone who would not approve of the behavior."[78] Bachman, Paternoster, and Ward, in a scenario study of sexual offending, found evidence of impact from risk of formal sanction, but only where respondents failed to find the described assault innately morally reprehensible; otherwise, moral inhibitions were considerably stronger than either formal sanctions or the disapproval of others.[79] As suggested by Williams and Hawkins, moral repugnance for such *mala in se* crimes—where that repugnance is felt—may make formal sanctions unnecessary.[80]

Nagin and Paternoster reinterpret old arguments about "present orientation"—the idea that some sorts of people are too impulsive, self-involved, and focused on immediate gratification to respond to deterrence—in light of such findings. Such people are not unresponsive to incentives, they argue. Rather, or significantly in addition, such people have made smaller investments in what Nagin and Paternoster call "personal capital." They have worked less hard than others at their education, careers, and social relationships (and, plausibly, at building a self-image characterized by and valued for good behavior); they thus have less at stake in these areas. "We believe," they argue, "that the reason persons with poor self-control commit crimes at a consistently higher rate than others is because they have less to lose."[81]

Other sorts of research are in broad alignment with the findings of the perceptual deterrence literature with regard to the salience of informal sanctions. Studies of desistence from crime, for example, "highlight the significance of social ties, such as marriage, employment, military service, and parenthood, and broader emotional and psychological processes of maturational reform."[82] These are not usually interpreted in deterrence terms, but such ties and processes can also be viewed as enhancing personal capital; the likelihood and salience of losing it though offending; the development and inculcation of orientations incorporating shame, guilt, and long-term orientations; and the development of relationships with others who encourage good behavior and discourage bad behavior. Research on adolescent drug use shows that the "social meaning" of drugs is highly correlated with trends in usage; while both perceptions of heath risks and of social disapproval matter, for marijuana and cocaine (but not alcohol and cigarettes), perceptions of social disapproval are inversely related to use even after controlling for health risks.[83] Again, while not usually viewed through a deterrence lens, this sort of finding is consistent with a personal capital/informal sanction framework.

4 Initial reflections
From within the traditional framework

Where, then, does this leave us?

First, it is clear that there is reason to think that deterrence matters a lot. While the failure of deterrence, or more accurately of particular deterrence regimes and policies, is visible all around us—each crime is evidence— deterrence is clearly operating, and might well be made to operate more. Beyond this, specifics are greatly lacking. What constitutes "a lot," and where its boundaries lie, is very murky. Matters have not advanced much since Cook, over twenty years ago, wrote that the evidence showed only that "a wide variety of crimes are deterrable, and there are no types of crimes which have been demonstrated to be undeterrable."[1] While research has given us a wealth of tantalizing data points, those points fail to cohere into a clear picture of how deterrence is actually operating in the world. Much of our thinking about this in practice returns to the most basic of first principles. Are people rational, or not? Do they care about consequences, or not? Would they commit the crime if a police officer were standing next to them?[2]

Second, it matters a good deal what we mean by "rational." Do offenders carefully calculate the costs and benefits of particular crimes? If not, what sorts of "calculations" do they undertake? Are there types of offenders who think in persistently particular ways? What sorts of "standing decisions" or "rules of thumb," if such there are, govern offenders' actions? About these questions, it is fair to say, we know almost nothing. Deterrence, the literature often reminds us, is a *subjective* business. But the veil of subjectivity is rarely lifted.

Third, the normal public, political, and policy equation of deterrence with the impact of *formal sanctions* is clearly mistaken. This mistake has two quite distinct components. One is the usual *restriction* of formal sanctions to include only arrest and sentencing. Formal sanctions include a good deal more than that: simple discovery and contact with authorities; bail and bond levels and conditions; probation and parole conditions and their enforcement; warrants and their execution; fines; asset forfeiture; service obligations; and more. About how offenders regard these sanctions we know essentially nothing. The second is the *exclusion* from our normal conversations of what the deterrence literature calls *informal sanctions*: self-perception, the perceptions of others, the various other elements of "personal capital." There is good reason to believe that these dimensions are in fact more powerful than formal sanctions and can be expected to operate more reliably.

Fourth, we err when we equate sanction *severity* with the *magnitude of formal sanctions*, and especially with arrest rates and sentence length. Subjectivity, again, is all here. An arrest can be catastrophic for one offender, so much so that what happens afterward is of marginal significance, or so mundane for another that even repeated arrests are inconsequential. Probation supervision that disrupts everyday life can mean more than a prison sentence. A prison sentence may be more attractive than life on the street. A ten-year sentence may mean little more than a five-year one. We know enough only to know that these things are true; we do not know enough to parse out their impacts, or rankings of their impacts, for different offenders and classes of offenders.

Fifth, and perhaps most dramatically, we err in neglecting the role of *information* and *communication*. The logical point here is a central one: What is not known cannot deter. We have strikingly little information about what is known; what little we have suggests it does not accurately reflect reality. Beyond this logical point are several nearly as salient practical ones. It matters how information moves around. It matters how it is viewed by its recipients. It matters what adds, or detracts, from its credibility and weight. We know, once again, almost nothing about these things. But there is no reason to believe that offenders are well informed, and good reason to believe that they are not. There is no reason to believe that the "messages" authorities seek to send get through, or that what does get through is interpreted as intended. There are tantalizing instances suggesting that clear, credible messages can have considerable impact. There is virtually no systematic exploration of this process, or of the deliberate use of communication to create deterrence.

Finally, it is clear that what authorities *do* matters. As the "experiential effect" suggests, if the idea that authorities will sanction offending promotes deterrence, learning that they will in fact not do so, or will do so to a lesser extent than expected, undercuts it. Promising breathalyzer tests deters drunk driving; not delivering them eventually vitiates that deterrence. "[I]f the first task of the threatening agency is the communication of information," in Zimring and Hawkins' classic formulation, "its second task is persuasion."[3] And in the matter of persuasion, deeds, as much or perhaps more than words, signify.

5   Crime and criminal-justice practice

The context of deterrence

How do these issues play out in practice in the real settings in which crime takes place and criminal justice agencies and practices work to address it? It is primarily the role of criminal-justice authorities to produce effective deterrence regimes (above and beyond, at any rate, those produced by natural social processes). What sort of regimes are these authorities and their practices in fact producing?

Offending

We begin with the observation that in many settings, criminal offending is not at all unusual, and even serious and violent criminal offending is in some settings very common, and sometimes common enough that it approaches the normative. Freeman, using official crime data, estimated that for one year in the late 1980s 14 percent of men age sixteen to thirty-four were arrested, with 2.3 arrests for each person arrested, and 25 percent committed crimes, with 6.6 crimes for each person who committed a crime. For black men in that age group, 35 percent were arrested, with 2.3 arrests per arrestee, and 68 percent committed crimes, with 5.7 crimes per person.[1] He notes further that in 1987, 41 percent of the young men in the National Longitudinal Survey of Youths reported having committed a serious crime, and another 17 percent a lesser crime.[2] Esbensen *et al.*, in surveys of youth conducted to evaluate the Gang Resistance Education and Training Program (GREAT), found that after four years of data collection beginning in the seventh grade, only 12 percent of the sample had *not* initiated general delinquent behavior.[3] In Baltimore, a 1992 survey of poor, minority nine- to fifteen-year-olds showed that 9 percent had been involved in drug trafficking; among the thirteen- to fifteen-year-olds in the survey, 15 percent had. In a similar study in Washington, DC, 17 percent of sixth/seventh-grade boys and 30 percent of seventh/eighth-grade boys had been asked to get involved in drug trafficking.[4] A national household survey in 1975 showed 28 percent with histories of domestic violence, 16 percent in the last year; in another survey, 34 percent of ever-married women reported having been attacked by a male partner.[5]

A vast criminological literature shows that offending tends to be concentrated by person, group, and place.[6] To take but one example, a study of homicide in Baltimore linked most homicides to some 325 drug groups, from a few rather sophisticated drug organizations to a large number of loose neighborhood groups. Some 59 percent of the incidents occurred in or near a street-level drug market and about 46 percent of the suspects and 37 percent of the victims were known members of a drug organization or some recognized neighborhood criminal network. A close examination of criminal history data revealed that 74 percent of the victims and 87 percent of the suspects had adult or juvenile criminal records or both, and 53 percent of the victims and 68 percent of the offenders had been under either adult or juvenile court-ordered supervision. Among those with criminal records, victims averaged about eight prior charges and offenders nearly ten prior charges; these prior offenses included a wide range of violent, drug, and property offenses.[7] As this example suggests, the dominant findings from this literature show that chronic offenders commit a wide variety of offenses; that offending and victimization tend to be closely associated; that violent offenders tend to commit a wide variety of nonviolent offenses as well; that groups of various sorts play a prominent role in such offending; and that high-crime neighborhoods and hot spots within those neighborhoods also figure prominently.[8] Amongst such persons, groups, and places, the prevalence, incidence, variety, and presentation of offending can be extraordinary. Ethnographers of high-crime areas and groups describe settings in which drug and alcohol use, drug-selling, violence, intimate violence, sexual assault, weapon carrying and use, theft, and other crimes are routine, open, and expected.[9] Dembo *et al.* found that 67 percent of the young drug dealers they interviewed had killed or hurt someone.[10] One Washington, DC high school lost six school athletes to gun violence in one year, and twenty-one in a twenty-five-year period.[11]

These high-crime settings are not limited to the urban, "underclass" areas and populations with which they are popularly associated. To take an example with extreme contrast, *police departments* can themselves become such settings. The Knapp Commission investigation of the New York City Police Department in the early 1970s revealed thoroughgoing corruption, with established and deeply embedded structures and rules for extorting payments from vice organizations and city contractors, and more opportunistic extortions from defendants and others.[12] The Mollen Commission investigation twenty years later found less structured but arguably even more serious offending to be widespread in certain precincts, with teams of street officers routinely committing thefts, robberies, and sexual assaults; colluding with drug dealers; abusing drugs; perjuring themselves; and assaulting members of the public.[13] Other such examples in police departments abound. The recent disclosure of sexual abuse in the Catholic Church is another such instance; the sexual offending in question was also widespread, well-known within the hierarchy, and actively concealed by the Church's bureaucracy.[14] Much "routine" abuse and violence experienced by adolescents in school constitutes, under criminal law, stalking and assault, but is rarely treated as such. Research has shown that bullying at school is widespread and is often not addressed by teachers and administrators.[15] A survey by the Defense Department's Inspector General showed that 12 percent of recent female graduates from the US Air Force Academy had been victims of rape or attempted rape while at the Academy, a conclusion not challenged by the Air Force, which confirmed its agreement with its own information. Rape victims were regularly punished for minor associated infractions, such as drinking, while the rapes went uninvestigated and the rapists unpunished.[16]

Businesses and industries can also become such high-crime settings. The savings-and-loan crisis of the 1980s is an example of a fundamentally, even paradigmatically, mainstream, conservative business sector that was overrun with criminality. An atmosphere of moral hazard created by regulatory changes unleashed a wide range of misbehavior, from what Zimring and Hawkins characterize as "culpable negligence"[17] to outright banditry by "Texas cowboys, California sharpies, Beltway whores, and assorted mafiosi."[18] Estimates of the cost of the crisis range from more than twice that of the Apollo space program to nearly half that of the Korean War.[19] Studies of the garbage-collection industry in and around New York City[20] and of the post-war heavy electrical-equipment industry provide more examples of "willful, blatant [...] flagrant" and concentrated criminality.[21] So too do the more recent examples of apparent criminality at Enron, WorldCom, and other firms, in which networks of insiders colluded with outside auditors to defraud the public.

Less rigorously, it is the ordinary experience of most people that offending, including "serious" offending, is widespread. Most people know, or have known, persons who deal, or use, drugs; who have assaulted, or been assaulted by, spouses or intimates; who have assaulted, or been assaulted by, persons in other settings; who have committed larceny or fraud (shoplifting, theft from the workplace, tax offenses, misbilling, and the like); who have been the victim or perpetrator of sexual assault; who have bought sexual services; who have driven drunk; who have bought or sold stolen goods; who have perpetrated insurance fraud; and the like. Tax fraud is, or at least was, so common that Inciardi reports an extortion racket in which con artists pose as auditors in order to shake down taxpayers.[22] Sparrow reports that in 1986 the Internal Revenue Service, aware that many filers were claiming nonexistent dependents, began requiring that dependents' social-security numbers be provided; the number of dependents claimed promptly dropped by 7 million.[23] When I taught at Harvard's John F. Kennedy School of Government, I regularly asked classes of graduate students whether they could buy drugs at school. Typically, two-thirds said that they could do so immediately; nearly all the rest could do so with some slight effort. Some criminality is so brazen, and still so low-risk, that perpetrators literally *advertise:* prostitution services, for example, are to be found in any yellow pages under "escort services," something known to many in the public and well-known to law-enforcement agencies, but about which action is almost never taken.

Getting punished

If offenders and potential offenders believe, as Jensen put it, that "you can't get away with it," this should affect their behavior.[24] One problem with deterrence, then, is the fact that to an extraordinary degree, you *can* get away with it.

It is a commonplace in criminal justice and criminology that most crimes are never even reported. Even for relatively "serious" crimes such as rape, robbery and burglary, from half to two-thirds go unreported.[25] In a recent study of assault on adolescents, 86 percent of sexual assaults and 65 percent of other assaults were never reported.[26] One study of domestic violence showed that women reported only 10 percent of violent incidents.[27] Less than 5 percent of "serious" crimes are reported in progress.[28] Even trained professionals required by law to report offenses do not do so reliably; only about one-third of child-abuse cases and one-half of child sexual-abuse cases known to such professionals and subject to mandatory reporting laws are so reported.[29] Schools can become, in effect, safe havens for bullies and worse; 66 percent of victims in a survey of middle- and high-school students reported inadequate responses by school professionals to the bullying that they witnessed.[30] As one child beaten by a group of boys daily at school for over a year told psychotherapist Terrence Real of his teachers, "they watched."[31] The police criminality uncovered in the Knapp and Mollen investigations, and in many similar instances, was flagrant, widely known inside the department, was not acted upon, and was actively concealed by large numbers of people. Less "serious" crimes, and consensual crimes such as vice, drug transactions, trafficking in stolen property, and the like are reported at even lower rates, sometimes approaching nil. Crime not reported cannot be met with formal sanctions; to the extent that informal sanctions need to be activated by a formal criminal justice response, they also cannot be activated. Much crime by middle- and upper-class offenders—domestic violence, drug, vice, fraud, and similar offenses—fits this frame. Such offenders commit such crimes with little concern about being caught and punished (though not without some respect for the risk of sanction; middle- and upper-class people smoke marijuana, but they no longer, for the most part, do so openly in public).[32]

In general, those crimes that are reported usually do not result in an arrest. Even for the more "serious" FBI index crimes, only about a fifth is so "cleared."[33] A long line of research on detective work shows that for the most part, in essence, there is no such thing: If somebody at the scene doesn't know what happened, the case will remain uncleared.[34] Even very serious crimes often go uncleared. In Washington, DC, for example, only 45 percent (ninety-nine of 220) of 2002 *homicide* cases in the city's four most violent police districts were cleared; in one district, the clearance rate was only *28* percent (sixteen of 57).[35] In these communities, one thus has a one-half to nearly three-quarters chance of getting away with murder. In an analysis of homicide in Boston, Bernstein found that, especially where black victims were concerned, clearance rates were very low—31 percent over six years—and that as of 2005 not a *single one* of twenty-two homicides involving a black victim committed in 2002 had resulted in a homicide conviction.[36]

Jacobs reports that the street drug dealers he studied in St. Louis were confident, with some reason, of their ability to evade police attention.

> The average heroin dealer, for example, is arrested only once every twelve months. Many are never arrested during the course of a year's selling. For curbside crack sellers, only one arrest occurs for every 200 transactions. Among drug-market participants in general, rates of arrest range from one in every 353 crimes to one in every 413—unimpressive at best.[37]

Mieczkowski reports that for the crack dealers he studied in Detroit, "typically, the law enforcement policies and mechanisms of a community are unimportant," and cites Johnson *et al.* in suggesting that low-end crack dealers "may carry out 1,500 transactions a year."[38] Wright and Decker examined the criminal histories of their ethnographic sample of active armed robbers. Of eighty-six, only three (4 percent) had never been arrested. But twenty-eight (33 percent) had no *armed robbery* arrests.[39] Jacobs' similar study of armed robbers who preyed on drug dealers found them to be very little concerned about arrest. "That's [the possibility of arrest is] so freakish," one said. "I mean, it's never happened to me."[40]

Even for many crimes known to police, an arrest will not take place. Elliot reports on a number of studies of domestic violence that suggest that even for felonious assaults where police find offenders at the scene, arrests are often uncommon.[41] Letkemann, writing in a "crime as work" tradition going back to Sutherland, found in his ethnography with thieves, safecrackers, and robbers that many had high, and justified, confidence in their ability to avoid sanction. They were both *known* and *safe:*

> The amateur criminal's central concern is to avoid detection. My own data suggest the importance of distinguishing between detection and conviction. The amateur criminal's central concern is to avoid *detection*; the experienced criminal is concerned that he avoid *conviction*. Experienced criminals indicated a general disregard for anonymity. They didn't particularly mind if the police "knew" they had pulled a particular caper. The important factor for the experienced criminal was that "they have nothing on me." That is, there must be no evidence that will "stand up" in court. They are aware that their particular methods of

operation and their technical skills and patterns do away with their anonymity, and that the police will "know" who did it.[42]

The description—though the social settings and methods, skills, and patterns are very different—applies equally to more modern criminal settings such as drug trafficking and drug robberies, where research has shown deliberate, complicated and frequently successful behavior to insulate offenders from sanction for what are often quite flagrant crimes.[43]

Arrest rates for less "serious" crimes can be even lower. "The 'overreach' of the criminal law," writes Sherman, "has long made it necessary for police to ignore many, and perhaps most, violations of the criminal law."[44] Simon and Burns note the flagrant "metal men" in Baltimore, who steal with such impunity that they line up in public at vendors to have their goods weighed by scrap vendors:

> A police cruiser passes them on Baltimore, turning at Gilmor, but the two barely tense. Time has taught them that once on the street, they are invisible. [...] At first, it seemed incredible to Gary that he could drag large, stolen appliances from one end of the neighborhood to the other without going directly to jail, but over time, he had learned to gauge the priorities of the rollers working Fayette Street. Most of the police were about the drugs; they lived off the corner arrest, and for Gary and Tony, there would always be more risk when they went down Vine Street to cop than when they broke into someone's home.[45]

Police frequently respond to known prosecutorial charging practices, such as discretionary office guidelines on the volume of drugs necessary for a trafficking charge; persons found in the possession of lesser quantities will often have their drugs seized but will not be arrested for trafficking. They also frequently respond to customary local sentencing practices, such as the diversion of those convicted of drug possession to treatment programs; feeling, as many officers do, that such programs are inconsequential, they will also pass on the opportunity to arrest such offenders for simple possession. Implicit local understandings effectively allowing certain crimes are sometimes reached. Jacobs reports that in St. Louis, for example, statutes require possession of more than 35 grams of marijuana to bring a felony charge, but that in practice district attorneys usually require "considerably more" than that to actually press a case.[46] It is not unusual for police officers to be expressly directed not to make arrests for some offenses, as, after the Knapp Commission scandal in New York, patrol officers are directed not to involve themselves in drug and vice enforcement out of concern for corruption control.[47] Policy decisions in the wake of scandal or misbehavior, such as the suspension of service of search warrants, can have the effect of putting whole classes of offending, such as indoor drug trafficking, off limits. Agency practices can mean that even offenders known and wanted by police get no particular attention: Police departments, for example, routinely hold large numbers of arrest warrants and make little or no attempt to serve them unless the offenders in question come to their attention in other ways, as during a traffic stop.[48] And when arrests are made, the immediate impact may be regarded by many offenders as meaningless. "Ain't nobody afraid of the cops," one Rochester offender told the author. "You're back on the block the same day."[49]

The same basic pattern holds for offenders on probation and parole. "Supervision" in community corrections is a term of art; whatever is in fact going on, it does not rise to the level of supervision. Caseloads per working line probation officer of as much as 200 are not uncommon. Joan Petersilia's account of probation in Los Angeles County is telling:

> In 2000, its 900 line officers were responsible for supervising 90,000 adult and juvenile offenders. Since the mid-1970s, county officials have repeatedly cut the agency's budget, while the number of persons granted probation has grown. As a result, 70 percent of all probationers in Los Angeles are now supervised on automated or banked caseloads—no supervision, services, or personal contacts are provided.[50]

The Los Angeles example is not so extreme as one might think. Probation agencies routinely sort their caseloads in ways that mean that many probationers never see a probation officer at all; most report rarely; and "high risk" probation status means that probationers are required to visit their probation officers in his or her office two or three times a month, rather than once, or never. The use of the term "supervision" in such settings is obviously inappropriate.

Even for those who are, to some extent, supervised, probation regimes are often thin and inconsistent. Langan found that half of probationers did not comply with the court-ordered terms of their probation, and that only half of even known violators went to jail or prison for noncompliance.[51] Many probation regimes incorporate mandatory drug testing; missed and failed tests, however, typically result in no sanction, or to an increase in essentially illusory "supervision" conditions, or to treatment regimes with similarly low accountability.[52] Boston's much-heralded "Operation Nightlight," in which teams of probation and police officers conducted nighttime home visits with high-risk probationers, responded to violations in widely disparate fashion: Some of those found absent when their conditions required them to be at home would be arrested, while others would find chocolates on their pillows and a note directing them to get in touch with their supervisors.[53] Herrell found that even in the Washington DC court system, which pays an unusually high degree of attention to drug-testing, offenders were sanguine about the consequences of dirty tests.[54] Perhaps most dramatically, probation agencies generally take no active steps to seek out supervisees who abscond: Most, but not all, agencies will issue warrants for absconders, but very few take any active steps to locate them.[55] A review of domestic homicides in one jurisdiction of the author's acquaintance revealed that domestic violence offenders put on intensive probation but who never even reported to their probation officers were put on "inactive" status—a step not communicated to the courts. There is very little evidence that probation reduces offending or improves outcomes for supervisees. Petersilia and Turner studied intensive supervision programs (ISP) in California—probation regimes that give supervisees a great deal more attention than is usual—and found no reductions in recidivism.[56]

Parole, while typically a tighter regime than probation, displays fundamentally the same dynamics, with rather dire effect. A 2005 study by Solomon *et al.* using data from fifteen states found that, after controlling for individual-level characteristics of offenders released from prison, parole had what was in practical terms no meaningful impact on subsequent rearrest: Failure rates for both parolees and nonparollees were equal and high. "Specifically, when all other variables were controlled for, the predicted probability of rearrest for mandatory parolees and unconditional releasees was identical at 61 percent," they wrote.[57]

When arrests are made, prosecutions, and prosecutions directed to the highest possible sanction, are not certain. The extent to which prosecutors deviate from stereotypical punitive, adversarial positions is so great that when it was first discovered through American Bar Foundation research in the 1950s, corruption was presumed: Only improper political influence, it was thought, could account for the departure from anticipated practice.[58] In fact, as is now well understood, many factors press against a single-minded push for sanctions, and for maximum sanctions. Charging practices, perhaps especially in busy urban jurisdictions, result in many charges ultimately being dropped through the practice of pursuing, for many crimes, only one of several offenses charged. This is so routine it is rarely commented upon even within law-enforcement circles. A person arrested in connection with armed robbery with a firearm may be charged with a number of distinct offenses: armed robbery, illegal possession of a firearm, illegal discharge of a firearm, aggravated assault, possession of narcotics, and resisting arrest. In practice, only one such charge, and not necessarily the one with the highest associated penalty, is often the matter of a disposition, the remainder being dropped after arraignment or during plea-bargaining. Prosecutorial discretion on such matters is generally, in practice, entire and can lead to remarkable disparities from case to case, from time to time, and from jurisdiction to jurisdiction. In Richmond, Virginia, for example, federal prosecutions for illegal possession of a firearm, with concomitant exposure to substantial federal minimum mandatory sentences, more than tripled between 1997 and 1998, entirely the result of a change in charging policy by the office of the US Attorney.[59]

A startling number of criminal cases are simply dropped altogether by prosecutors. Many cases are deemed not to be prosecutable due to evidentiary or procedural concerns. Necessary police work does not get done; witnesses cannot be located, fail to appear, or change their minds; critical legal standards for such things as police stops and searches are deemed not to be met. Some of this is inevitable and justifiable; some of it is clearly not. In San Francisco, for example, violent-crime investigators lacked radios, phones, and cars; they did most of their investigations in their offices, without going into the field to visit crime scenes and interview witnesses; and they dropped cases when victims failed to return phone calls.[61] The collective impact of these factors can be substantial, even for "serious" crimes. A Vera Institute of Justice study of felony assault arrests in New York City showed that only 10 percent of cases were carried through to a disposition.[62] In Wright and Decker's sample of armed robbers, twenty-three (26 percent) had armed robbery *arrests*, but no armed robbery *convictions*.[63]

Where sanctions are imposed, severity—even relative to the statutory exposure—is also not certain. On the order of 90 percent of all criminal cases are discharged through plea-bargaining. Research has shown that the prime driver of plea-bargaining is the notion of a locally applicable "market rate" for given offenses.[64] Such rates are, almost by definition and certainly in practice, below statutory maxima. They are clearly, in many cases, insufficient to deter. One of Wright and Decker's armed robbers told them:

> [If I get caught, I'll probably be sentenced to] about ten years [probation]. I would probably do about a hundred and eighty days' shock [incarceration], let me out, put me on some papers. When you get caught, it depends on what kind of weapon it is. Since it's my first offense, my first time going to jail, period, they'd put me on a hundred and eighty days' shock and then put me on papers and let me out.[65]

Offender understandings like these may or may not, as we have seen, be accurate. The author has, in field work in New York State, been briefed by confident young offenders on state law that gives them a "YO" pass for their first felony offense: they think, and act as if, their first felony arrest comes free. They are, unfortunately, wrong. The "youthful offender" status to which they refer is discretionary, not automatic, and can still carry a sentence of up to four years in prison.

Simon and Burns report that the Baltimore police make nearly 20,000 drug arrests annually; that fewer than 1,000 of these defendants will get prison time; and that fewer than half of those will get a sentence of more than a year. "In short, for the vast majority of those arrested, the threat of incarceration is limited to a night or two in jail until a bail review hearing or, in the rare event that a money bond is set and a defendant is unable to pay, a month or two of pretrial detention."[66] Gibbs estimated that at one point murderers in South Carolina faced only a 22-percent chance of imprisonment.[67] Peter Reuter and David Boyum have estimated that the risk of going to prison for a cocaine transaction in the USA is 1 : 15,000.[68]

The gap between statutory maxima and penalties actually imposed can be enormous. In Washington, DC, a jurisdiction with one of the highest homicide rates in the country and where federal sanctions for gun possession start at five years and rise sharply from there, half of all dispositions for illegal possession of a firearm are sentences to probation.[70] "Split sentences"—a term of imprisonment plus a term of probation—frequently amount in practice to probation alone, with the imprisonment component restricted to pre-trial time served or contingent on later processing of probation violations, itself an uncertain prospect even in the face of clear violations of probation conditions.[71] A person currently under probation or parole and arrested on a new charge will frequently be discharged by prosecutors to the probation or parole authorities rather than tried on the new charge; their exposure is then generally limited to whatever remains of the sentence for the prior offense, without any certainty that a violation proceeding will in fact be pursued, or imposed by the bench if it is pursued.

Sentences to probation for new convictions are frequently imposed even for "serious" crimes; the conventional idea that community supervision is reserved for minor and nondangerous offenders is simply not accurate. Nor is there consistency to whether jail, prison, or community supervision is assigned. In a study of California probationers, Petersilia and Turner concluded that about a quarter of "those granted felony probation are indistinguishable in terms of their crimes or criminal record from those who are imprisoned (or vice versa)."[72] In Texas—a state which uses the death penalty more frequently than any other—9 percent of murderers sentenced in Dallas County were allowed to plead to a special probation program; if they completed their probation period successfully, their records were cleared of the homicide charge. The rate of sentencing to probation was twice that of sentencing to death.[73]

New offenses by persons on probation are frequent. Langan and Cunniff report for one sample of felony probationers that

> within three years of sentencing, while still on probation, 43 percent of these felons were rearrested for a crime within the state. Half of the arrests were for a violent crime (murder, rape, robbery, or aggravated assault) or a drug offense (drug trafficking or drug possession). The estimates (of recidivism) would have been higher had out-of-state arrests been included.[74]

One study of 155 homicide victims age twenty-one and under in Boston between 1991 and 1995 identified 125 known homicide offenders age twenty-one and under associated with those victims. Nearly 60 percent of those offenders had probation histories, and 25 percent were actually on probation at the time they committed their homicide.[75]

If one takes a slightly broader look at the nature and behavior of the probation population, matters often look still worse. It is well known that many persons on probation are chronic offenders and that the offense for which they are currently serving a probation sentence is not necessarily a good guide to their prior or future offending. Serious violent offenders, for instance, are rarely specialists: They tend to have long and varied criminal careers encompassing high rates of offending for a wide variety of offense categories. One cannot thus conclude that an offender on probation for a minor offense is not a high risk for future violent offending.

Such disparities and inaccuracies in sentencing are well known and have fueled efforts to reduce judicial discretion through mechanisms such as sentencing guidelines and mandatory minimum sentences. Efforts to reduce judicial discretion, however, often serve to enhance the salience of prosecutorial discretion, as crucial decisions formerly made by judges are instead made by prosecutors. Federal guidelines on sentence mitigation, for example, can mean that serious offenders able to cooperate with prosecutors by sharing information will receive lesser sentences than objectively less serious offenders with nothing to offer.[76] Other studies have shown discretion moving to the probation officers who write the presentencing reports on which guideline sentences are based.[77]

Finally, there is a well-documented tendency for high sanctions to be reduced in practice through the exercise of discretion throughout the criminal-justice process, what Ross calls "the neutralization of severe penalties," the idea that "sharp increases in formal penalties tend to be subverted by contrary adjustments in the behavior of those who apply the law."[78] When faced with outcomes that seem too high, for whatever reason, police arrest less; prosecutors drop cases, charge lesser crimes, and plead more leniently; judges sentence less severely; probation and parole officers decline to pursue violations. Some federal prosecutors have undercut mandatory drug sentencing by instead charging offenders with less severe crimes such as wire offenses.[79] Federal three-strikes prosecutions, while frequently open to prosecutors based on the law, are, as has been noted, rarely brought. Police officers have registered their distaste for domestic-violence policies requiring mandatory arrest by arresting, in practice, both offenders *and* victims.[80] Federal prosecutors pursuing gun and low-level drug cases—"street" crimes addressed under federal law but not traditionally the purview of the federal bench—frequently report pressure, both explicit and implicit, from federal judges to cease and desist.

None of this means that offenders face no risk of sanctions, or that the sanctions they do face do not shape their behavior, or that sanction risk is never consistent and predictable. Nor do these dynamics necessarily extend to *informal* sanctions—shame, guilt, and the opinions of peers can still operate regardless of official action—but to the extent that informal sanctions are predicated on arrest, conviction, and other formal steps, they too will be undercut.

It may well mean, however, as Sherman argues, that offenders typically face a "high certainty of low risk of punishment for most offenses,"[81] and that this holds true even for "serious" and violent crime. Looking, again, to Wright and Decker's sample of armed robbers, nearly 60 percent had *never* been convicted for that offense.[82] It may also mean that that sanctions lack coherence, consistency, and—crucially, from the standpoint of deterrence— predictability. Fagan found no apparent logic in the sentencing of drug offenders in New York. "Neither offense nor offender characteristics combined with charges to influence sentencing outcomes [...] The most severe sentences were not reserved for the defendants with the most serious charges. Lacking a calculus for assigning punishments, sentencing of drug offenders appeared to be a random process."[83] Another, qualitative study of drug enforcement in New York during the same period paints a picture of what can fairly be described as chaos; not even the authorities knew, or understood, or very much controlled what was going on.[84] Cook found that the prosecution and sentencing of armed robbers failed to incorporate any heightened focus on those who caused their victims nonlethal injuries.[85] As has been noted, federal law permits the prosecution of many gun crimes, but most such crimes are not so prosecuted. It is the author's experience from years of working closely with police and prosecutors addressing gun violence and gun trafficking that even seasoned professionals cannot predict whether federal prosecutors will agree to pursue a given gun offense; prosecutors themselves are often unable to articulate the grounds on which they accept some cases and reject others.

Punishment can thus be unpredictable, in both directions: Offenders can face unknown, and even unknowable, chances that any given offense will result in lenient or punitive treatment. They can face extremely misleading cues from their own experience and that of those they know or about whom they hear: Whatever the true, probabilistic risk, the example of someone who was treated softly or harshly may strongly and inaccurately influence risk perceptions. These perceptions may attach to particular kinds of offenses, or they may be much broader: A "pass" on a gun case, for example, may influence beliefs about future gun cases, or beliefs about violent crimes, or beliefs about the general seriousness and competence of the authorities. It means that offenders will routinely be exposed to great variance in the way similar offenses are handled. It means that offenders are routinely exposed to instances in which authorities know of offenses and there are no formal consequences at all, including instances in which arrests are made and formal proceedings initiated and parallel instances in which probation and parole violations are known to authorities and no action is taken.

6 The criminogenic implications of official practice

Criminal offending, then, is in many settings common and subject to surprisingly little risk. What risk there is is often poorly understood by offenders and potential offenders, and all but impossible to predict. We usually think of this in simple and straightforward ways: Authorities are not effective, or serious, enough; or offenders are too resistant, too serious, too disinterested in their own welfare. Zimring and Hawkins distinguish three categories of failure that are germane here: (1) a general *failure of enforcement,* in which enforcement is attempted but does not succeed; (2) the failure to even attempt enforcement for a particular offense, which creates *general immunity* for that offense; and (3) the failure to attempt enforcement for a particular classes of person, which creates *status immunity* for those persons.[1] All three are at work in the above examples. Since we rarely expect offenders to become less active, we generally look to authorities to become more so. When, as often happens, that fails, the same equation still applies, if at a higher level of official effort: Offenders are seen to be resistant. Deterrence, in this framework, is a largely static equation: Authorities take offenders pretty much as they find them, and do or do not get their attention and shape their behavior. In keeping with our deeper notions about criminality, the roots of offending are located in the character of offenders and in social and community conditions. Official enforcement action engages with those roots, and wins or loses.

In this framework, enforcement efforts are purely *subtractive:* They can *take away* from offending but cannot *add* to it. Offending and potential offending are taken as endogenous. Enforcement failures fail to control, but this means only that offending is not reduced, or is reduced only somewhat, from otherwise natural levels. We do not much entertain the idea that enforcement efforts can be *additive,* or criminogenic. This is inaccurate; they can be. There are a number of important ways in which official behavior can encourage offending and, in particular, can undercut deterrence.

Inaccurate and misleading signals

Offenders are routinely exposed to misleading "signals," both explicit and implicit, from authorities about how offending will be handled. This is true of both statutory steps, such as three-strikes laws—if such steps are presented as promises to offenders that they will be treated in specific ways, as they usually are presented, those promises are often, arguably usually, broken—and of discretionary enforcement policies such as "zero tolerance" strategies or the federal firearms prosecution programs: simple and direct promises which are not, in practice, carried out. Zimring, Hawkins, and Kamin, for example, looked at California's much-touted three-strikes law and found that it had little actual impact on the odds of imprisonment for eligible defendants.[2]

If, in Zimring and Hawkins' phrase, such promises are "advertising," it seems likely that they would be found improper under established regulatory criteria for commercial advertising: that there is "a representation, omission or practice that is likely to mislead."[3] The US Department of Transportation's "You Drink and Drive, You Lose" program,[4] for example, features television spots of drivers pulled over, breath-tested, and arrested, along with an ominous voiceover saying, "No matter where you drive, if you drive impaired, you *will* be arrested." This is, of course, not true. The National Commission Against Drunk Driving estimates that the arrest rate for drunk driving is one in 2,000 incidents, and that 80 percent of chronic drinking drivers continue to drive even after having their licenses suspended, with a low probability of being caught doing so.[5] A pamphlet issued by the District of Columbia's Metropolitan Police Department as part of the national "Click It or Ticket" campaign says that the police will have "NO EXCUSES—ZERO TOLERANCE" for not wearing seatbelts; drivers are told bluntly that "YOU WILL BE PULLED OVER" if out of compliance.[6] This is, of course, also not true, or anything close to true.

As with many other false promises by authorities, the hollowness of such threats is evident to most people with ordinary social experience and is particularly well understood by those with experience of offending and likely to offend again. The same can be true of very serious threats to very serious offenders.

Project Exile, Richmond, Virginia's very well known and frequently replicated attempt to deter gun homicide by promising federal prosecution for gun-carrying and use, provides a case in point. Federal law provides for a five-year mandatory minimum sentence for those convicted of illegal possession of a firearm if they have a previous felony conviction (requisite additional predicate felonies can bring fifteen years; threatening the use of or actually using the gun, or the presence of drugs, can also increase sentences). This law, too, is relatively rarely applied: Federal prosecutors have usually not so charged many or most felons open to it, leaving those cases to local prosecutors and usually substantially lower penalties.

In the mid-1990s, at a time when Richmond was one of the most violent cities in the country, Project Exile sought to use these federal laws much more fully and, in a very rare example of strategic communication aimed at serious crime, to promote deterrence by informing offenders about what was going on. Police officers passed out business-size cards on the street with the stark warning that "an illegal gun will get you five years in federal prison." Billboards and placards on city buses drove home the same message. The Martin Agency, a Richmond advertising firm, developed television spots with grainy footage of ominous prison cells and slamming doors. Richmond Police Chief Jerry Oliver explained that "It was niche marketing to the bad guys [...] They all know the name Exile. We hit on a label that explains what it does, which is get them out of the community."[7] Federal law enforcement told Congress the same thing; Andy Vita, the Assistant Director for field programs for the Bureau of Alcohol, Tobacco, and Firearms, testified before the Senate Judiciary Subcommittees on Youth Violence and Criminal Justice Oversight that

> It was a simple premise: "Anyone caught with an illegal gun in Richmond will go to Federal prison for the minimum mandatory sentence of 5 years. Period. This criminal forfeits the right to remain in the community and is 'exiled' for 5 years. Using existing Federal law, prosecute all felons-with-guns, guns-used-in-drug-trafficking, and gun/domestic violence cases in Federal court."[8]

The problem was that it wasn't true, or even close to it. It could not have been true, no matter how hard federal prosecutors had tried. Not all those who carry guns illegally have prior felonies; they are simply not covered under the federal statute. But beyond that, in practice no federal prosecutor takes all the cases that he could take. Some cases look weak on evidentiary grounds. Office guidelines lead prosecutors to reject some cases because they don't seem serious enough; because the gun carrier is open to more serious penalties on other charges—there's little point in making a five-year gun prosecution when the defendant is facing thirty-five years on a narcotics-trafficking charge; because it's easier to do something else, like let the defendant's parole officer violate him, because of the gun, and send him back to prison to finish out a prior sentence (which might in fact be longer than a new gun sentence); or because given the facts of the case the defendant faces more time on a state charge. Both internal and external pressures can inhibit prosecutions: Most US attorney's offices have relatively small staffs of lawyers who are used to working relatively high-status, long, complicated cases, not plowing through vast numbers of street-level cases, and to exercising a great deal of discretion over the cases they take. The judges they appear before are used to much the same thing; neither line prosecutors nor federal judges necessarily like the shift, and in Exile both pushed back against the new policy. Defendants suddenly facing large sentences, perhaps to be served in far-away federal prisons in New York or Utah, demand trials rather than accepting plea bargains, slowing the process and creating more pressure to somehow divert cases.

Project Exile was announced early in 1997. In the year between August 1, 1997 and July 31, 1998 the Richmond Police Department submitted 1,114 crime guns associated with named offenders to the Bureau of Alcohol, Tobacco, and Firearms for tracing. Those guns are a not-unreasonable, and almost certainly low, proxy for gun-possession offenses in Richmond.[9] By way of comparison, at around that time Project Exile could claim on the order of 140 federal gun convictions a year.[10] This is not an exact calculation, but we are clearly talking a small fraction of possible cases—under 20 percent, probably under 15 percent, very likely less than that.

When authorities in Richmond and in Washington promised the community and the streets that they would put all gun offenders in federal prison, they lied. This is routine with such programs. At the same that the state of Maryland, building on Richmond's Exile, was launching a state-wide version with advertising saying "Get caught with a gun, say goodbye for five years," US Attorney Rod J. Rosenstein was reporting that "the vast majority" of cases would remain in Maryland state courts.[11] This is invariably true when authorities declare "zero tolerance" or promise severe sanctions for something: gun crime, drug crime, gang crime, accounting fraud. I have come to think of these declarations as "aspirational": Authorities want it to be so; they think it should be so, they want offenders to think it will be so and to act accordingly. But what they are promising is not and cannot be true.

In a very rare piece of research on the reaction of serious offenders to false promises, John Klofas interviewed inmates in Rochester, New York about Rochester's "Exile" program, which also made such promises and also had had no apparent effect on homicide and shootings. He found that inmates knew the program well and understood the link between gun-carrying and high federal sentences, which they thought severe. Further, about 20 percent actually knew someone who had been prosecuted under the program. At the same time, many knew of people who had been caught with guns and had *not* been so prosecuted, therefore thought the program arbitrary and the penalties uncertain, and therefore did not think the program served as a deterrent. They were inclined to think of actual prosecutions not as the playing out of statutory and institutional factors but as the result of authorities' personal bias and racism, which made them angry.[12] Here the law was arguably stiff, policy steps had been taken to increase its application, those steps had—unusually—been communicated to offenders, the program had in fact been implemented, and, still, apparently, little deterrence was created, and may have been actively undercut.

The same is true of the more implicit messages embedded in routine enforcement practices. This is a different matter than the objective, and very often low, probability of sanction for a given offense. This is a matter of the *credibility* of the authorities. It is the regular experience of many offenders that consequences are promised, explicitly or implicitly, and not delivered; this is often the case, as has been noted, even after detection, after arrest, and after sentencing to probation or release to parole. That damaged credibility may not alter the actual exposure offenders face; it may well, however, alter how they *perceive* that exposure, and how they *interpret*, in that light, the intentions of authorities and actual enforcement. It may lead them to underestimate, on the basis of concrete experience, their future risk of sanction.

Offenders, writes Matza—speaking of juvenile delinquents and jail, but in a statement more broadly applicable—"typically learn that there is a large quota of chances—each solemnly described as the final one—before the weighty sanction of incarceration is forthcoming."[13] As one offender in Jacob's ethnographic study of street drug-dealing in St. Louis told him about selling marijuana, "They [police] catch you with a gang of dope [crack], they send you up to penitentiary. They catch you with blunts [marijuana], they say, 'Don't let me catch you with no more of this.' Then they let you go."[14] The dealer did not draw from these experiences the lesson that he had really better not sell marijuana; he drew from them the lesson that "Weed ain't that illegal like dope is."[15]

Mention was made earlier of a study of serious gun offenders, sentenced to a federal minimum mandatory sentence of fifteen years, which showed that many did not believe, *even after being convicted and incarcerated*, that they would serve out their terms.[16] The statute can only be employed if the accused has a criminal record that includes three serious prior felonies; in practice, such offenders tend to have extremely extensive records and to have had a great deal of contact with police, prosecutors, judges, and probation and parole. One possible explanation of their disbelief lies here: that their long, concrete experience with authorities had shown them so consistently that official representations were false that the current one, too, was presumed to be hollow.

And it may lead offenders to frame actual sanction, when it comes, as unfair or biased, as we saw with offenders' views of federal gun prosecutions in Rochester. It is conceivable, in that case, that an actual *increase* in sanction risk for firearms offenses, because its application was seen by offenders as contrary to official representations and, beyond that, unfair, led to lower credibility for authorities and therefore to *lower* levels of deterrence. "Publicity without substance," as Zimring and Hawkins put it, "may decrease the credibility of legal threats in general among some potential criminals."[17]

Randomness, permission, and corruption

It is an objective fact that the likelihood of sanction for many offenses is quite low. How that fact is interpreted by offenders is an important matter. A low likelihood can, for a variety of reasons, still generate deterrence, even considerable deterrence. But there are a number of ways that any such impact can be blunted, and even reversed.

One is that sanctions are robbed of their meaning because they seen as *random*. If an event is not only low probability but also unpredictable, it may not seem that there is any way to avoid it, and no connection between action and reaction: We worry about being struck by lightning in the rain, and take steps to prevent it, but if lightning strikes were as common in clear weather, what would we do to avoid them? Studies of speeding show just this dynamic: The offense is so common and sanction so unpredictable that enforcement has little meaning.[18] This may also happen with more serious offenses, as with street drug dealing, which is frequently flagrant, known to authorities, and still subject to relatively little enforcement. Where it does, it may undercut any deterrent effect from the actual sanction risk.

Worse is that real enforcement patterns are seen as indicating *permission* to offend. Offenders routinely experience situations in which authorities know of their crimes and do not act. Police officers drive by drug dealers; men who hit their wives and girlfriends are visited by police but not arrested; probationers and parolees flagrantly violate the conditions of their supervision and find no action is taken. If arrests are made, prosecutions are often not made, and so on. It is but a short step to a conclusion that such offending is being tolerated. That step is often taken. Elijah Anderson, for example, in his ethnographic study of inner-city Philadelphia, notes that police regularly ignore flagrant street drug-dealing—a situation repeated in many other cities—and interprets it as official tolerance.[19] In, again, Rochester, where police attention to crack houses is very high, without much reducing the problem, Klofas found that incarcerated drug dealers "believed that drug houses only stay open as long as the police allow them to."[20] The movement toward mandatory arrest for domestic violence was fueled by concern that offenders, victims, and witnesses such as young children were learning from police inaction that domestic violence was not a real crime and a desire to create an unequivocal statement by authorities that it was.[21] On a lesser level, this is of course the routine experience of most drivers: When a patrol car travels with ordinary traffic down the highway at 15 miles per hour over the limit, the conclusion is drawn, almost always correctly, that the offenses being committed are really acceptable.

This perception, whether accurate or not, can be very meaningful. The "signal" that offending is tolerated by authorities is powerful. Cook and Goss report on experimental evidence on the point:

> Sigelman and Sigelman [...] watched more than 700 drivers in Lubbock, Texas to see if illegal right turns on red were contagious. Some of the time, they stationed a man in an Air Force ROTC uniform at the street corner to represent an "authority figure." Curiously, they found that illegal turns were not contagious (to a statistically significant extent) when there was no authority figure present. But when he was at the intersection, a follower was significantly more likely to "catch" the preceding car's law-breaking behavior. This finding was counterintuitive. The authors hypothesize that the authority figure, in ignoring the car's illegal turn, "endowed such acts with legitimacy" in the eyes of the follower.[22]

And where such perceptions are at work, actual enforcement action will be seen as unlikely; where they occur, they are more likely to be seen as unpredictable, random, and—as violations of a tacit understanding—illegitimate and unfair.

Worse yet is that real enforcement patterns are seen as indicating *official corruption*. Again, offenders—and others—routinely experience situations in which authorities know of their crimes and do not act, or at any rate do not act effectively. It is but another short step to a conclusion that such inaction is being, somehow, purchased. (This was in fact the first academic response to the discovery, through the American Bar Foundation's "law in practice" research of the 1950s, of such things as the exercise of prosecutorial discretion through plea bargaining: Only malfeasance, it was thought, could explain the departure from idealized adversarial practice.) This conclusion is very common around persistent, visible urban crime such as drug-dealing, street gun violence, and the like. It is routine to hear, in such communities, the obvious fact of official incapacity in the face of such offending explained in terms of corruption. Similar thoughts, frequently expressed, are that "there are no coca fields" and "there are no gun factories" in such communities, that the police could stop the flow of drugs and guns if they chose, and that their failure to do so in only explicable through corruption.[23] The author, in his fieldwork, has heard these thoughts expressed in essentially identical terms by young drug dealers and elected officials.

Here the undercutting of the normative sanction structure is complete. The law becomes viewed as an opportunity for profiteering, and often as one deliberately constructed for that purpose. Enforcement actions are seen as illegitimate, coercive measures to control markets or exact tribute. Failure to take enforcement action, or to take enforcement action that actually addresses the underlying problems, is further evidence of corruption. Both particular enforcement regimes and the standing of authorities are damaged.

Scholars in a variety of settings have consistently found that perceptions of fairness on the part of those subject to rules and enforcement action are central to their willingness to accept authority. "Research has found that people obey the law not just because they are afraid of being punished or because they believe the law is morally right, but also because they believe the law and its enforcement is impartial and being fairly administered."[24] Those who feel that they are being treated equally to other individuals and groups, and that their own contacts with authorities are handled reasonably, are more likely to see rules and sanctions as legitimate, even when they disagree with the outcome, and to comply, both immediately and over time. A seminal assessment of these dynamics was that "there is a demand that the rules be legitimate, not only in emanating from established authority, but also in the manner of their formulation, in the way they are applied, and in their fidelity to agreed-upon institutional purposes."[25] For deterrence to be as effective as it can be, offenders should believe that the rules to which they are subject flow from rightful sources, are imposed on them in fair and respectful interactions, and serve purposes widely viewed as moral and correct. They very often do not believe these things.

Stigma and damage to personal capital

In deterrence terms, and more broadly in law enforcement and many policy conversations, arrest and any subsequent sanction are often taken as unalloyed goods: They are held to have some deterrent effects; they demonstrate the capacity and seriousness of the authorities; they underscore the social stands embodied in the law; and the like. On this account, there is only gain. This is clearly not true. Arrest and other enforcement action can do severe damage to an individual's personal capital. To the extent that personal capital and its loss is a factor in subsequent offending behavior, that damage can promote offending and undercut deterrence.

This is most clearly understood with respect to impact on employment and earnings. Grogger showed that arrest has negative impact on future employment and can explain a good deal of the difference in persistent joblessness between blacks and whites.[26] Waldfogel found large effects from conviction on subsequent employment and income, with the largest effects for those with better education and more responsible jobs.[27] Nagin and Waldfogel found effects from conviction, but not from self-reported criminality, suggesting that it was the effect of the enforcement action that mattered (perversely, the wages of convicted youth go up for a time relative to their unconvicted peers, as they take relatively well-paying but unskilled and dead-end entry-level jobs; this can mean that both for these offenders and their peers, the first signal around the cost of sanction can be positive).[28] Freeman found "massive long-term effects on employment" from jail and probation, but lesser effects for being stopped by police, being charged with a crime, and being convicted without jail or probation.[29]

Other impacts are less direct and less well understood, but still plausibly quite meaningful. Nagin and Waldfogel found dramatic impacts of conviction on college and plans to go to college.[30] Enforcement action against school-age offenders can interrupt their educations and make finishing school more unlikely.[31] Wilson has identified criminal records and their impact on employment prospects as a factor in making young men less "marriageable," a fact implicated in a variety of urban social ills.[32] Incarcerating parents damages families in a variety of ways, including lowering parental control over youth and increasing the draw of making money illicitly.[33]

The primary implication of all these effects is clear: Whatever the appeal of future crime, and whatever the deterrent impact of future official action, the former will go up and the latter will go down as work becomes less remunerative, individuals have less reason to invest in personal capital, and ties to conventional others weaken. The impact of present enforcement may well be to reduce permanently the deterrent value of subsequent sanction risks.

Community-level damage to social capital

These individual-level effects can also have broader implications at group and community levels. Clear *et al.* found in a study of Tallahassee, Florida counties that once levels of incarceration passed beyond a certain point, approximately 1.5 percent of the population, additional incarceration led to more, not less, crime. Their explanation was that the "coercive mobility" of incarceration burdened and destabilized families and neighborhoods and increased social disorganization, just as other mechanisms of high mobility have long been known to do.[34]

> Qualitative research in similar neighborhoods showed that while residents reported positive outcomes from the incarceration of neighborhood offenders, they were generally more focused on problems caused by incarceration: For instance, family members had to support the additional financial burden of paying for phone calls from inmates, traveling to visit them, and financially supporting them on their return to the community. Residents suffered from other effects, such as problems associated with the stigma of incarceration in the family and the neighborhood, in addition to problems with self-esteem and attenuated social relationships. Many residents reported withdrawing from community life in the aftermath of a family member's incarceration. Thus, it seems likely that high incarceration rates concentrated in certain communities could increase social disorganization by depleting the already limited resources of community members and by damaging the social networks that serve as the basis for social capital and ultimately provide private and parochial social control.[35]

Precipitating offending

Enforcement action can spark offending in quite direct and immediate ways. Normative aspects of the idea of "cause" confuse here; to the extent that "cause" carries the freight of moral or legal culpability, we hesitate to say that enforcement "causes" crime. Still, if taken as simply descriptive, the basic dynamic is often quite clear. Street enforcement pressure can disrupt stable local arrangements; Simon and Burns describe the effect of a street crackdown on drug markets in Baltimore:

> [P]ressed by the police, the sprawl of the neighborhood drug bazaar is quickly compressed, so that more and more players—touts, slingers, stickup boys, burn artists—are hustling in a smaller place. There is a crossing of the corners' electrical currents: Dealers are more volatile than usual, the fiends more desperate and nervous. Violence picks up.[36]

Removing leaders in criminal groups, a routine objective in law enforcement, can create chaos as discipline in the group is eliminated and remaining players jockey for position. Eliminating a strong criminal group can cause group-on-group competition for its trade and turf. Groups weakened but not eliminated can become prey for competition or old antagonists. Police officers involved in a gang suppression operation in Boston, which resulted in the gang literally being disarmed, report gang members imploring them not to leave the area for fear of still-dangerous rivals.[37] These phenomena have apparently received little formal study; it is telling that they are taken for granted—though usually discussed privately—amongst working law enforcement.

The erosion of stigma

Where enforcement efforts are simultaneously intensive and ineffective, sanctions can reach a level of social density such that their meaning is vitiated and even inverted. "If crime is stigmatizing, then as the number of criminals rises, the average criminal becomes a 'normal' member of society," write Glaeser *et al.*[38] When arrest, conviction, probation, and incarceration become normal, they become, at least to some extent, drained of their power to stigmatize. They may become normative, taking on the status of a "rite of passage" or a marker of toughness and accomplishment. In such a situation, the deterrence value of formal sanctions—the direct cost to offenders of official action such as arrest and incarceration—will be reduced, and the impact of many informal sanctions—guilt, shame, the disapproval of friends and family, and the like—will be reduced and may transmute to pride, approval, status enhancements, and encouragement to offend. As a boy told Ricardo of urban drug-dealing, "Even though it might be illegal in the government, it's not illegal on the street."[39] Stanton and Galbraith found that young drug dealers in Baltimore tended to see themselves as likely to be arrested, to not see arrest as a serious outcome, and to believe that "kids respect a guy who has been picked up by police."[40] Anderson, in his work in Philadelphia, found that "the word 'incarcerated' is a prominent part of the young child's spoken vocabulary. In such communities there is not only a high rate of crime but also a generalized diminution of respect for law."[41]

Trappings of the drug trade such as beepers, used to make connections with buyers, became status symbols.[42] "Straight" youths and those who sought to do well in school were abused by their peers.[43] Drug dealers importuned "decent" kids to join them.[44] Nonoffenders took on the trappings of offenders, further undermining prosocial norms:

> Yet many ghetto males are caught in a bind because they are espousing their particular ways of dressing and acting simply to be self-respecting among their neighborhood peers. A boy may be completely decent, but to the extent that he takes on the *presentation* of "badness" to enhance his local public image, even as a form of self-defense, he further alienates himself in the eyes of the wider society.[45]

Xiaoming and Feigelman found, in a survey of African-American adolescents, that 57 percent of boys involved in drug-dealing reported that "kids respect guys picked up by police."[46]

Not all of this is attributable to the failure of enforcement strategies. To the extent, however, that enforcement strategies simultaneously fail to control crime and contribute to the perception of criminal sanctions as normative—a far from unusual situation—deterrence will be undermined.

A further development along this chain is a social and political critique that casts authorities in the role of systematic oppressors, enforcement actions as acts of oppression, and those subject to such actions as oppressed. Linking criminal justice strategies to the history of slavery and institutionalized racism in America, Wacquant argues that

> we first need to break out of the narrow "crime and punishment" paradigm and examine the broader role of the penal system as an instrument for *managing dispossessed and dishonored* groups. And second, we need to take a longer historical view on the shifting forms of ethno-racial domination in the United States. This double move suggests that the astounding upsurge in black incarceration in the past three decades results from the obsolescence of the ghetto as a device for caste control and the correlative need for a substitute apparatus for keeping (unskilled) African-Americans in a subordinate position—physically, socially, and symbolically.[47]

On these views, enforcement actions directed toward minorities, especially in troubled urban communities, are of a piece with other historical and current official actions in the service of or reflective of racism, such as slavecatching, police strategies to restrict vice to minority neighborhoods, police strategies to keep minorities geographically contained, Jim Crow legislation, official actions to support and perpetuate civil-rights abuses, police participation in lynchings, racial profiling, and the like.[48] Evidence of criminality in majority society—always ample—is seen as underscoring a simple but profound racial power imbalance expressed in part through criminal justice institutions. Poor male African-Americans interviewed by Whitehead, Peterson, and Kaljee

> believed that white men "rip people off" and engage in both legal and illegal hustling for much more money than do African-Americans; but, whereas African-American men are likely to be jailed for hustling, white men are rewarded, even for illegal hustling. These sentiments may be best summarized by the following comments: [...] "Those hustling on Wall Street and Capitol Hill...we are no different from the Boeskys, the Oliver Norths, the George Bushes [...] they all hustle."[49]

An arrest thus become an act of political oppression, a sentence creates a political prisoner, and committing a crime can be viewed as something close to, or in fact, an act of political resistance.[50] One black prisoner, the Infamous Pistol Pete, writing from the federal prison in Otisville, New York referred to himself and his fellow inmates as "we the few honorable men" and "real soldier[s] wounded behind enemy lines."[51] Stigma is reduced, neutralized, or converted to standing. So advanced is this process in some urban minority circles that there are now several glossy mass-circulation magazines devoted to "thug life." One, *F.E.D.S.*—for Finally Every Dimension of the Street—bills itself as covering "Convicted Criminals, Street Thugs, Music, Fashion, Film, Etc";[52] it features articles on gangs and rap artists (with a heavy influence on their histories of street crime) and offers a legal-advice column.

One way of framing these processes is that what are usually viewed as "unconventional" attachments become conventional, and vice versa, with many of the complicated dynamics that produce social control in conventional circles operating in similar ways to support deviance and undercut conventionality. The idea of "social disorganization" as productive of offending is often fundamentally misleading, as many sociologists have commented; frequently, offenders and communities with high rates of offending in fact have their own distinctive, if oppositional, forms of social organization.[53] In a graphic example of this process, the Infamous Pistol Pete, in his communication from Otisville, urged women in the community not to sleep with "the heartless and soulless" men who cooperate with law enforcement; "all this jail shit," he wrote, "is going to show our kids and the rest of our loved ones that loyalty and honor is to be applied in their lives, whether they are free today or locked down tomorrow."[54]

Self-control and backlash

The exercise of authority can weaken internal control; when the exercise of authority and the application of sanction are seen as unfair or disproportionate, it can provoke active resistance. There is much psychological evidence that where internal constraints are, or might be, sufficient to prevent certain actions, the presence or exercise of sanctions or sanction threats undercut those constraints (a phenomenon closely connected to that of "overcompensation," in which rewarding behavior that was initially self-motivated serves to weaken those motivations).[55] Further along this spectrum, offending can be *provoked* by the perception of the unfair prospect or exercise of sanction. Makkai and Braithwaite found, apparently paradoxically, that for some corporate managers, stronger sanctions produced *lower* levels of compliance. Their fieldwork suggested that "highly emotional managers tend to be insulted by deterrence threats," interpreting them as signs of procedural injustice and lack of trust.[56] Their humiliation is "transform[ed] into anger and defiance."[57] Another result can be various forms of disengagement, expressive less of anger than of demoralization and withdrawal; noncompliance is then to be seen less as "a rational playing of the regulatory game as dropping out of the game."[58] The comment of one such manager—"When they keep on treating you as unprofessional, untrust-worthy, you end up deciding if they want to treat me like a businessman who only cares about the bottom line, then I'll be a businessman"[59]—is strikingly similar to that of a gang member whose attempt to leave went unac-knowledged by authorities and who subsequently told Skolnick *et al.*, "If I'm going to be identified as a gang member anyway, I might as well really be one."[60] These phenomena are closely related to what psychologists call "reciprocity motives," in which actions costly to the actor are motivated by negative feelings toward another party. Examples are common; typical ones include consumers who refuse to buy goods from companies they dislike, even though other products cost more; industrial sabotage; and punitive strikes by union members.[61]

These dynamics can undercut the most basic workings of criminal justice and deterrence processes. Norms against relying on or cooperating with police—to "stop snitching"—have become so deeply embedded in some black American communities, along with closely related phenomena such as witness intimidation, that it has become extremely difficult to investigate and prosecute even very serious crimes. Those involved, as both victims and wit-nesses, refuse to report crimes, cooperate with investigators, or give testi-mony at trial. In Baltimore, prosecutors arrest witnesses to homicides and nonfatal shootings in order to make them appear at trial.[62] In some high-crime cities in New Jersey, authorities are deliberately withdrawing from prosecutable homicide cases for fear of retaliation against witnesses, settling instead for lesser charges, provable without witness testimony, involving guns or drugs; the Governor of New Jersey has instructed police and prosecutors to avoid involving witnesses in cases against gang members.[63] These are not steps calculated to enhance deterrence.

Crime as social control

Where authorities are not viewed with confidence, are not seen as legitimate, or are not regarded as effective, people will to some extent take matters into their own hands. Some of this is legal and legitimate; people can move, invest in "target hardening" and alarm technology, and buy and carry weapons legally. Some of it is not and itself constitutes criminal offending. As Black points out, "This is especially clear in the case of violent modes of redress such as assassination, feuding, fighting, maiming, and beating, but also applies to the confiscation and destruction of property and to other forms of deprivation and humiliation."[64]

Both violence and property crime are in fact common in this context. A father whose son was killed on the streets of Philadelphia seeks out the per-petrators with a gun; he fails to find them before he calms down, but friends of his son do find them, and people are shot.[65] A rape victim robs the drug dealer who attacked her.[66] A man sold bad dope robs the dealer who burned him.[67] A carpenter refused payment by a landlord robs him at gunpoint.[68] Such exchanges can become iterative dynamics, as in the gang-on-gang or group-on-group "beefs" that currently characterize much urban violence. In many such beefs, the "launching" incident becomes immaterial and even forgotten; what is important is each side's felt necessity to avenge or equal a prior incident, exact payment, or establish dominance.

Some of this is a product of the inability of offenders to seek recourse for harms that arise out of prior illegal activity, such as debts and thefts connected with drug activity, vice, and the like, which are not legally actionable.[69] In Klofas's focus groups with offenders in Rochester, fourteen of twenty-one males and three of eleven women had been robbed of money or drugs; none had reported the robberies to police.[70] Some of it is a product of the unwillingness of offenders to seek official help with what would in fact be actionable offenses, such as a gun assault committed in the course of a drug transaction. Some of it is the product of official inaction or incapacity, even when their help is sought; the Philadelphia father whose son was killed, for example, knew who had done it, but authorities either could not or did not make the case. "The judicial system—they do not represent us," he said.[71] Jacobs found that "even murdered [drug] vendors are unlikely to elicit a vigorous response [from police]; 'dirtbags' and 'shitbums' deserve whatever fate befalls them."[72] Inside the Los Angeles Police Department, such crimes are (or at any rate were) sometimes informally tagged as "NHI": No Humans Involved.[73]

Victims can also find themselves occupying such positions of more-or-less official disregard by dint of race, ethnicity, class, or status. Black notes that "lower-status people of all kinds" have traditionally been accorded less protection by authorities; "the problems of these people seem less serious, their injuries less severe, their honor less important."[74] In one study of women who had killed abusive mates, all reported calling for police help at least five times before the homicide.[75] A significant amount of crime as social control, then, arises from gaps in, and the ineffectiveness of, official crime-control strategies.

It is possible to view much of what goes on in high-crime urban communities through this lens. Anderson identifies the most salient aspect of these neighborhoods as a "code of the streets":

> The code of the streets is actually a cultural adaptation to a profound lack of faith in the police and the judicial system—and in others who would champion one's personal security. The police, for instance, are often viewed as representing the dominant white society and as not caring to protect inner-city residents. When called, they may not respond, which is one reason many residents feel they must be prepared to take extraordinary measures to defend themselves and their loved ones against those who are inclined to aggression. Lack of police accountability has in fact been incorporated into the local status system:

the person who is believed capable of "taking care of himself" is accorded a certain deference and regard, which translates into a sense of physical and psychological control. The code of the streets thus emerges where the influence of the police ends and where personal responsibility for one's safety is felt to begin.[76]

The more normative crime as social control becomes, the less standing adheres to official strategies and to authorities. In "code of the streets" communities, the reversal has reached a point that standing now attaches to crime as social control—as embedded in the code and its manifestations, such as conventions around "respect"—and those who practice it, and stigma has become attached to the police and other authorities, and to those who would mobilize or cooperate with them.

"Nested" offending and criminogenic dynamics

Criminal offending, uncontrolled, often creates conditions facilitating further criminal offending. Here, again, the various connotations that attach to concepts of causation make us reluctant to say that the failure of official crime-control strategies "cause" these further crimes. But, and also again, it is frequently the fact that if the initial problem had been addressed, the subsequent problem would have been avoided.

Some of these dynamics are simple and straightforward. If loan sharking were prevented, there would be no predicate for assaults on defaulters. If prostitution were prevented, there would be no rapes of prostitutes or badger games played on johns. If street drug markets and crack houses were prevented, there would be less opportunity to rob drug dealers. If drunk-driving were prevented, there would be fewer hit-and-run accidents. Such "nested" offending, which operates along basic victim/offender/opportunity dimensions, is very common.

Some such dynamics are far deeper and more complicated, and can be very significant. Here, while victim/offender/opportunity dimensions may also operate, more intricate and often iterative influences are also at work. It is a feature of such dynamics that what is "cause" and what is "effect" become very difficult to characterize. Zuckerman, for example, describes some of what happens when mothers are drug addicts:

> Other problems associated with heavy use of drugs or addiction, such as depression or violence, also impair parenting ability and adversely affect children. Depression may precede or be a consequence of drug use. Depression itself, without drug use, has been shown to adversely affect parenting and to result in negative consequences for children. Drug and alcohol use increase the likelihood that a woman will be a victim of violence. Additionally, children of drug users are more likely to witness violence in their homes and to be victims of violence. Concern is

mounting that this exposure to violence has serious and long-term implications for children's development, including an inability to pay attention and function in school, impaired emotional stability, and a disoriented perception of the future.[77]

Here, drug use becomes drug addiction; drug addiction causes personality changes in the mother; the mother's behavior increases her likelihood of being a victim of violence and perpetrating violence on her children; the personality changes and the violence harm the children; a chaotic home exposes the children to further harms, including additional violence; all these harms damage the children's life prospects. At all of these points, criminal justice interventions, including deterrence regimes, are possible and are in fact essayed; their failure, therefore, is implicated in what actually happens. We can easily imagine other factors also at work: the introduction of the children to antisocial and dangerous men; eased entry for the children into offending circles; the communication of antisocial norms; the mother's difficulty in pursuing legitimate work, and the additional burden of financial deprivation; the stress of difficult children on the mother, should she try to clean up; the establishment of negative views toward the police and other authorities through repeated, unhelpful, and unsatisfactory encounters; and so forth.

One important feature of such dynamics is that they can be viewed as an *interplay between authorities and offenders* in which the actions of each affect the environment, incentives, and behavior of the other. Neither offending nor enforcement seems wholly independent: There is, rather, an intricate dance being conducted. If the authorities were more effective and controlling drug markets, the mother would be less likely to become a drug addict. If there were fewer drug addicts, the markets would be easier to control. If authorities pursued less profligate and more effective enforcement strategies, their standing in the community would improve and neighbors would be more likely to call when the children were being abused. A better-behaved mother and less traumatized children ease the struggle with addiction. Less active drug markets would mean fewer chronic offending men for the mother to associate with. Better men, or fewer bad men, in the house would mean better examples, or less harm, to the children. More children exposed to less harm in the community means better-functioning schools. Children doing better in school, with real prospects for a successful future, mean less work for the police. Less work for the police means better productivity on remaining problems. And so on.

The interplay of crime and enforcement

The underlying point we see in all these categories is that, in deeply meaningful ways, and in contrast to the way in which we usually think about deterrence and other enforcement strategies, these are *not* static equations:

authorities do *not* simply take offenders pretty much as they find them. The roots of offending are often correctly located in the character of offenders and in social and community conditions, but the character of offenders and social and community conditions *are themselves shaped* in powerful ways by the actions—both successful and unsuccessful—of authorities.

This is perhaps nowhere more powerfully demonstrated than in the example of the crack epidemic. Crack had an almost unimaginably destructive impact on inner-city communities. Jacob writes:

> In St. Louis and other metropolitan areas, urban drug markets came to be controlled by self-employed, freelance sellers—some gang affiliated, others not. Intense competition and turf wars soon defined the scene as the urban drug landscape experienced rapid deregulation and destabilization. Epidemic levels of homicides and assaults resulted, not surprisingly given the drug's pharmacology, fights over territorial boundaries, and sellers bent on propagating a fearsome "don't mess with me" reputation. Community institutions were woefully unprepared for the crisis. Social controls, both formal and informal, broke down. Coupled with a high level of residential mobility and loss of economic opportunity, the wholesale destruction of communities and individuals took on a life of its own. Once peaceful neighborhoods were transformed into urban badlands that persons traversed at their own peril.[78]

And so it was; this is the familiar story of "what crack caused." But it also possible to tell the story in terms of the *interplay* between the drug epidemic and particular enforcement approaches. Police failed to control the street markets that were a signature of the epidemic—despite isolated demonstrations that controlling them was possible—which led to the formation of youthful "crews" that battled for turf and became enmeshed in standing violent vendettas. Losing control of the streets drove out businesses and many residents; with them went much local social capital and informal social control. The loss of economic opportunity and what Anderson describes as "decent" culture made the drug business more attractive and less stigmatized, and promoted the emergence of a "respect" culture as traditional markers of maturation and accomplishment became unavailable. The wholesale arrests practiced by police did little to reduce trafficking but tagged vast numbers of young men with criminal records, alienating them and their families and peers and lowering their utility in making ordinary investments in school and entry-level legitimate work. The volume of enforcement swamped prosecutors, undercutting sanctions and communicating to offenders that authorities were not serious. Indiscriminate street stops in the name of drug enforcement fueled the perception and reality of racial profiling. Widespread and meaningless probation regimes fed disrespect for the authorities and failed to curb drug use by supervisees, one of the few real demand-side opportunities in drug enforcement.[79] Addiction, unaddressed, tore families apart. The dangerousness of the streets and the lack of effectiveness of police fed "the code of the streets," which in turn cut off the citizen–police contacts crucial to solving violent crimes, prosecuting murderers, and the like, and promoted the use of private violence as social control. High levels of violence and recidivism among young black men fed majority concern about "superpredators" and statutory action to enhance drug penalties, leading to, among other things, the notorious powder cocaine/crack sentencing disparities, seen in the affected communities as further evidence of racist intent. The opportunities provided by drug markets created new classes of armed robbers preying on street dealers and drug houses; largely unaddressed by authorities, they promoted defensive gun acquisition and use and fueled the code of the streets. Some police officers—frustrated, enticed, or both—chose perjury, brutality, and corruption, confirming residents' worst suspicions and tarring their legitimate peers. Desperate attempts by authorities to stem the violence, such as the "stop and frisk" strategies employed in many cities, alienated both the offenders and nonoffenders who were swept up in them; unconstitutional and ultimately unsustainable, they were often publicly condemned and abandoned. Communities deeply disenchanted with the authorities saw acts and failures to act alike as evidence of malevolence; many in majority circles, at the same time, saw the offending and deviant culture through racist lenses.

Violence and death became so commonplace in some offending circles that young male offenders, especially, felt that they were at very high risk and unlikely to live very long. There is every reason to believe that this belief drove antisocial behavior like fathering children out of wedlock, taking pains to establish a violent reputation, joining gangs for self-protection, and gun carrying, and undercut what would normally be viewed as severe criminal sanctions: Why worry about a three-strikes conviction or a federal penalty for carrying a gun, which might be imposed a few years from now, when one faced objective dangers today and reasonably expected to be dead by then? All these behaviors can be seen as, at least in part, *responses* to the failures of enforcement strategies. They were more often viewed from the outside, however, as indicative of deep failures of community and character, evidence of a "culture of violence" and the emergence of "superpredators."

We see here a blending of what are generally seen as distinct and often competing frameworks in which to locate offending. "Criminal justice" frameworks look at the character and choices of offenders, emphasize individual responsibility and accountability, and look to enforcement regimes to produce, among other things, effective deterrence. "Root causes" frameworks look at social and community conditions, emphasize collective responsibility and accountability, and look to social and cultural regimes to produce, among other things, low rates of offending. It is recognized that social and community conditions affect the character and choices of offenders, and criminal justice is usually seen as *reacting* to those effects. It is also true, however, that criminal justice actions *themselves* affect the character and choices of offenders—that is, criminal justice does not only react to these dimensions—and that crime and criminal justice actions *themselves* affect social and community conditions. Crime is not just a *product of* but also an *input into* "root causes" conditions, and criminal justice does not only *react to* but also helps *produce* social and cultural regimes. The actions authorities take and do not take—arresting a drug dealer, failing to arrest a domestic violence offender—and its successes and failures—clearing a homicide, failing to eliminate street drug markets—can all have complicated effects, both positive and negative—often some of each—for individuals and communities. Realistic assessments of criminal justice strategies must take all these effects, and their subsequent interplay, into account.

7 Reflections II

Amending the deterrence framework

What, then, does all this tell us about how we might address deterrence?

Our previous conclusions are underscored. Deterrence does matter a lot. If deterrence strategies can be made more effective in addressing crime problems that matter to individuals and communities, some of the criminogenic dynamics just sketched might be weakened. The same holds true, of course, for strategies other than deterrence. But deterrence has a special place here because when it is effective, it can operate without other aspects of criminal-justice strategies, such as arrest and conviction, which can themselves be costly both immediately and in the long run. It matters that we understand how offenders think: If the stiffest sanctions we promise are meaningless in practice because previous experience with enforcement has robbed them of all credibility, that is something we had better address. We are right to attend to informal sanctions and, beyond that, to attend to the impact on informal sanctions of formal actions: If our enforcement practices are destroying the prospects that young offenders can ever achieve legitimacy and making the authorities anathema in the eyes of the broader community, that is also something we had better address. We would do well to sort out what seems severe from where offenders stand: If we can reduce gun-carrying among drug dealers as effectively by beefing up probation regimes as by delivering draconian prison sentences, the former would surely be preferable. And the role of information and communication remains central.

In line with this, and in addition, there are ways in which it might make sense to expand the traditional deterrence framework. We might, especially, move from a focus on *individual offenders* to include groups, networks, places, and other collectivities, and move from a focus on *individual offenses* to include the *criminogenic dynamics* that produce patterns of offending and crime problems.

Beyond the individual offender

Deterrence theory is rooted in traditions of moral philosophy and economics that concern themselves primarily with individuals and their decisions. Utilitarianism, from which deterrence theory emerged, addresses the moral obligations and behavior of the individual actor. The branches of economics and the economic theories of utility that have mostly informed modern deterrence theory, also emerged historically, from utilitarianism and have done likewise. Both frequently consider the individual in relation to other individuals and to various groups and collectivities, but their focus remains one of explaining the thinking and the behavior of individuals. Criminal-justice theory and practice is likewise primarily about individuals, their actions, and their legal accountability. Groups and collectivities play a role, for instance in the legal constructions of joint liability, conspiracies, gangs, and the criminal liability of corporations, but criminal justice is overwhelmingly about individuals. A robber prosecuted for the armed invasion of a crack house will be prosecuted as an individual, or with the partners he happened to be with on the occasion and who also happened to be caught. No mention at trial will be made of the fact that he, or they, were part of a larger group specializing in such robberies; those facts will not be affect the disposition of the case; no sanction will accrue to the group as such. Even prior offenses will usually not be admissible at trial. Those investigating and prosecuting the case may understand the larger setting quite well, but their recognition is unlikely to have any legal significance.

Even actions directed at, and because of the actions of, groups may not show any sign of this in formal legal proceedings: Enforcement directed at a drug gang because of persistent violence will present itself—absent the relatively rare steps of a conspiracy prosecution or formal legal gang certification—as a series of unrelated arrests and prosecutions for drug-dealing, gun possession, probation violations, and the like. Police, prosecutors, and probation officers will know of the gang focus; defense lawyers may know, but may have no legal grounds to even raise the issue; judges quite often will not know, since the matter will never be raised formally. Indeed, individual defendants—and other gangs still on the street—may themselves not know what has really happened.

There are good intellectual and legal reasons for this. Once sufficiently steeped in traditional deterrence theory and its practical manifestations, in fact, thinking otherwise can seem incoherent: A gang, after all, does not pull a trigger; a person does. A fraternity does not commit date rape; a person does. The criminal law likewise directs our thinking powerfully toward the individual. We do not, usually, indict the fraternity for the rape a member commits. At the same time, however, this way of thinking is thoroughly out of alignment with many of the ways we think about crime and criminal offending, and many of the ways—particularly some of the newer and more promising ways—in which we have learned to address it. It is also thoroughly out of alignment with the ways in which criminal justice is in fact often practiced. Recognizing this raises interesting possibilities for framing and practicing deterrence.

Sociology and criminology

In particular, perhaps, the focus on individuals and the framing of deterrence around individuals stands in contrast to core sociological and criminological traditions, frameworks, and analyses of crime, offenders, and offending. These ways of thinking are, of course, overwhelmingly about collectivities and processes within collectivities. This point is partly an analytic one, and trivial at that level; sociology and its branch, criminology, are by definition about collectivities, and any substance addressing crime must therefore also be. But there is a good deal more to it than that.

The key points can only be sketched here, as much of both criminology and sociology—and many related disciplines—have bearing. The most important point is actually quite simple: *Collectivities*, not individuals, and processes involving collectivities are at the center of some of the most powerful ways we have to understand and address crime. Crimes, viewed as events, frequently involve groups of some sort: In large settings such as societies, cities, communities, and neighborhoods; as cooffenders in crime incidents; as gangs, drug groups, corporations, and the like with which offenders and victims are involved; as networks of various sorts; in markets, as for drugs, stolen goods, sex, and other commodities and services. The boundaries between such categories, as with the difference between a gang and a drug crew, are unclear and vexing, and overlap between such categories is frequent: An armed robbery by a pair of stick-up boys in a drug house can represent, for example, the victimization through cooffending of members of a drug crew operating in an illicit market. Backing off from such empirical and analytic headaches, however, the main issue is clear: Such collectivities matter a great deal. Nearly as important, and secondary perhaps only as a matter of logical and causal precedence, are *dynamics* within and between such collectivities. We will touch on each in turn.

Collectivities

There are a variety of social, group, and similar settings for crime and criminality. The individual's propensity to offend is often viewed as heavily influenced by society and social setting. Personality itself, Sutherland argued, could be viewed as "the product of group relationships rather than of the presence of specific individual traits and characteristics."[1] Core drivers of offending have been located in the relationship between the individual and others. The theory of "strain," or the failure to achieve conventional goals as a precursor to deviance, rests on the idea of socially defined convention.[2] Such a fundamental criminological idea as that of anomie, as Sampson and Bartusch point out,

> refers to a state of normlessness in which the rules of the dominant society (and hence of the legal system) are no longer binding in a

community or for a population subgroup. Anomie in this sense is conceived as part of a social system and not merely a property of the individual.[3]

Sutherland's idea of "differential association" located offending in the influence of group norms on individuals, arguing that "society has become organized in such a way that a premium has been placed both on refraining from crime and on perpetrating crime," with the result that there are "'rules for crime'" as well as "'rules against crime.'"[4] And so on: Theories about crime are overwhelmingly theories about collectivities and dynamics within those collectivities.

Such dynamics manifest themselves at various levels of collectivity. Culture and subculture inhere to places, and we think about crime as such. We recognize differences amongst nations: America is violent, has a severe drug problem, and features high levels of firearms crime; the Balkans suffer from interethnic strife; Colombia from violence and political corruption connected with narcotics-exporting networks. We recognize similar differences amongst cities: Chicago and LA have problems with gangs, Baltimore with drug crews and a heroin epidemic that has lasted some four decades, Rochester with street drug markets atypical of cities its size. Within those cities, there are neighborhoods that are high- and low-crime; within those neighborhoods, there are "hot spots" of particular crime activity. These are differences that are not entirely, and probably not primarily, about individuals and differences amongst individuals. A Colombian boy transplanted to East Los Angeles is less likely to get involved in narcoterrorism and more likely to get caught up with Crips or Bloods; move him to Beverly Hills, and those dynamics diminish, while those connected with prescription drug abuse and insider trading go up. As we have seen, opportunities vary similarly: There are tough boys in every community, but there are not street drug markets in every community, and so the possibility of becoming a drug robber varies dramatically from place to place.

Groups of various kinds, and group-like associations, figure prominently. Legal entities such as corporations can be held criminally liable.[5] Groups can be constructed legally, as in conspiracy or federal Racketeer Influenced and Corrupt Organizations (RICO) prosecutions. Most attention, however, has been given to what might be considered "found" groups—those that seem to manifest themselves when one looks at offending and how it occurs. As noted, the right categories here, and the boundaries between them, are not always obvious.

The simplest—though still not a simple—collectivity is found in *cooffending*: more than one person committing a crime together at the same time and in the same place. Cooffending is particularly salient where younger offenders are concerned; most juveniles commit their crimes in the company of others (though Reiss points out that this does not mean that an equivalent share of crime *incidents* involve cooffending, as a large proportion of offenders can be involved together in a smaller proportion of individual crimes).[6]

Cooffending drops off sharply by the early twenties; this period of prevalence for cooffending, however, includes the peak offending portion of the typical criminal career.[7] The mere fact of cooffending raises serious issues for thinking about crime control in general and deterrence in particular and can make the ways in which we usually describe and think about these issues deeply flawed. If, for example, a group of five offenders is involved in a gun assault, and the assault goes unreported, it is one offense but five offenders that receive no official attention; if the assault is reported and one arrest is made—which is sufficient to formally "clear" the case—four offenders receive no sanction; if that offender is sentenced to prison, the crime-control value will be nil if the other four continue to offend as before, or recruit another offender to round out the group.[8] Cooffenders tend to commit crimes at higher rates than solo offenders.[9] They tend toward more extreme behavior; groups, and especially larger groups, of armed robbers, for example, are more violent than solo actors.[10] The pairings and larger groups involved in cooffending are unstable, shifting a great deal over even short periods of time.[11] Within that shifting landscape, some offenders stand out as particularly active, committing large numbers of crimes with large numbers of accomplices, who themselves tend to be higher-rate offenders.[12] Warr found evidence of "instigators"—more active offenders taking leadership roles—and "joiners" in such groups.[13] While cooffending drops off amongst older offenders, it does not disappear; however, there has been no systematic study of cooffending in older offenders.

The idea of cooffending is itself incident-based: that is, the phenomenon and its analysis is rooted first in a crime event, then in the individuals active together in that event. Such a focus can lose important connectivities between events and individuals. A gang feud, for example, involving two gangs with ten people each and three shootings perpetrated entirely by one gang, could incorporate three different victims and three nonoverlapping groups of three cooffending aggressors per shooting. Reviewing those incidents would not reveal any connection between the victims or between the groups of aggressors. The next level of analysis, therefore, turns to such groups. *Gangs* have been most studied. Central to such studies has been a persistent difficulty in defining satisfactorily what is and is not a gang and what constitutes membership in a gang.[14] Different definitions can lead to widely varying accounts of the role of the gang in offending and in the incidence and prevalence of gang crime and crime by gang members. Despite such difficulties, certain findings consistently stand out. Gangs are associated with, and beyond that play some kind of causal role in, very high levels of offending, including violent offending.[15] Gang members commit a wide variety of offenses, what Klein calls "cafeteria-style" offending.[16] Gang members tend to be high-rate offenders before, during, and after their spells in gangs, with the highest rates occurring during gang participation. Offending can take on distinctive *meaning* within gangs, with criminogenic implications. As Skolnick *et al.* report,

To advance one's position in a gang, it is important to show that one is willing to take risks, is fearless, is willing to hurt and be hurt, and can be trusted. Drug-related activities—especially intergang violence for black gang members—present some of the most risky, and therefore the most highly valued, of gang activities.[17]

There is an embarrassment of riches on the subject of the high rate of gang offending. To take but a few, Thornberry and Burch, using self-report surveys, found that gang members—30 percent of their sample—committed 86 percent of serious delinquent acts, 69 percent of violent offenses, and 70 percent of drugs sales.[18] Recent city-level studies have shown that gangs representing, typically, under one percent of the population were responsible for at least 60 percent of youth homicides in Boston, and at least half of all homicides in Minneapolis, Baltimore, Indianapolis, and San Francisco.[19] In Cincinnati, research showed that sixty-nine groups with no more than 1,000 members—representing 0.3 percent of the city's population—commited 61 percent of homicides in Cincinnati, were involved as victims in 45 percent of homicides, and were involved as offenders, victims, or both in 73.5 percent of all homicides.[20] Research in Sweden showed that one gang in the city studied comprised 13 percent of the population of offenders but accounted for 42 percent of all suspected crime.[21] Gang turf in Boston represented less than 4 percent of the city but produced about a quarter of its serious crime.[22] While the processes underlying these findings are obscure, there is broad agreement that gangs are somehow distinctive; as Klein and Maxson put it, "qualitatively different precisely because of their involvement in a confrontational world of crime and violence."[23]

If it is not clear exactly what make a group a gang, it is entirely clear that not all offending groups, or groups of offenders, are gangs, and that even the idea of "group" sometimes implies more cohesiveness than is warranted. The crack-dealing "crews" that are a feature of the post-crack-epidemic American urban landscape, for example, fail to meet the threshold of many definitions of "gang" and are themselves nonetheless more cohesive than many of the episodic alliances of crack-house robbers Jacobs describes, the loose affiliations of safe-crackers described by Letkeman,[24] the structure of burglars and burglary described by Shover,[25] or the world of fairground hustling and confidence men described by Inciardi.[26] Neither cooffending nor gang frameworks fit much of what is known about even the more structured kinds of white-collar crime; a savings-and-loan fraud, for example, may have few or no literal instances of cooffending—in that the fraud is constituted of a pattern of behavior rather than an incident located in space and time—nor the sorts of relationships or broad landscape of multiple kinds of offending typical of gangs. Even gangs-qua-gangs, as has been noted, often seem to dissolve upon close examination; Jacobs, for example, notes that drug-dealing by gang members is largely independent and person-by-person, but that the same members may come together for other purposes. "Everybody got they own hustle, but when we gangbang, we gangbang together," one dealer told him.[27] Such presentations cause endless theoretical and practical problems; is such dealing "gang activity"? If not all offending by "gang members" is "gang crime," what defines which is which? If a clique within a corporation commits fraud, is the correct unit of analysis the individuals, the group, or the firm?

One solution to this has been to elevate the idea of *network*. Waring argues that all forms of criminal organization can be viewed as networks:

> This is because cooffending—whether in the form of a vial of crack for money, or contract fraud against the federal government committed by a Fortune 500 company—always is organized in the form of a network, although these networks may, at times, also incorporate elements of other forms of social organization. Perhaps more importantly, coof-fending is never organized either as a pure market or as a hierarchy or other formal organization, although at times cooffending networks may incorporate or imitate specific elements characteristics of these other forms.[28]

Offenders cannot submit their resumes to other offenders, advertise for help, or unionize; they could, but do not, hold elections for executive positions. In the absence of such techniques and possibilities, less formal, more face-to-face, and word-of-mouth processes dominate. Thus, a "gang" is one form of offending network which may crystallize for particular purposes such as collective violence and which can facilitate more autonomous offending such as drug-dealing. Networks of networks are also common. Many individual acts of cooffending represent momentary groupings drawn from larger offender networks. Larger and more organized gang structures, such as the People and Folks in Chicago; Crips, Bloods, and Mexican Mafia in California; and the Latin Kings, are often large networks of smaller nodes— "cliques" or "sets"—with very loose connections to other such nodes. Kennedy, Braga, and Piehl described youth homicide in Boston in terms of more or less standing hostilities and alliances among an overall network of sixty-one street gangs.[29] Sarnecki's research in Sweden suggested that coof-fending by the most active of gang members formed a national network linking *all* the major Swedish gangs.[30]

The "crime as work" literature describing the landscape of more-or-less professional robbers, burglars, fences, and fraud and confidence grifters also fits this framework, with shifting informal relationships between individual offenders and amongst shifting and opportunistic groupings of offenders. Such networks can have remarkable diversity and scope; Klockars' ethno-graphy of a fence describes him as central to a network that extends over many states and includes professional thieves, shoplifters, store owners, other fences, truck drivers, addicts, police officers, judges, society women, and others.[31] Letkemann's ethnography with thieves suggested that they themselves defined a "professional" thief as one who—in addition to basic technical compentencies—had connections with fences, without whom the pursuit was not viable.[32]

The ways in which deterrence has formally been framed and analyzed have tended to limit consideration to those cases in which such collectivities are vulnerable to formal legal sanctions for particular offenses. This is in practice very restrictive. Klockars' fence was vulnerable to prosecution for a variety of crimes; he and those with whom he committed particular crimes were similarly vulnerable for those offenses; others in his network were similarly vulnerable for any crimes they might have committed alone or with others. But the network *as such* had no legal existence, had committed no actionable offense, and thus faced, as such, no formal sanction. A street drug crew—as recognized by its members, its rivals, and the community in which it operates—will similarly typically face no formal exposure *as a crew*. Each member may, for individual drug sales, acts of violence, illegal possession of firearms, and the like, and subgroups may, if together they commit crimes like drive-by shootings for which joint liability legally obtains. But the crew as such has no legal existence and faces no legal risks.

Deterrence theory has thus traditionally been silent. Given the habits of mind of traditional thinking about deterrence, it has often been silent when it might have spoken; writing about corporate crime, for example, Paternoster and Simpson took the position—despite the fact that corporations very often *are* legally liable for criminal acts—that "while not denying the fact that corporations do at times take on the characteristics of acting agents responsible for their actions, we hold that the decision to break the law is made by *individuals*."[33]

Beyond this, even within the bounds of traditional deterrence theory, this is unduly restrictive, since informal sanctions may be brought to bear on a collectivity even where formal sanctions cannot. Girls may shun all the members of a gang, and local businesses refuse to employ them, as a result of acts committed by a single member. When Arthur Anderson accountants were seen to be complicit in the Enron scandal, market forces effectively put the entire firm out of business. Beyond this, however, the real workings of enforcement authorities are often predicated on the existence and actions of collectivities. To take an extreme example, the mafia had no formal or legal existence, and was as such never subject to enforcement or sanction. The network of networks which made up the mafia, however, was the focus of exhaustive attention by authorities and was eventually effectively crippled. Some prosecutions were against individuals for individual crimes; some were directed at groups, in part through new law such as the federal RICO statute written expressly to address the collective nature of the crime in question (even RICO, however, addressed only pieces of the larger network). Lesser examples, such as coordinated local attention to the actors in a particular offender network through the prosecution of individuals for discrete offenses, are common: A gang killing by an individual, for example, may lead authorities to seek opportunistic cases on drug, weapon, and any other charges obtainable against all the members of the gang in question. High-profile incidents often lead to such actions; the killing of a police officer is nearly certain to do so, one reason such attacks are generally viewed as out of bounds by even the most hardened offenders. Deterrence theory has been largely silent on these possibilities and their implications, matters to which we shall return.

Dynamics involving collectivities

If collectivities matter, and can be the object of deterrence, then dynamics within and between collectivities also matter. Here too key themes can only be sketched. But the main points are both simple and profound. People acting in the company of others behave in distinctive ways for distinctive reasons. Collectivities shape, as well as are shaped by, the characteristics and behavior of their participants. The actions of both collectivities and the individuals in them are often best understood in terms of these dynamics; these dynamics, for their part, can be the focus of, or suggest opportunities for, deliberate intervention.

The range of these dynamics, and the enormous amount of thinking that has been brought to bear on them, defy tidy categorization. For our purposes, and unsatisfactory a schema as it certainly is, two main areas emerge. These are *the creation of understanding, meaning, norms,* and *roles*; and *contingent and nonlinear dynamics*.

The creation of understanding, meaning, norms and roles

People care about what those around them think, and about what they *think* those around them think, and about the consequences of disagreeing and being seen to disagree. In a classic experiment by Asch, subjects in a laboratory setting were exposed to deliberately incorrect group opinions about the relative length of lines drawn on display cards. Some subjects were profoundly influenced by the group, overruling their own correct judgments in favor of the expressed consensus. One actually perceived the line as the group falsely described it; most either doubted their own perception or knowingly overruled it in favor of the group's, experiencing, as Asch wrote, "one imperious need: not to appear different."[34]

This sort of influence figures prominently in much sociology, social psychology, cognitive science, and the like. Understandings of the world, on this view, are in important ways constructed through interactive processes. The results matter. "If men define situations as real, they will be real in their consequences," wrote sociologist W. I. Thomas.[35] There are limits to this, of course. A woman who decides that she is a witch and can fly will not be able to do so. But if her peers decide she is a witch and that witches shall not be suffered to live, her burning will be real enough. The group that burns her, though acting in concert, may well contain individuals who feel differently (it may, in fact, be comprised *entirely* of individuals who feel differently, a bizarre but entirely realistic possibility we shall explore shortly). It may go through a period of conflict, lack of cohesiveness, and indirection before moving with purpose. Particular participants may take on new roles, and new relationships, which may or may not last. The understandings, ideas, and actions evidenced during the process may or may not persist. These may all take place across large populations, in smaller populations, and in small groups, and over different spans of time. These processes are often extremely volatile, and small changes in how they play out can lead to dramatically different outcomes.

These are not matters of simply summing and dividing, reconciling, or negotiating over individual propensities. Group processes often have importantly different outcomes than the characteristics and interests of participating individuals might suggest. Groups tend to move away from neutral positions, a phenomenon called *extremism,* and further tend toward more extreme responses than the individuals in them, a phenomenon originally called *risky shift* and then, in recognition that such shifts could occur toward cautious as well as risky responses, *group polarization.*[36] Group polarization can then produce changes to group members' original positions: individuals tend to rationalize their own behavior; groups are more inclined to do so and are even more so inclined when in conflict with other groups.[37] At the individual level, this is a key feature of *cognitive dissonance* theory and research. People dislike inconsistencies between their attitudes and their actions. "When such cognitive dissonance occurs, one will alter one's cognitions to restore a consistent relationship," writes Hass. "How one has behaved in the past (or, more precisely, a cognition about past behavior) is very difficult to change; thus a person is more likely to change her or his attitude to be consistent with the behavior."[38]

People look to others for cues about how to think and act, a process called *social comparison.*[39] Laboratory observation of delinquent youth has shown very direct processes of reinforcement for misbehavior, with—after controlling for other influences—violence-promoting effect.[40] Cook notes that "potential criminals make judgments on the basis of direct observation of the extent of criminal activity in the area: if 'everyone' is doing it, it must pay."[41] McCord's "construct theory" argues that "motives are not purely private events," and that participation in groups affects "how a person reasons about the world," creating "grounds for delinquents to see criminal behavior as appropriate in a wide variety of circumstances."[42] As one career offender told Letkemann about his boyhood initiation into break-ins, "[a]nd these guys were kicking joints in and everything; like, from school, and we were getting razzed about being sissies, so we acted, or reacted, I guess, and we got to be pretty tough eggs ourselves during the next, well—in my case, the next forty years, or thirty-five."[43]

In a graphic example of how fundamental, and often overlooked, such dynamics are, Skolnick *et al.* note that they operate even with respect to addiction. The draw of addictive substances is often held to be essentially self-explanatory, but they note that

> [D]rugs do not necessarily offer pleasure, at least initially. First use may be unpleasant, even painful. Thus, many readers of this report who have never used heroin or cocaine may well be familiar with effects of cigarettes and alcohol. Cigarette smokers rarely, if ever, begin a smoking pattern because cigarettes initially offer pleasure. On the contrary, a smoker's first cigarette usually induces coughing, nausea, dizziness, and so forth. Similarly, few first-time users of alcoholic beverages find the taste of whisky, beer, or wine pleasurable and often describe the initial taste as harsh or bitter.
>
> The moral of the story? *Initiates who smoke or drink must learn to define the experience as positive.* ...Initiates have to learn, and are taught by peers or role models, to ignore initially negative sensations and to *appreciate* the experience of smoking or drinking alcohol.[44]

Such dynamics can also influence the *form* of offending. In explaining the prevalence of crack houses over street markets in Detroit, Mieczkowski noted the contribution of the social stigma that had become attached among crack users to buying on the street. The most productive and highest-quality drug-acquisition patterns involved buying powder cocaine and "rocking up" one's own crack, a process that involved buying from houses and exercising some planning and self-control. Thus, controlled users stigmatized street transactions as being associated with "fiending": acute, high-rate, compulsive crack use. Buying from the street was a sign that the user was growing imprudent and wasteful. In effect, "only a fool or a fiend" would buy from a street vendor.[45] More generally, research on the effect of "source characteristics" on attitudes and behavior has demonstrated that people often "strive to dissociate [themselves] from individuals or groups [considered] unattractive."[46]

Individuals act, in many settings, in the knowledge that their attitudes and actions will be evident to their peers, and that such evidence can be consequential. Zimring and Hawkins explicitly raised this issue in connection with deterrence:

> [W]hen group values are in conflict with those that underlie the legal threat [...] the visibility of an individual's response to a threat results in pressure to defy the threat in order to preserve or secure standing with the group. Against the prospect that deviant behavior will result in punishment, the threatened individual must balance the likelihood that failure to defy a threat will lower his standing among the group and result in his being branded disloyal or cowardly. There are probably also some situations where failure to conform to the group expectation is threatened with more tangible discomforts.[47]

They note as well that such processes can operate in the other direction, with deterrence threats providing a reason to avoid offending: an "instrument for the rationalization of conforming conduct."[48]

Concrete examples of offender-group norms against offending are relatively rare, but far from unknown. One notable example is offender-group norms around drug use, or certain kinds of drug use. The "crime as work" literature mentions this in more-or-less "career" circles of safecrackers and robbers, who eschewed heroin addicts and alcoholics as unreliable and dangerous.[49] These circles also, Letkemann reports, ostracized rapists.[50] Gangs frequently stigmatize and punish the use of crack by members.[51] Skolnick *et al.*, in their study of the early crack market in California, found that self-reports by gang-involved drug dealers showed no regular crack use, with real risks perceived for doing so. As one of their interviewees said,

> I never use cocaine; it's not real when they say that a person that sells ends up using his drugs; that's not true, he's like an outcast [...] you get beat up, dogged out, nobody respects you anymore; it turns you scandalous; the shit will make you steal from your mama.[52]

Johnson, Golub and Dunlap report that in New York City, crack users are regarded as so unreliable within drug-dealing networks that they are "not trusted as sellers and were fortunate to occasionally perform low-level distribution roles."[53] They argue that the negative examples of crack users have led the next age cohort to eschew crack and many of its associated behaviors, especially violence and gun-carrying. In its place has evolved a new set of norms revolving around group use of marijuana "blunts." Such groups, they report, have conduct norms that

> discourage rapid ingestion of alcohol and displays of drunken comportment, including aggressive language and threatening or violent behavior. If one consistently and rapidly consumes large quantities of alcohol, acts drunk, or is violent toward others, that person will be sanctioned and if necessary excluded from the blunt-sharing group at future times.[54]

Cook *et al.*, in their ethnographic study of illicit gun markets in Chicago, found that gangs imposed strong controls against their members' trafficking in, carrying, and using guns in order to avoid arming rivals and drawing police attention. Such controls extended to fines, beatings, expulsion, and even turning offending gang members over to police.[55]

Less rare are examples of "tangible discomforts" visited by groups of offenders in support of offending. Decker and Lauritsen report that it is a commonplace belief in gang circles in St. Louis that one must kill one of one's parents in order to leave a gang, a belief that is clearly mostly, if not entirely, a myth but nonetheless inhibits gang desistance.[56] Police officers who refuse to participate in or cover up police corruption often report both bureaucratic and individual responses damaging to their careers and to their personal safety, such as poor reviews, transfers, an inability to find partners, harassment, the denial of backup, and physical attacks.[57] A variation on this theme is what might be termed "coercive solicitation" by groups, as when gangs threaten or attack individuals who have not or will not join with them. Yet another variation is practiced by *other* groups, who may treat everybody from the neighborhood or turf of a rival group as a member of that group, or refuse to recognize that an individual once a member of a rival group has separated from it. The same can be true of police and other authorities.[58]

A great deal has been written about the ways in which groups, including offending groups, and individuals in those groups act to undercut the legitimacy and influence of others, including authorities: what Sykes and Matza, in connection with juvenile delinquents, called "techniques of neutralization."[59] Much, even most, of their argument is applicable to broader offender circles. Central is the idea that offenders mobilize many of the core ideas and norms of *conventional* culture, including many essential to the actions and the legitimacy of authorities. The subculture of delinquency, on this analysis, is far from wholly distinct from conventional culture. "It is partially incorporated and partially alienated," writes Matza.[60] He describes, in essence, a kind of mental aikido in which the precepts of conventional culture are, sometimes somewhat modified, deployed in the service of the unconventional. Offenders acknowledge their offending but escape accountability on the legalistic premise that a particular offense has not been properly proven. The persistent attention of authorities is recast as prejudice. Disparity of treatment from offense to offense and offender to offender is read as unreasonable and arbitrary injustice. The patent inability of authorities to know of and act against a great deal of offending is taken as evidence of incompetence or corruption. Incidents of corruption, brutality, and the like are evidence that the authorities are really just another kind of criminal. Traditional virtues of loyalty and valor are mobilized to justify and honor associations of offenders and violence. Clear evidence of misbehavior of "legitimate" persons around, for example, crimes of vice shows that the law prohibiting such crimes are unreasonable. The recognition in law and custom of the legitimacy of self-defense is expanded to include pre-emptive strikes.[61]

Central to all this is what Matza calls "the situation of company."[62] These and other aspects of delinquent acts, roles, norms, and culture—and, again, of many older offenders and settings involving older offenders—are worked out over time *in association with others*. It is worth quoting Matza at length on this point.

> A distinctive feature of the subculture of delinquency is that its beliefs are imbedded in action. This is partially true of all traditions but never as much so as in delinquency. We speak of the delinquent code as if it existed somewhere clearly displayed. There are such patent codes in modern society. Their hallmark is that they are written. The code of

delinquency is relatively latent. It is not written, except by sociologists, nor is it even well verbalized. Delinquency is well characterized as a relatively inarticulate oral tradition. Its precepts are neither codified nor formally transmitted. Rather, they are inferred from action which obviously included speech. An ideology of delinquency in the sense of a coherent viewpoint is implicit in delinquent actions, but this ideology is not known to delinquents. They are not conscious of an ideology because they have not bothered to work it out. Thus, they infer ideology from each other. This is the primary relevance of the situation of company. Mutual inference is accomplished through concrete verbal directives, hints, sentiments, gestures, and activities. But as long as the subculture is inferred, it is not taught in the usual sense of the term. Instead, it is cued. Each member of the company infers the subculture from the cues of others. The company is in a state of acute mutual dependence since there is no coherent ideology which may be consulted. There are only specific and concrete slogans. But there is no explicit general theory.[63]

The situation of "company"—groups, networks, collectivities, and associated processes and dynamics—is on this account central to understanding much offending. There very much are ideas, norms, rules, expectations, demands, and the like that obtain around offenders. They are virtually never formalized and codified. There are no texts that define "respect," or set out when violence must be used to redress disrespect. There was no charter establishing the tiers of payoffs, and rules for buy-ins and buy-outs, that characterized corrupt police "pads" in the Knapp Commission-era New York Police Department. There was no formal call for rioting in the wake of the Rodney King verdict, or deliberation in support of the idea that looting and violence constituted an "insurrection." No written code—any longer—defines when it is acceptable to hit one's wife; no written code ever defined when it was *expected* that one would hit one's wife. The "blue code of silence" exists only in the hearts and minds of police officers. The "code of the streets" exists, as such, only in Anderson's books. But all these things were, or are, very real.

The study of *collective behavior* is of particular use here. Collective behavior, a branch of sociology, addresses "those forms of social behavior in which usual conventions cease to guide social action and people collectively transcend, bypass, or subvert established institutional patterns and structures."[64] It has been brought to bear on political campaigns, social movements, natural disasters, riots, crowds, lynchings, fads, the adoption of new products, technologies, and medical treatments, and the like. It focuses on "emergent norms," indications of salient features of a situation, the involved actors, and appropriate and inappropriate behavior. The central process in collective behavior is thus "the construction of a dominant definition of a situation through symbolic interaction."[65]

Collective-behavior theory suggests several key roles and processes that commonly shape emergent norms. One central role is that of the *model*, and one central process that of *keynoting*. In uncertain situations, an active individual (or, though the theory does not address it, perhaps an active group) can create meaning and define what will be appropriate action. Such an individual or group can be a model for less activist participants. By their words or actions they frame, or keynote, directions for thought, understanding, definition, and behavior.[66] Familiar examples include the first person to get up and leave a room when a fire-alarm sounds and the first driver to take to the shoulder during a traffic jam. Such first moves are often followed by others. This has been demonstrated with regard to violence and aggression, a phenomenon sometimes called "disinhibitory contagion."[67] *Release theory* suggests that this pattern is general, driven by a process in which "the discovery of a single group member [...] who endorses high risk-taking *releases* the more cautious members from the assumed social constraints holding them back from risk taking."[68] As this suggests, "keynotes" that emerge in undefined situations are likely to be on the extreme side, as those who act strongly in such settings tend to hold both extreme and intense positions.[69] There tends to be more susceptibility to the suggestions of others in more uncertain situations, and a greater tendency to reach a group norm.[70]

These constructs help address, for example, the vexing problem of gang "leadership." There is usually none, in the sense of being clearly defined, elected, or appointed; one generally looks in vain for such persons or roles. This does not mean, though, that there is no leadership, or nothing similar to leadership. Rather, says Klein and Maxson, "It changes by activity and time period, is to be found in each age-graded subgroup, and is closely related to clique structures." They even use the same language: "In many ways," they write, "gang leaders are more often modeled than followed."[71]

These processes can occur in what are termed *compact crowds*—actual aggregations of individuals in more or less direct contact—or in *diffuse crowds*, which are more widespread. (Those who first sparked the street rioting in Los Angeles after the Rodney King verdict constituted, in all likelihood, a compact crowd; those who learned about their actions while watching television in other cities and followed their example constituted a diffuse crowd.) Crowds can take in and give off information in various ways, including direct contact and mass communication; one core concept here is that of the *interaction net*, in which networks of groups both shape and pass on information and behaviors. The networks-of-networks that comprises the basic structure of much criminal offending will frequently constitute such an interaction net. This is almost certainly, for example, how the technological innovation of crack cocaine—a new way of creating smokable cocaine base—spread across the country in the late 1980s; it is probably also a general explanation of how such offenses as savings and loan frauds and exotic accounting frauds move within white-collar circles.

Such networks can shape both *behavior* and *meaning*, as was evident in the massive post-war electrical equipment antitrust violations. Clusters of businessmen in large American firms such as General Electric carried out a complex price-fixing scheme for some years; executives at twenty-nine companies were eventually indicted.[72] Their "interaction net" carried out the conspiracy, socialized new executives into the criminal enterprise, and framed and sustained the idea that what was going on was not truly wrong. "Illegal? Yes, but not criminal," said one participant to a Senate subcommittee. "I didn't find that out until I read the indictment. [...] I assumed that criminal action meant damaging someone, and we did not do that."[73]

A crucially important feature of such collective behavior is that some, or even all, of the participants can reach and sustain incorrect conclusions about the views of other participants. This phenomenon of "pluralistic ignorance" is one of the oldest findings in social psychology: It refers to the situation of each person in a group believing that each other person in the group believes something that they do not in fact believe.[74] In a band of citizens preparing to burn a witch, each individual may simultaneously believe that there is no such thing as a witch, but that all others in the group do so believe; each individual will tend to go along with what is in fact an utterly false group consensus, and the group will therefore resolutely follow a path none of its individual members supports.

Matza, again, is particularly insightful about the situation of pluralistic ignorance in group-based offending. The "culture of delinquency" is not explicit and textual; it is implicit and to a considerable extent inferred from the actions of others.

> Each member believes that others are committed to their delinquencies. But what about each member, what does he believe himself? [...] Possibly, he is transformed in the situation of company to a committed delinquent by dint of the cues he has received from others. Possibly, however, each member believes himself to be an exception in the company of committed delinquents. The intricate system of cues may be miscues. Since the subculture must be constructed from the situation of company, it may be misconstrued.[75]

It may, moreover, be cued on the basis of extreme behaviors by outlying members of the group—keynotes and models—whose examples then assume normative status. Matza notes that the extreme "status anxiety" and "masculinity anxiety" prevalent in offending circles inhibits opposing and confronting, or even articulating reservations about, the behavior and norms of such outliers.[76]

Others have framed these dynamics in terms of "referent informational influence"[77] and "the inductive aspect of categorization."[78] Both refer to processes in which "group members seek out the stereotypic norms which define category membership and conform their behavior to them. It is, in effect, a process of self-stereotyping."[79] Quite informal and fluid groups may thus act with remarkable cohesion.

A cycle is easily imagined in which what was extreme become modal, aspirational and competitive pressures produce a new extreme, the new extreme becomes modal, and so on. In theory, many participants may have private reservations about the outcome; in theory, *all* participants may have private reservations about the outcome. Without something to correct the pluralistic ignorance, what is hidden may remain so, and the process may continue.

These processes are supported by a consistent tendency of individuals to commit what has been called "fundamental attribution error": to interpret others' behavior in terms of free choice and settled aspects of character rather than external forces and internal pressures such as shame and embarrassment.[80] If we see everyone in a room sitting quietly while a fire alarm rings, we tend to think they know something important about false alarms and are confidently waiting this one out; we tend not to think that they are scared witless but afraid to look stupid. When everybody in the room would rather leave but each thinks he is the only one, we are operating in pluralistic ignorance. Situations of both kinds are very common.

Perkins, discussing these dynamics in the context of alcohol and drug abuse, identifies three driving factors also generalizable to other settings. One is, as just noted,

> the general social psychological tendency to erroneously attribute observed behaviors of other people to their disposition, and to think the behavior is typical of the individual when the action cannot be explained by the specific context or put into perspective by knowing what the other person usually does most of the time.[81]

The second is that social communications processes highlight the extreme. "[T]he tendency is to recall the most vivid behaviors and then conversation gravitates to the extreme incidents, in the end making them seem more common than is really the case."[82] The third is that "cultural media reaffirms and amplify these exaggerations," something that is true of a wide variety of offending and other extreme behaviors outside the realm of substance abuse.[83]

These are powerful dynamics, and ones that profoundly influence both offenders and authorities, and their views of one another. Authorities, faced with an outbreak of drive-by shootings, will readily conclude that they are dealing with stone-cold superpredators; they have no way of knowing that the shooters have never done such things before, did not want to do them this time, acted in abject fear of both their enemies and their friends, and hope fervently never to have to do anything similar in the future. Authorities will remember the drive-bys, and discuss them; they will not similarly remember the vastly more frequent occasions in which street tensions did *not* lead to violence (the ludicrous but frequent comment in law enforcement and other circles that guns have become the "method of choice" in settling urban disputes is a testament to the power of this mistaken inferential process; were it true, there would be virtually nobody left standing). Film, rap, and the like reinforce these conceptions. Offenders, for their part, faced with authorities driving by open-air drug-dealing, will readily conclude that they are dealing with police officers who are racist and corrupt; they have no way of knowing that the officers loathe drug-dealing and its impact on the community, have been enjoined from street drug enforcement by their superiors and been chastised by the district attorney for clogging the calendar with arrests the bench will simply throw out. They will remember, and discuss, these and other incidents of mis- and malfeasance by authorities; they will not similarly remember occasions in which authorities acted to protect them and the community. Film, rap, and the like reinforce these conceptions. Such confusions, of course, virtually never get aired or addressed, still less resolved.

Research into norms associated with alcohol and drug abuse on college campuses and in similar settings has revealed striking examples of pluralistic ignorance and related dynamics. One of the first studies into such norms found that three-quarters of students believed that one should never drink to intoxication or that intoxication was acceptable only in limited circumstances. Yet, almost two-thirds of those same students thought that their peers believed that frequent intoxication or intoxication that did interfere with academics and other responsibilities was acceptable.[84]

Subsequent research found the same sort of "reign of error"[85] to hold at each of 100 campuses studied, for other drugs, for all gender and ethnic groups, in a variety of on-campus settings, and in high schools and statewide populations of young adults.[86] Beliefs—however misinformed—about *others'* drinking are strong predictors of *personal* drinking.[87] Perkins describes what follows:

> Students who are ambivalent about drinking or using other drugs and prefer to abstain feel pressure to indulge because they erroneously perceive that "everyone" expects it of them. Students who, left to their own inclination, would choose to drink only a moderate amount of alcohol with limited frequency are likewise nudged along to drink more heavily by their mistaken notion of what most other peers expect them to do and what they think most others are doing at parties and other social settings. Thus students with relatively moderate attitudes sometimes take risks with their drinking that they would not otherwise take, thanks to their distorted perception of norms. Finally, students who do have a permissive personal attitude, and who are thus personally prone to frequent drinking or taking risks with other substances, can do so without reservation, naively thinking they are part of the majority. Perversely, other students give them the license and encouragement to do so because most other students hold the misperception of what is

normative as well, even if their own behavior does not reach the falsely perceived standard. Overt peer opposition to destructive behavior declines in the face of misperception. Students become less willing to speak out against abuse and less willing to intervene when a peer is about to engage in risky behavior because they think they are the only ones who are concerned or uncomfortable with the actions of a peer.[88]

Offender groups and norms may lend themselves disproportionately to such dynamics, particularly where young people are involved. Matza, again talking about delinquents and delinquent groups but again often generalizable to many other offender settings, argues that

> The stress on valor is usually connected with a high evaluation of loyalty. Both are among the traditional martial virtues. They are bound together by a conception of reputation. Reputation reveals a concern with how one appears before others, and the urgency of maintaining it depends on the depth of belief in group solidarity. Thus, valor is most assiduously pursued in groups that celebrate the precepts of loyalty. However, the celebration of group solidarity and loyalty may not reflect actual group relations. Unstable and shaky groups may come to stress loyalty and solidarity and thus mask the brittle bonds that tie it together. Just as outlandish youth may become the prime exponents of the virtues of manliness, conflict-ridden companies may develop harsh and totalitarian expectations of loyalty. The demand for total loyalty is made not because it has been or can be gained, but, instead, because the company has been so discontentedly accustomed to losing membership.[89]

The parallels with, for example, what Anderson describes as "code of the streets" communities are striking. The "respect" culture that dominates in such communities is simply a particular—if very powerful and pervasive—manifestation of a concern for "reputation" in a very broad "situation of company." Indeed, one realistic—if stunning, and tragic—way of looking at those communities is as places in which many of the norms and dynamics once restricted to relatively small populations and groups of young delinquents have come to apply to much of the population all of the time and most of the population some of the time, and with far less stratification by age.

A modern, unusual and strikingly similar account comes from offenders themselves. A group of life inmates at Pennsylvania's Graterford maximum-security prison has for some years been conducting a self-study that locates the roots of their own crimes squarely in norms and group processes. These norms and processes constitute what they call the "culture of street crime." This culture, they argue, is to a considerable extent independent of core community and social structures and influences: it is a stand-alone force. "Clearly, one cannot disregard the role that a society rife with poverty, unemployment, racism, and discrimination plays in pushing people toward the criminal underclass," they write. "Yet, even under the most favorable circumstances, many young people in each new generation fall into this street crime culture."[90]

We did what they did, they say, because we held wrong ideas together:

> The present-day street crime culture consists of a group or groups of individuals who live outside societal norms. They have their own values, codes, practices, and principles that are oftentimes in direct opposition to the larger society, although many of the negative characteristics displayed by this culture, such as self-focus and greed, are also common to the mainstream culture.[91]

We wanted prosperity, but we did not want to work:

> Moreover, most of those who are driven by this part of the culture have less than an adequate appreciation for wealth earned by labor or the traditional aspects of employment. Because members of this culture desire more than what traditional employment can provide, they turn to hustling, most often through illegal activities, and, more than likely, drug-dealing. They also crave the power, influence, and respect hustlers in the street crime culture receive from having expensive cars, the latest fashions, and flashy jewelry.[92]

And we had, and encouraged in each other, a distorted sense of ourselves as men:

> The paramount need in the street crime culture [is] for respect, proving one's manhood and being viewed as courageous. [...] When a member of this culture feels disrespected or his manhood is challenged, he feels justified in exacting justice through the barrel of a gun. It is this psychology of the survival of the self that causes innocent victims to get caught in cross fires, and young men to lose their lives through death or incarceration. These individuals who are afflicted with this inordinate desire not to be shamed or have their manhood tested make up the larger segment of this factor.[93]

A critical feature of all such analyses is that it can be profoundly misleading to infer *underlying individual characteristics and attributes*—character, disposition, norms, preferences, and the like—on the basis of *behavior*. We recognize this in many familiar settings: When a nightclub catches fire and those inside, in a rush to escape, clog the exits and die, we do not attribute either the rushing or the deaths to sudden and simultaneous individual suicidal impulses, or to a collective urge toward self-destruction. We recognize, instead, ordinary people in an extraordinary situation; the dire collective consequences of individually rational decisions, such as wishing to be the first out the door; group processes, such as the spread of panic, imitation of the first to run, and the like; the meaninglessness, and beyond that the cost-liness, of individual restraint and good sense in such a situation; and the vanishingly small likelihood that the group will, under such circumstances, behave calmly and deliberately—though doing so would clearly be much the safest thing to do. It is a feature of collective behavior, as Granovetter notes, that "[C]ollective outcomes can seem paradoxical—that is, intuitively incon-sistent with the intentions of the individuals who generate them."[94]

It is thus easy to make serious misattributions on the basis of behavior. Bennett, DiIulio, and Walters, looking at the dramatic rise in youth and juvenile homicide in the late 1980s and early 1990s, concluded that the vio-lent offenders responsible were "radically impulsive, brutally remorseless" "super-predators" driven by a "violent, hair-trigger mentality" in pursuit of "sex, drugs, money."[95] In fact, inquiries into the conduct of such offenders consistently show that their violence is often driven by accurate perceptions of high levels of risk from other offenders;[96] that violence is frequently motivated by complicated "scripts" involving street norms and rational concerns about self-protection;[97] that "ordinary" disputes take on special meaning and require special responses in such settings;[98] and that those involved can dislike what is going on, often profoundly, without feeling any capacity to change or escape it.[99] Rob Garot, interviewing young men in an extremely violent urban area, found frequent examples of this:

ANTOINE: So he just kept on trying to fight me. So I have to stick up for myself. 'If you wanna fight me, come on man. I ain't fittin' to sit up here and let you punk me.' So he got up in my face and he swung on me. So I just slammed him on a car [...]. I just started chokin' him out. All his friends were laughin' at him. And they told me, 'I see that you ain't a punk.' So they just wasn't gonna mess with me. Period. I had to stick up for myself and I had to fight. But you know, I don't like fightin' period.

RG: Right.

ANTOINE: This was in front of a lot of people, so you can't just punk out here.[100]

Khalil Sumpter, who shot and killed two students at Thomas Jefferson High School in New York City in 1992, later wrote that

My situation was based on my belief that my life was in danger. [...] In East New York there was an unwritten set of rules or codes that many young people abided by, young black men in particular. I didn't make any of these codes, for lack of a better term, but the way of thinking for most young men was either abide by these laws or become consumed by them. As stupid as these laws are, that was the norm at the time.[101]

In the strictest and most immediate sense, such actors "want" to do what they do: Sumpter did in fact shoot two people, and chose to do so. In less strict and immediate senses, things may be a good deal more complicated. It is common for people to choose to do things they do not really want to do. In ordinary life, we recognize this as unremarkable: People get up and go to work when they would rather not, stay home and study when they would rather not, say no when they would rather say yes, and yes when they would really rather say no. The same is also clearly often true with offenders and offending. What appears to be the result of character, desire, and design may be importantly the result of context; what appears to be the grounded result of individual intent and disposition may be a heavily contingent result of group dynamics.

And—and this is crucial—we may see offenders committing very serious crimes and resisting all efforts to prevent them from doing so, while in fact they may not want to be doing so at all. This is utterly counterintuitive, entirely possible, and a matter to which we will return.

Contingent and nonlinear dynamics

"Context," in thinking about offending, is, of course, traditionally the province of root causes analyses. "Context" in this framework describes broad social and community conditions, shaping individuals and their opportunities, incentives, and disincentives in sweeping and fundamental ways. "Context" has also, more recently, been framed in a much more proximate and "situational" fashion, with attention to quite particular features that may facilitate or inhibit offending, such as vehicular access to street sex markets or walking access to opportunistic residential burglaries, and the presence or absence of formal and informal "guardians."[102] Both are powerful and evocative frameworks, with strong theoretical and practical contributions to thinking about crime and crime control.

Another frame for context might be seen to operate in territory between these two: less fundamental and sweeping than root causes, but more so than most situational analyses; less particular and contingent than most situational analyses, but more so than root causes. Anderson's "code of the street" can be seen through this lens. The code has come to obtain in many urban communities. It emerged from particularly distressed times in distressed communities, and thus seems well situated in root-causes dynamics. Two features of how the code has developed, however, suggest that the story is both less and more than that.

On the "less" side, the crack epidemic pushed many such communities over the edge; troubled as they might have been in the early 1980s, they were truly desperate five and ten years later, with much of their precipitous decline attributable to the dire and complicated fallout from crack. But crack may be viewed as something of a historical accident: not a well-determined product of core social forces, not inevitable even in hindsight, crack was a technological innovation that happened to emerge at a particular time and place. It would not have taken the social trajectory it did without preexisting conditions in urban America. Nor, however, would urban America now look like it does had crack not emerged. We would, to take one very concrete example, almost certainly not have had the youth violence epidemic that began in the mid-1980s.[103] The code, as Anderson describes, developed in the particular circumstances of the crack epidemic in these neighborhoods. It may be regarded, then, as in a considerable part the product of forces that were both powerful and in important ways *accidental*.

On the "more" side, the code has taken on a life of its own, as have many products of the crack epidemic. Norms around respect, including expectations of and behavior around violence, have become "decoupled" from crack and the epidemic.[104] Drug markets were established and persist. Gangs and other offending groups and networks flourished and continue to do so. The use of firearms soared, dramatically changing risk and the incidence, prevalence, and meaning of various forms of risky behavior. Opportunities for offending, such as the armed robbery of street dealers and drug houses, emerged. Fundamental socioeconomic shifts occurred, and continue to occur. These things are now persistent features of the affected communities.

It becomes, in such accounts—perhaps especially with dynamics as powerful as that of the crack epidemic—difficult to sort out what seems a deep, "root" cause, what is more accidental and contingent, and just when the latter may transform itself—as often happens—into the former. Cook, for example, has suggested that the decades-long history of New York as a troubled, high-crime city—and, for many, an exemplar of the root-causes diagnosis—may be characterized as the product of two stacked drug epidemics: heroin beginning in the 1960s, cocaine in the 1980s.[105] There is nothing simple or superficial about a major drug epidemic, or about its community impacts. Nonetheless, such factors remain manifestly distinct from more rooted factors. Poverty, racism, inequality, class, inadequate and failed services, social dislocation: Such things are always with us, and always have been. Crack, still less a crack *epidemic*, has not. Status, and concern about status, and violence have always been with us; it took the intersection of deep social and community factors and the crack epidemic to produce the code of the street.

As hard as it is to sort out the different factors and their interplay, there is a difference. Some feel fundamental and structural; they *cause*, in the "root" sense of the word. Others feel far more contingent, at least in their initial manifestation. They do not so much cause, in that sense, as *precipitate* what follows. And, of course, even within these unsatisfactory distinctions are further, similar distinctions. The crack epidemic would have been quite different without the open-air markets that generally characterized it (and which, by accident or policy, were much less prevalent or deliberately prevented in some places[106]) and which fostered easy access by users, the entry of youth into trafficking, gang and group formation, turf and other violence, gun-carrying and use, robberies, and much else. If we take, on this frame, the crack epidemic as more or less a given, street crack markets were at least somewhat more contingent: and precipitated a good deal.

These sorts of notions have received a good deal of attention at both general and more particular levels. Much of the collective behavior and social-psychology literature noted previously fits this framework. One can readily frame the emergence of street crack markets, for example, in terms of collective uncertainty around what would and would not be acceptable in the early stages of the crack epidemic; the "keynote" example of the first street sellers; the spread of that behavior along networks; the reinforcement of street selling behavior in light of the failure of police to act, or act effectively; emergent definitions (and quite possibly some degree of pluralistic ignorance) of what would constitute normative behavior in those settings; attribution error off all sorts; and the like.

In particular, the ideas of "contagion" and "epidemic" have been mobilized to capture the various ways in which ideas and behavior can spread rapidly. These ideas can be more evocative than they are precise, with actors, ideas, information, behaviors, influences, vectors, and pathways playing shifting and inconsistent roles, and the core notions, as Levy and Nail said of contagion, "subject to imprecise, inconsistent, and incongruous usage."[107] Many, if not most, analytic frameworks and key findings can be collapsed into more general frameworks and findings from other fields. When we talk of a teen fad, or crack dealing, as being "contagious," we do not mean that there is a literal physical carrier that infects new persons with the behavior; we mean, rather, such things as that particular behaviors are modeled, that models are followed, that group processes influence individuals, that processes and effects seem more nonlinear than linear, and so on. Much of the literature of contagion and behavioral epidemics thus involves explaining these processes in terms of established disciplines. Collective behavior theory, indeed, considers the "deviant epidemic" to be a special case of general collective social processes.[108]

It may be, then, that the principal virtue of ideas like "contagion," "epidemic," and the like in these settings is to draw attention to the extent to which offending—like other behavior—can be, as has been noted, *contingent*, and can both come and go in distinctly interactive and often *nonlinear* ways, and, further, to draw attention to the ways in which offending can be driven by factors importantly separate from either root social and community conditions on the one hand, or the character of individual offenders on the other. We are not used to thinking about drug-dealing and carjacking in the same ways in which we think about hula hoops and body piercing—as, in essence, *fads*, or something very much like them—but there are important ways in which they can be very similar.

Holden, for example, examined aircraft hijackings of the late 1960s and early 1970s and concluded that publicity regarding successful hijackings accounted for about half of "transportation" (i.e., diversions to Cuba) and nearly 90 percent of "extortion" (ransom) hijackings.[109] Phillips and

Carstensen found that teen suicides "clustered" imitatively after television stories about suicide.[110] The author has suggested that the wave of school shootings of the late 1990s and early 2000s—invariably attributed to deep structural factors in families, schools, and communities, broad influences like media violence and popular culture, and personal attributes like metal illness—represented similarly imitative behavior, with a relatively small population of "susceptibles" nationally being moved to action by the relentless media coverage of each event.[111] Such coverage is routinely followed by numerous less serious "copycat" incidents; detailed examination of more serious ones, such as the shooting at Heritage High School in Georgia a month after the Columbine shootings, have shown clear evidence of imitation.[112] Violence in general has been typed as a "contagious social process" by Loftin, who notes that violence is spatially clustered, reciprocal (with prior violent *victimization* the best predictor of violent *offending*), and tends to escalate sharply in particular places and at particular times.[113] "[V]iolence spreads," Loftin writes, "because offenders and victims are part of social and moral networks."[114]

Much has recently been written on this process in connection with the homicide "epidemic," particularly amongst juveniles and youth, of the late 1980s and early 1990s. A great deal of it—the role of gangs and groups, the extreme concentration of violence in particular places and amongst chronic offenders, "respect" norms, violence "scripts," the social meaning of firearms and firearms use, and the like—fits Loftin's "social and moral network" framework. From where we stand now, it can also be noted that that "epidemic" of violence—as with others—both *rose* and *fell* sharply, with the rapid decline as well as the rapid increase difficult to explain on the basis of core structural and characterological factors. Interpersonal normative shifts amongst both adults[115] and youth[116] have been suggested as causal in both directions. Drug use and drug epidemics are often strikingly stratified in ways that are, again, difficult to explain in terms of structural, characterological, opportunity, and other such factors. In the late 1980s and early 1990s, for example, fully a quarter of male arrestees in San Diego tested positive for methamphetamine, more than five times the typical rate in other cities; nearly 20 percent of arrestees in Chicago for heroin, but less than 2 per cent in Miami; PCP (Phencyclidine) rates in Washington DC were five times as high as any other city[117] (PCP was evidently suppressed by the crack epidemic, but has recently begun, according to police observers, to reemerge; PCP has traditionally been and generally remains essentially unknown in most American jurisdictions). The recent epidemic of methamphetamine was for years confined largely to California and the upper Midwest; it has since spread widely in rural areas but is largely unknown in urban settings, except amongst networks of gay men, a problem socially and behaviorally separate from the rural epidemic. Network ties and social norms have repeatedly been implicated in both the rise and fall of drug epidemics. Heroin epidemics tend to self-control as longer-term users become first less-appealing and then unappealing models to potential new initiates.[118] The same process has been described with respect to crack in New York City.[119]

And so on. There is no shortage of such examples, and of at least glimpses of the processes behind them. It is exceedingly difficult, at the same time, to model those processes in detail, or to say with certainty that some sort of "contagion"—rather than social structure, personal characteristics, opportunity, variations in the actions of authorities, and the like—is at work. Nonetheless, it seems hard to argue that these sorts of processes are not often quite important and powerful

It is then important to note several key aspects of such processes. These begin with their core *contingency*, their *instability*, and their frequent *nonlinearity*; and their frequently misleading appearance of what might be called *rootedness*.

Contingency, instability, and nonlinearity are closely related and are best addressed together. "Contingency" can be taken to apply to several central aspects. It pertains to more or less *proximate causal factors*: the invention (or not) of crack, the broad availability (or not) of guns, the development (or not) of easy home syntheses of methamphetamine; easy access (or not) to such syntheses via the Internet. It pertains to how those proximate causal factors are *socially processed in the relevant populations*. Many seemingly promising opportunities for widespread offending simply never catch on. "Ice," for example, an extremely potent smokable form of methamphetamine, appeared in Hawaii in the late 1980s, sparking mainland concerns of a new drug epidemic; it never materialized. Ice did, however, become epidemic in the Philippines.[120] There are no technical or trafficking features that would explain these and similar disparities in drug usage: Ordinary methamphetamine and ice are the products of largely similar syntheses, and there is no reason to think that it would be difficult to make or traffic either in any given place (the same is true for PCP). "Blunts," on the other hand—marijuana rolled in the casings of cheap cigars—did become epidemic in the USA, something it is hard to explain on the basis of anything other than fashion. "Ram-raiding"—robberies conducted by crashing stolen vehicles into businesses—is a major problem in the UK and Australia but is all but unknown in the USA, except among certain gang circles in California and the Southwest, where it is a favored method of breaking into gun shops. Carjacking, viewed by many in law-enforcement circles as a singularly stupid crime, since it involves a public, violent confrontation for a goal that can easily be accomplished quietly and surreptitiously, enjoyed a brief vogue in the USA in the late 1980s, one quite possibly sparked by news coverage of several notorious incidents, and then largely died out—but it became and remains epidemic in Puerto Rico. Many large American cities suffered heroin epidemics beginning in the late 1960s: In most of them the epidemics waned, but in Baltimore, for some reason, it never did.

Contingency also pertains to how, within types and patterns of offending, particular *manifestations* develop. New York City once had active street sex markets, with famous concentrations around Times Square and the Holland Tunnel; driven by heavy street enforcement and the potential of the Internet, brothels have recently reemerged. Drive-by shootings were a central feature of the youth violence epidemic in southern California, but were relatively rare even in other cities with high levels of youth gun violence. Many cities have extremely active street drug markets; relatively few, however, have the severe problems with "stick-up boys" that, for example, St. Louis, Rochester, and Baltimore do.

As these and other, similar examples suggest, such settings, processes and patterns are often extremely *unstable*. Poor urban America was, in hindsight, ripe for some sort of drug epidemic in the late 1980s. And, in hindsight, the crack epidemic looks inevitable, but as has been noted, it was not. When crack hit, however, it spread—socially and geographically—with enormous speed. Equally interesting, though, is that it is also in many places *receding*: not at the pace with which it hit, but nonetheless. In such places, the impact of official action pales next to that of local social processes: What is most important is not exogenous but endogenous.[121] In those places there is, then, instability in two directions: from low levels of offending to high, and from high to low.

The same thing happened with the youth violence epidemic. No one saw it coming, but it arrived and grew with historic speed. Once it was entrenched, many saw it as inevitable: the inexorable result of structural factors, character, and the like.[122] The resulting projections, as of a wave of remorseless "superpredators," were often dire in the extreme. At which point it largely went away. In some places, like New York City and Boston, deliberate enforcement interventions played a part in the reductions. But in others— perhaps most notably Los Angeles, whose police department was quite clearly at very low ebb in the wake of the Rodney King and other scandals— considerable reductions were also seen. These reductions, in turn, were again frequently explained in terms of changes in basic factors, making it difficult to explain why in many places violence promptly began to edge up again. The same thing is true of the limited, but fascinating, pictures of offending and offender culture available to us through ethnographic studies. The worlds of safecrackers, "rounders," networks of bank robbers, con artists, and circus grifters portrayed by Letkemann and Inciardi in the "crime as work" literature of the 1970s are all but unrecognizable now: the crime types, offender types, network structures, and governing norms have receded enormously or vanished altogether. Crime, it is fair to say, is always with us, but particular crimes and particular sorts of criminals clearly are not. The idea that urban police officers would routinely hear the sound of safe-cracking explosions, as one of Letkemann's sources described,[123] is as foreign today as the idea that urban police officers would routinely hear the sound of gunshots would have been then.

These processes are also quite clearly frequently *nonlinear*, both in the sense of very rapid, akin-to-geometric increase (and sometimes reduction) in offending, and in the sense of sudden changes in states. This is part of the appeal of notions like "contagion," "epidemic," and "tipping."[124] Offending sometimes moves fairly smoothly and gradually over time, as happened, for example, with the slow reduction in adult homicide victimization in the 1980s and 1990s.[125] But it often does not, as happened with youth violence, which saw a striking increase and a considerable decline over the same period. That such movements are steep does not, of course, make them nonlinear. The intriguing idea here is that there is some sort of process of influence or effect, or involving sudden discontinuities, that would make for large, or larger than expected, or more or less bimodal, outcomes.

These are not hard to find. To take a common example, a highway full of cars stopped by an accident will often wait patiently until someone takes to the prohibited shoulder, at which point others will frequently follow. There is nothing mystical about what is happening. At the same time, such processes can be extremely complicated. When one car moves, generally others also will. That is, still, often not enough to lead to a wholesale departure. At some point, the trickle may become a cascade: The situation has "tipped." Why, and why then? Has a group norm that "shouldering" is acceptable emerged? Has a trooper present failed to intervene, signaling that shouldering is approved? Has the chance that that trooper will apprehend any given shoulderer dropped so low as to be inconsequential? Are drivers unwilling to see others profit while they do not? Are drivers fundamentally competitive, and unwilling to "lose" to others? Has the constant temptation to shoulder undergone "restraint reduction" through the early examples? Does the insight that "early adopters" will travel quickly while late ones will be not much better off than before drive the process? Is there a local "script," known to local drivers, that says, this is what we do in circumstances like these, and which is then learned by other drivers present? Do many of the offending drivers privately believe that what they are doing is wrong, and pluralistically justify the common departure from a common norm?

Such nonlinearities are thus common, easy to recognize, and extremely difficult to explain in any depth. Part of the problem in sorting out what is really going on is that there are *too many* such explanations, all of them plausible, many or all of them quite possibly at work simultaneously, in ways generally too subtle and complex to understand very clearly.

As with notions of "contagion" and "epidemic," the main value at present of recognizing such nonlinearities may be to underscore that these sorts of dynamics may produce, or influence heavily, behavior that we generally assume to be produced by far more fundamental social and personal factors. Urban youth violence may not be produced—proximately—by core community forces, or reflect the emergence of "superpredators;" it may, instead—to use Schelling's term in his pioneering work on tipping—reflect "micromotives."[126] Why exactly did young minority males start carrying guns in the mid-1980s? Did those initially choosing to carry guns see their actions in terms of aggression, protection, business, or status? How did those assessments change as guns and gun use became more common? At what point did *not* having a gun make one stand out? How many such gun carriers, and how many using their guns, did it take to create a sense that the streets had become much more dangerous? How did such carrying and use affect norms around conflict and "respect," and vice versa? How, and how much, did it matter that authorities seemed unable to stop what was happening? None of these are questions for which we have very good answers, still less how they all interacted. We can be satisfied, however, that all mattered. It is not at all difficult to posit a nonlinear process in which many young offenders, looking at one another, reached a point at which they decided to arm themselves and to use their guns in particular ways. It is not at all difficult to imagine a street dynamic in which an emergent norm that one must be perceived as slightly more dangerous than one's peers could lead to a dizzying positive-feedback escalation of violence. It is not at all difficult to believe that many young men might act violently while wishing that things were otherwise. And it is not at all difficult to see how easy it would be to characterize that violence as the product of individual depravity or community collapse.

Granovetter shows that even when analysis is limited to varying distributions of initial preferences and to dynamics involving those preferences—that is, without attention to the emergence of *new* preferences—such processes can be strongly nonlinear; often puzzling and counterintuitive; have dramatically different outcomes based on small differences in initial conditions; and present outcomes that appear to, but do not necessarily, represent deep differences in the dispositions and intentions of individuals and groups.[127] He presents the following illustration. Situation 1 is a crowd of 100 people, with an evenly stratified willingness to riot: one person who will riot spontaneously, a second who will riot if one other person does, a third who will riot if two others do, and so on. Situation 2 is exactly the same, except that the second person requires two people to riot, rather than one. The implications are obvious and fascinating. Situation 1 ends in a riot; in Situation 2 almost nothing happens. Granovetter writes, "Newspaper reports of the two events would surely be written as, in the first case, 'A crowd of radicals engaged in riotous behavior'; in the second, 'A demented troublemaker broke a window while a crowd of solid citizens looked on.'"[128]

In such "situations of company"—not Granovetter's term, but appropriate—small changes in the distribution of initial preferences—equivalent to "a minor fluctuation in the composition of a crowd, or to some change in the situation which altered the distribution of thresholds a bit"[129]—gives rise, mathematically, to strikingly discontinuous outcomes, showing that "two crowds whose average preferences are nearly identical could generate entirely different results."[130] Similar results follow from positing greater influence on individuals from those they view as friends (and, by implication, from those viewed for other reasons as having particular standing, and in the reverse from those viewed as having low standing).[131]

Connolly and Aberg have derived similar results in viewing speeding as a contagious process. They frame a model in which 10 percent of a population of drivers will speed unconditionally, a second 10 percent who will speed if they see more than 10 percent of others speeding, and so on. Given this distribution, they show, everybody speeds (in fact, this result seems to require 10 percent plus one additional speeder).[132] We now begin again with this all-speeding condition. Convert the 10 percent unconditional-speeders to compliers, and, by the same logic, the entire population will comply. They note, as well, just how nonlinear these results are. Convert all but one of the unconditional speeders and the outcome is 90 percent plus one driver speeding, "while a tiny extra effort that converted this last holdout would have a huge effect on overall speeding levels, cutting them from over 90 percent to 0."[133] They, too, show distinct "tipping" points, thresholds above which populations of speeders will tend to draw in more speeders, and below which speeders will tend to drop out.[134]

It is not hard to frame similar dynamics around the aspects of collective behavior, norms, the reading and misreading of norms, communication, networks, and the like described above. In processes involving groups, networks, cultures, and subcultures, it will matter what sorts of behaviors are modeled and keynoted; the standing, or lack thereof, of those who do so; the way their behavior is understood and misunderstood by others; the way those others understand and misunderstand the views and actions of their peers; the manner, speed, and extent of the way information about behavior and norms is communicated; the extent to which all these aspects are open to outside influence; and a host of other such factors. Following Phillips and Carstensen, a suicide advertised by television news can become a miniepidemic of suicide; without the news, it will not be. Within the crack epidemic emerged street markets; had the first of those markets been dealt with effectively by the authorities, or defined as unacceptable by the community, the rest might not have followed. Any such enforcement or community intervention would have been easier before protrafficking norms were established amongst a critical population of young people than after. Such norms may be strong and persistent, as is suggested by the resilience of street dealing behavior, or they may be far more superficial than that, with pluralistic ignorance and fear of losing face driving what appears to be settled disposition and action. Efforts to address the behavior may meet with no success and still be only a short distance away from "tipping" the problem rather dramatically. In an environment in which the problem persists, there may be "equilibrium" points at which the problem manifests itself at quite different levels.

And all of these factors can be interactive. As street markets emerged, official or community action that contained them would have meant fewer offenders to "keynote" the behavior and its acceptance. Less acceptance

would make it easier for a community to maintain a stand against street markets. A smaller problem would mean fewer arrests for street dealing, less tension between the police and the community, fewer opportunities to view the police as helpless and even corrupt, less erosion of the stigma of criminal justice sanction, and the like. Less hostility to the police would make it easier for the community to take a stand against street dealing, and less opportunity for the mistaken interpretation by young dealers of community silence as approval for their actions. A smaller market might raise risks and lower profits to dealers, and be less visible and attractive to outside buyers. There might be a threshold of activity and visibility below which outside buyers will not know, or be willing, to do business, making the market very much easier to address and much less of a magnet for young dealers. Fewer young dealers may mean more young people in legitimate entry-level jobs, reducing the cachet of dealing and of pluralistic ignorance and emerging norms operating in support of dealing. And so on, in what might be and probably are very complicated ways.

Kleiman has identified a particular nonlinear dynamic operating between authorities and offenders that he calls "enforcement swamping."[135] In any enforcement regime for any given type of offense, he argues, there will be a threshold in the number of violations below which the expected value of offending is negative, and above which it is positive. Below the threshold, it will be rational for potential offenders to refrain from offending; above it, it will be rational to offend. Below the threshold violations will tend to diminish, the likelihood of sanction will increase, and expected value will decrease, and so on: The authorities are operating from a position of strength, which should naturally increase. Above the threshold, violations will tend to increase, the likelihood of sanction will decrease, and expected value will increase: the authorities are operating from a position of weakness, which should also naturally increase. Here, too, small changes in the position of authorities and offenders, and small changes in the behavior of authorities and offenders, can result in large changes in outcomes. These outcomes can include stable positions at opposite poles—sustained high levels of offending and sustained low levels of offending—without, importantly, any differences at all in the underlying propensities of offenders or capacities of authorities.[136]

Revisiting some core frameworks addressing offenders and offending

A number of traditional and more recent sets of ideas that seek to address crime and criminality can be viewed in these terms: as processes that combine, often in very complicated ways, social processes in collectivities with nonlinear dynamics. Labeling theory, for example, portrays a social process in which a relatively small initial act—a minor delinquency, for instance—acts on both the delinquent and those in the delinquent's environment in a "cascading" fashion. The young person is taught to think of himself as an offender; the finding of delinquency forecloses legitimate opportunities and makes illegitimate ones more attractive; adults in key roles, such as teachers, consciously or unconsciously act so as to undermine; all of these factors can reinforce one another. Classic theories of delinquency put, as has been discussed, groups and group processes at their core. Insights into the behavior of offenders who are generally considered more or less as individuals—burglars, armed robbers—consistently feature the direct or close influence of groups, networks, and related processes. Studies of burglars, for example, regularly highlight the facilitating role of fences and loose affiliations among offenders.[137] Armed robbers frequently cooffend; frequently prey on victims such as drug dealers who are themselves heavily influenced by, and available because of, groups and network dynamics; and, as has been noted, are frequently motivated by norms that emerge from particular settings of company. Studies of adult gun offenders highlight the mutuality of influence by which risk and fear drive gun-carrying and use.[138] Accounts of the etiology of domestic violence and sexual assault feature the central role of modeled behavior and the often unintended influences of actions by authorities (in which both action and inaction can, depending on context, have criminogenic effect).[139] It is in fact hard to find theories or descriptions of offending in which groups, networks, norms, and associated dynamics do not play a central role.

Some more recent frameworks also very much fit this mold. Wilson and Kelling's "Broken Windows" theory, for example, posits a dynamic process by which low-level offending and disorder affects both offenders and nonoffenders in ways which can lead to communities "tipping" into high-crime states."[140] The similar ideas of "disorder and decline" suggest complicated process in which crime and disorder trigger, at the neighborhood level, changes in social control, criminal opportunities, the functioning of key institutions such as schools, demographic patterns, the use of public space, and the like—all of which are mutually influential and can lead to substantial changes in the character of the neighborhood. Anderson's "code of the street" analysis is, in considerable part, an account of the iterative, recursive effects of offending and victimization; norms and behavior; community institutions; and family and other basic aspects of social structure.[141] Wilson's notion of the "underclass" and underclass neighborhoods, and especially of "concentration effects"—characterizable, again, as a complicated dynamic involving individuals, groups, networks, norms, families, community institutions, and social structures—fits the same pattern. Neither Anderson nor Wilson explicitly seek to explain offending; in both of their accounts, however, offending is both influenced by and influences other key factors and plays a central role in the community dynamics they describe. Even the relatively recent criminological recognition of "hot spots" and other place-based frameworks—most superficially about location as such— frequently turns out to be attending to particular presentations of offending that accompany these sorts of dynamics.[142]

Implications for deterrence

The implications for deterrence and deterrence theory are simple, but profound. Classical deterrence theory focuses on the individual offender and on the individual offense. Without losing sight of that, it is clearly possible to expand that focus to include *groups, networks, and other collectivities.* Beyond that, it is also clearly possible to expand that focus to include *collective processes and dynamics.*

Given the traditions and habits of mind of deterrence theory, this may appear to be either incoherent or a difference that makes no difference. Where offending is concerned, it is possible, surely, to reduce all group behavior to the behavior of individuals. In a gang beef, for example, in each of a series of shootings there is a person who pulls a trigger. We seek, of course, to deter those persons and those actions. This is simple and clear. If we do so, we succeed; if we do not, we fail. What is added—indeed, what might even be *meant*—by framing the issue as deterring the *gang*? And what do we seek to deter, if not the shooting?

Our ways of thinking about these questions are strongly influenced by a number of traditions. Deterrence theory emerges, historically, from utilitarianism, which as a moral philosophy treated individuals making individual decisions. The economic theories that followed used the same frames of reference, focusing on the choices of individuals around single acts. Most deterrence theory was developed, explicitly or implicitly, in relation to the exercise of authority by law enforcement authorities operating as a "criminal justice system," a strategic and legal framework that again focused almost entirely on individual offenders and individual offenses. Our shooter from above was prosecuted for the shooting, not for being a member of a gang: a nonoffense involving a collectivity with no legal standing or, often, even any recognized existence. What sanctions might be brought to bear were (for the most part) formal sanctions against an individual for a particular act. In our ordinary way of thinking, nothing else makes sense. We do not (the very rare RICO and such conspiracy prosecutions excepted) normally move from a shooting to the group or network with which the shooter is associated. Still less do we turn to, say, asset forfeiture—seizing property bought with drug money from another member of the gang—as a way to penalize the gang for the shooting: in part because our legal framework does not—apparently— allow for asset forfeiture in that situation (this is less true than it appears, as we shall see). And still less than that do we frame the use of asset forfeiture as a way of *changing norms about shootings*: to reinforce the notion, within this group that we are not really recognizing, that shooting is bad, will lead to consequences for the entire group, and ought to be frowned upon.

Except that, of course, sometimes we do exactly that. The clearest examples concern collectivities we do recognize, and relationships with those collectivities. "Organized" crime is such an example. The law allows for prosecution of members of some kinds of groups in particular ways. It is not illegal to be a "member" of a group called the "Mafia," but conspiracy, RICO, continuing criminal enterprise, and such legal avenues permit enforcement around groups and networks, and around multiple offenses and patterns of offenses. In some jurisdictions, such as the state of California, the existence of a gang can be formally certified, and offenses by gang members treated in distinctive fashion. Here, the appropriate fact pattern expands the usual enforcement and deterrence framework to include groups and their behavior.

However, groups are quite often recognized by authorities and treated as such *without such formal avenues being available or utilized*. A mafia "soldier" may get quite special attention from authorities simply because his behavior and the context of his behavior are of particular concern. His acts may get particular scrutiny, any cases special prosecutorial attention, probation and parole violations more likely to lead to revocation, and the like. All of this amounts to a special enforcement regime, and by extension a special deterrence regime, without any of it being formally recognized in law.

Within such informal regimes, particular acts may in turn get particular attention, sometimes as part of an explicit attempt to create norms within offender circles that will inhibit such acts. In dealing with networks of violent offenders, for example, the killing of nonparticipants frequently triggers exceptional attention to the network as a whole. When a gang member kills a rival gang member, authorities will pursue that case. When the same gang member shooting at the same gang rival kills a neighborhood child by accident, that shooting will tend to be pursued more vigorously, and it is far more likely that other members of the network will be targeted for special enforcement attention. Absent a fact pattern allowing some sort of collective prosecution, the other members cannot be implicated in the shooting. There may be, in any sense that has legal meaning, no "gang," no "members," and no "gang offense." Such are not necessary for action, however. Particular individuals are often known to be part of the group in question. They will often be open, as individuals, to enforcement attention for drug offenses, weapons offenses, special attention to open and old cases, probation and parole attention, and the like. One of the most frequent police responses is to maintain a sustained, visible presence in the area of the gang's operations; such a response may result in no arrests at all, but will inhibit drug-dealing and similar activities, and thus still impose costs. These official steps, again, take place well outside the statutory framework that appears to govern sanctions to individuals for homicide, and that frame the official deterrence regime for homicide. It is written nowhere that the penalty for a gang homicide may be that fellow gang members receive enhanced probation attention. Deterrence theorists have largely neglected such possibilities. Such strategies, however, are not at all unusual in practice. They are often mobilized explicitly to "send signals" about particular sorts of offending: that is, to deter, and beyond that to inculcate norms in offenders and groups of offenders.

Some such acts are celebrated in enforcement lore. The paradigmatic case is probably the prosecution of Al Capone on federal tax charges. Capone was famously violent, and the moving force in a network of particularly violent and active offenders. He could not be reached by authorities using ordinary means. The tax case was very much a means to an end. Nobody—authorities, Capone himself, or other offenders—ever thought that the government cared much about the tax evasion. All understood the core message: that the government would, in the face of certain kinds of egregious misbehavior, find a way to exact costs. The goal was both to incapacitate Capone and to deter other offenders from the acts that had drawn such special official attention.

Parallel acts are common in law enforcement. William "Billy" Johnston, a police officer who ran the Boston Police Department's Community Disorders Unit during a period of extreme racial tension in Boston, reports that he routinely employed such tactics in addressing neighborhood racial disputes. Black families moving into previously white neighborhoods were often attacked and harassed. Investigation would frequently show that the white perpetrators were also committing other offenses, frequently ones that would otherwise receive no attention. Johnston would speak directly to those perpetrators and inform them that if the harassment didn't stop, they would no longer be able, for example, to drink beer in public in the neighborhood. That, he reports, frequently took care of the matter.[143]

Given that such offenders were likely acting as "models" and "keynotes"—that is, taking key public roles in the framing of new norms in an uncertain situation—controlling their behavior quite plausibly had larger effects that rippled through the networks of which they were part and the neighborhood processes that was underway. It was explicitly part of Johnston's intent to "head off" or "nip in the bud" further and quite possibly catastrophic racial strife: that is, to prevent the situation he faced from reaching its tipping point, which could easily have resulted in race riot. We have, thus, the threat of enforcement for a petty crime being used strategically to shape behavior on a wholly different front, frame new norms, influence networks and contingent nonlinear dynamics, and prevent much more serious and widespread offending. Such frameworks for deterrence, while largely unrecognized by deterrence theory, are in fact quite common in practice within law enforcement.

8 Reframing deterrence

If we gather together the various strands identified thus far, we arrive at something like the following:

- Deterrence rests on the actual decision processes of offenders and potential offenders, regardless of whether those are what other persons would regard as "rational."
- Deterrence rests on the information available to and beliefs of offenders, not on the actual objective environment.
- Any sanction—formal or informal, internal or external—that attaches to behavior can serve to deter that behavior. There is good reason to believe that informal sanctions often matter more than formal ones. To the extent that offenders are influenced by personal and social capital, and internal and external norms, these dimensions—not only the imposition of formal penalties—can properly be considered part of the deterrence calculus and open to deliberate intervention.
- The severity of any sanction is entirely in the eye of its potential recipient. There is good reason to believe that the scale of severity as viewed by many offenders does not match the scale assumed by authorities and the public. There is good reason to believe that these judgments are different for different offenders.
- Offender knowledge about the risks that attach to various behaviors is crucial to deterrence. There is good reason to believe that such knowledge is deeply imperfect.
- The communication of sanction risk is crucial to deterrence. Such communication is very rarely pursued in a deliberate manner. Where deliberate communication is pursued, much of it is patently false.
- The behavior of authorities frequently sends misleading signals about the deterrence regime offenders actually face.
- The standing of rules and official actions in the eyes of offenders greatly affects the impact of sanctions and other acts by authorities. Where rules and actions are viewed as fair and reasonable, their impact is enhanced. Where it is not, their impact is vitiated and even perverse.

- The risks many offenders face for their behavior, even for very serious offending, can be strikingly low, even when that offending is well-known to authorities. Those risks can be very uneven and difficult to predict from offender to offender and for the same offender at different times.
- The imposition of sanctions does not necessarily result in even a small deterrent effect. Enforcement strategies can undercut deterrence through damage to personal capital, damage to social capital, the erosion and even inversion of stigma, precipitating offending, undercutting self-control and provoking backlash, and undercutting the legitimacy of authorities.
- The failure of enforcement strategies can create criminogenic dynamics which are often, but should not necessarily be, read as reflective of deep social and characterological factors.
- It is possible to consider the deterrence not only of individuals but also groups, networks, and other collectivities.
- It is possible to consider deterrence not only as a factor governing the decisions of individuals and groups, but also as a strategic intervention in group processes and dynamics.

One pole of our conventional framing of deterrence dynamics is considering the outcome of *predominantly ordinary criminal justice case processing activities*. From this vantage, deterrence is, or is not, the result of global statutory and operational policies: the impact of arrest, or mandatory arrest, on domestic violence, or the impact of the death penalty on homicide. The main concern is the formal penalties that attach to particular offenses, and the way the case processing machinery of criminal-justice agencies in fact imposes those penalties. The creation of special deterrence regimes is a commonplace in this way of thinking and operating; that is part of the intent, and perhaps the result, of attaching different penalties to different crimes, to sentencing enhancements for offenders with particular sorts of criminal histories, to restricting the discretion of police and judges through mandatory arrest and mandatory sentencing requirements, and the like. At the same time, once such regimes are created, their application is intended to become routine and conventional.

Another pole emphasizes the outcome of *discretionary decisions and activities*. A police department chooses to drastically increase its use of breathalyzer testing. Beyond that, it chooses to advertise its actions to the driving public. A federal prosecutor chooses to focus on gun-carrying cases (and, further, to advertise that fact). A police department chooses to enforce all available laws against even the pettiest offenses in high-crime neighborhoods as a way of regaining control of the streets. Here, while the limits of action are clearly set by law—authorities cannot impose legal penalties not permitted by statute—what seems to matter most is not what the penalties *are* but *how and why they are being deployed*. And even the law only limits the imposition of formal sanctions. It is entirely within the power of authorities facing an outbreak of, say, juvenile street drug-dealing to go to parents and say, here is what your son is doing, we strongly suggest you do something. It is even within their power to organize local churches to encourage community sentiment against street drug-dealing. Such regimes tend not to be routine and conventional but various sorts of special initiatives and projects. Their strength, if there is any, comes from the use of discretion to create distinctive deterrence regimes.

The boundaries between these two poles are not at all clear. The supposedly routine and conventional rarely looks to be just that upon close examination; in particular, the exercise of discretion is constant in even the most apparently ordinary workings of enforcement. Special deterrence regimes usually employ conventional sanctions in some fashion or other and can themselves become more or less conventional and routinized, as happened with Richmond's Project Exile. Still, the poles are real, and meaningful. There is a genuine difference between addressing a sizable street drug market through routine buy–bust enforcement and addressing it by announcing to dealers that on a date certain there will be a massive multiagency sweep (the example is real; in this case, the conventional did not work, and the unconventional did[1]). The main difference lies in the distinction between attempting to generate deterrence through routine case-processing activities, and attempting to generate deterrence, and other impacts via deterrence, through more customized activities.

A basic schema for considering such special deterrence regimes might include:

- attention to selected offenses and behaviors;
- attention to selected offenders;
- attention to selected "problems";
- a range of sanctions, both formal and informal;
- attention to offending individuals;
- attention to offending groups and networks;
- the framing of deterrence messages;
- the communication of deterrence messages;
- the establishment of more or less sustained relationships between authorities and offenders;
- clarifying, mobilizing, and altering norms;
- identifying and intervening in criminogenic dynamics.

These are not, clearly, neatly separated categories; overlap is frequent. At the same time, these categories reflect meaningful, and suggestive, distinctions in the larger deterrence enterprise.

Attention to selected offenses and behaviors

Special attention to particular offenses is of course routine in traditional enforcement and deterrence regimes. Such attention is often reflected in statute. It may indicate concern about particularly egregious offenses, as in some states' restriction of the death penalty to homicides involving police officers. It may reflect concern about what is revealed by the conjunction of lesser offenses, as in the federal sentencing guidelines' provision for sentencing enhancements when both illegal firearms and illegal drugs are found together. It may reflect a judgment about an individual's pattern of criminality, as is true of third offenses in three-strikes regimes. The criminal law can be regarded, in considerable part, as a set of social judgments about the weight that should be given to particular offenses and kinds of offenses.

A different kind of special attention is often reflected in the discretionary deployment of enforcement activity. Some such distinctions reflect, at least in part, more or less persistent judgments about the social and community costs of different kinds of offending. Police departments will often pay a great deal of attention to public prostitution, and virtually none to the escort agencies that advertise in the yellow pages. Prosecutors will pay a great deal of attention to street-corner drug trafficking, and much less to discreet trafficking in bars and high schools. The illegal sale of firearms to gang members may be a high priority, while the equally illegal sale of firearms amongst peer networks of hunters and collectors raises no concern.

A frequent variation on that theme involves particular kinds of offending in *particular settings or contexts*, which may or may not be persistent. Moderate levels of speeding are usually disregarded, but not near schools during school hours. Drunk-driving enforcement soars around national holidays and the Super Bowl. Attention to a wide range of low-level street offending is enhanced in neighborhoods that seem to be on the verge of "tipping" into rampant public criminality. Offenses associated with gang activity get special attention after an apparent gang homicide. Offenses that disturb the public and disrupt commerce get special attention as part of a community initiative to revitalize a flagging urban business district.

Authorities will often give special attention to offenses that seem to carry *special meaning* or have the likelihood of generating *special consequences*. Assaults on police officers and prosecutors are a classic example—they are, for a variety of reasons, typically treated quite differently to other assaults. Incidents of witness intimidation, seen to undercut the entire criminal-justice process, frequently get particular attention. Offenses seen as likely to provoke retaliation, such as a homicide or an assault involving members of rival gangs, may get special treatment. Offenses that may be the harbinger of new problems in particular areas will often get a heightened response: Police may tolerate streetwalking in urban "red light" districts but address it immediately in adjoining residential neighborhoods.

Authorities will not uncommonly focus on particular offenses entirely as a *means to an end*; in these cases, there is no great concern about the offense as such but a recognition of a larger opportunity presented by the offense. The use of "pretext" motor-vehicle stops as a means to seize firearms and drugs is one such strategy.[2] The offenses in question are traffic or vehicle code violations, but the official interest in those offenses stems almost entirely from the opportunity they give officers to invoke Terry searches.[3] The interest of transit police in fare-beating is another such example. Transit authorities have some intrinsic interest in preventing fare-beating, but a larger interest in the opportunity enforcement provides to arrest more serious offenders, seize weapons, serve outstanding warrants, and the like. Such strategies do not always involve petty offenders and petty offenses. It is not uncommon, for example, to hear federal prosecutors say in private that they have no interest as such in federal drug prosecutions and deploying often draconian federal drug penalties—they have given up the "drug war" as unwinnable—but that they readily and consciously use those tools as a way to solve violent crimes, dismantle violent organizations, and incapacitate violent offenders.

If there is reason to believe that offending in general, or some kinds of offending in particular, are "modeled" or "keynoted," and that the perceived official response to offending may signal to offenders and potential offenders the intention and the capacity of authorities to act effectively, then there might be reason to pay particular attention to *first instances*, or more broadly early instances, of given sorts of offenses. Drug epidemics, for example, might be averted if authorities responded effectively to the first manifestation of the trafficking of a particular drug in their jurisdiction. Both the supply-side and the demand-side aspects of epidemics proceed nonlinearly and through observation and imitation; those processes may be open to being interrupted early (and perhaps often) in ways that they cannot be interrupted later on. Likewise, different forms of drug activity may be open to a deliberate "first-instance" strategy. Street markets and problems associated with street markets were and are a distinctive feature of the crack epidemic. It is not altogether implausible to think that had authorities in given jurisdictions simply not permitted street markets—which always begin in particular locations and on a small scale—to take root, their subsequent cascade of problems might have been avoided. The same thing may be happening now with Ecstasy; once largely limited to face-to-face trafficking amongst middle-class students, rave-goers, and the like, several cities are now seeing street Ecstasy markets.[4] If Ecstasy breaks out as a widespread problem, this is how it may happen, and these markets are a critical opportunity to head that off. Similar dynamics may pertain with other sorts of offenses and issues concerning offending. Many urban jurisdictions now have serious problems with routine witness intimidation. This was once not true. In each jurisdiction, there were early examples that went unaddressed, and that may have modeled the behavior for future offenders and signaled to offenders and witnesses alike that there would be no meaningful response. In such instances, it is not only the *form* but the *scale* of the offending that matters. A few street dealers selling crack is something a good police department can address, if it chooses to do so. A city covered with street markets, and with buyers and sellers alike accustomed to those markets, is another matter entirely.

Given that authorities are often not operating from positions of strength—that they are, in Kleiman's framework, often operating on the wrong side of the enforcement swamping divide—there may often be reason to pay particular attention to *next instances* of particular offenses. There may be far too many instances of witness intimidation in a given jurisdiction to give heightened, effective attention to each one. If, however, authorities commit to give *the next instance that presents itself* an effective response, and if—crucially, and a matter to which we will return—potential offenders *know* of that commitment, the effect may be to deter each potential next instance, that is, to deter them all. Police and prosecutors may be unable to address each violent drug crew in their jurisdiction. But they may be able, rather easily, to dismantle *the next drug crew that shoots somebody.* If—and, again, crucially—all drug crews know that this will happen, the deterrence dynamic changes dramatically. This is a key aspect of Boston's Ceasefire violence prevention initiative and similar operations, which explicitly and openly bring special sanctions to bear on "next acts" of certain kinds of violence.[5]

It may also make sense to *openly vary* such special enforcement responses. Sherman has argued in the context of ordinary police crackdowns that the most productive approach may be to deploy enforcement across available targets in a serial fashion: the crime-control impact of each crackdown can persist for a time when the crackdown is over,[6] and telling each of twenty drug crews that two of them at a time will be chosen for special enforcement attention—on a schedule, and for a duration, of the authorities' choosing—could serve to dampen them all down, as long as the risk each faces is sufficient to influence behavior.

This discussion has taken place entirely, as is the convention, around examples of criminal offending. It seems incoherent that it should be otherwise. It is not; deterrence can occur, and in fact frequently does occur, around nonoffending behavior. It is perhaps easiest to approach this subject by first considering deterrence produced by other than formal sanctions. A gang member newly in love may—will, for the sake of example—face disapproval from the object of his affections for committing armed robbery and dealing drugs—both crimes. He may also, however, face disapproval and other sanctions for socializing with old companions, drinking, frequenting certain places, and comporting himself in particular ways. The gang member, his old friends, and his new friend will all understand exactly what is going on: He is being moved away from associations, actions, and places that are likely to lead to trouble. Offenders may, through such influences or through counseling, mentors, or simply changes of heart and mind, internalize these sorts of precepts, violations of which then manifest themselves as guilt and shame.

Such restrictions and deterrence dynamics often play a central role in probation and parole regimes. In such settings, what is ordinarily not criminal—associating with certain companions, staying out late, drinking—or is ordinarily a matter of personal discretion—going to school, getting a job, obtaining counseling—becomes by turn forbidden or obligatory. Something similar occurs in the in the civil restrictions that obtain through instruments such as restraining orders, which attach penalties to behaviors which are ordinarily unexceptionable.

These are formal influences directed at formally proscribed behaviors. It is not unusual to find formal influences directed at informally proscribed behaviors. It is a common, and clearly frequently justified, complaint of minority motorists that they are singled out for traffic enforcement, especially in majority neighborhoods or while driving expensive cars: the impact of which—intentional or not—may be to deter their presence in those neighborhoods and the manifesting of wealth. Groups of disorderly youth in a neighborhood park may face particularized enforcement of trespassing, underage drinking and open-container laws, with the explicit or implicit understanding that citation for such violations—criminal acts—is because of, and intended to deter, their presence and their noisy behavior: neither a criminal act.

Formal enforcement may also be brought to bear in order to deter actions that are clearly part of larger criminal dynamics but are not themselves criminal or actionable. As part of a broad strategy to reduce youth offending, authorities in Winston-Salem, North Carolina are focusing criminal sanctions on drug dealers who recruit juveniles as steerers and lookouts. It is not a crime to whistle when a patrol car drives down a street, nor is it a crime to give a child a pair of shoes to do so. All involved, however, understand what is going on, and that this is a critical moment in the launching of a criminal career. Authorities have therefore informed known drug dealers that this sort of thing will not be tolerated and will bring the attention of authorities to those aspects of the dealers' offending that *are* available: drug cases, outstanding warrants, probation and parole violations, and the like.[7] The penalty for socializing kids into offending thus becomes, potentially and for example, careful attention to a probation violation that would otherwise have been overlooked. The deterrence logic is clear and explicit.

Finally, authorities can act *to seek more information about the occurrence of selected offenses and behaviors*. The machinery of enforcement and deterrence can only be mobilized when authorities know that they have cause to act. Authorities can be greatly more or less activist about seeking such knowledge. In the case, for example, of a repeat domestic abuser, police can wait for his victim to call. She frequently will not do so. Police can also, however, work with medical and shelter providers to identify such high-risk victims, visit her regularly to assess her situation, and structure relationships with her neighbors, friends, and family to gather information about any violence.[8] Armed robberies of drug dealers are only infrequently reported to police, but knowledge regarding who is committing such robberies is often widespread in offender circles and is frequently known to line-level police officers. Mobilizing confidential informants to gather such information is possible and productive, as is creating internal procedures so that existing agency information is collected and can be acted upon.[9] Recruiting juveniles as lookouts is, as noted, generally not even criminal, but when it occurs and who is responsible is usually well known in the community and frequently well known to area police officers. Such information can be collected, and once collected can be acted upon.

Attention to selected offenders

The law, as has been noted, frequently makes important distinctions between offenders, particularly on the basis of offending history and key factors in the context of particular offenses. At the same time, authorities—and communities and peer networks—routinely differentiate between offenders in ways that the law does not. Beyond that, there are ways in which it might be sensible and productive to differentiate further.

The most common judgments made about offenders have to do with "seriousness." Particular offenders are thought to be particularly serious, usually based on the characteristics of an instant offense or series of offenses, a criminal career, or the role the offender is known to be playing in relation to other offenders. Some such characteristics are recognized in law. An assault, for example, can be charged as simple or aggravated. Particular criminal histories may allow charging as a "three strikes" offender or "armed career criminal." Federal drug laws allow a "kingpin" designation. Much information clearly relevant to questions of seriousness, however, is explicitly ruled out of consideration in prosecution and sentencing. Evidence of prior crimes is generally not admissible at trial. Sentencing may take an offender's criminal history into account but sequester information about even very serious juvenile offenses, and in any case remains limited to the statutory range for the offense in question. In both cases information not part of the formal record—for example, knowledge of crimes committed by the offender but not prosecuted or for which convictions were not obtained—is not admissible.

Such knowledge may greatly change the picture of an offender. It is routine, for example, for authorities to have certain knowledge of even very serious crimes and not be able to pursue them to an arrest or conviction. The information implicating the offender may not be admissible, as when it was obtained by illegal means such as an improper search. It may have come from a source authorities are unwilling to use as an affiant or a witness. It may have been developed in the course of an investigation focusing on other offenses and other offenders, which authorities are unwilling to compromise. It may be part of a case in which witnesses are unwilling to come forward, for example because they are intimidated or because they are also offenders. The crime in question, for example a shooting in the course of a drug house robbery, may never have been reported. An offender may be known to have committed a serious offense but to have pled to a substantially lesser charge, which will then be the matter of record. Limits imposed by resources and operational policies may inhibit the pursuit of offenses and offenders that are in principle open to enforcement. As a result, it is common for the picture of an offender held by experienced enforcement personnel, and knowledgeable figures in communities, to be very different from those suggested by formal records. This may operate, as well, in the other direction. A historically serious offender may be known to have calmed down, or reformed, or succumbed to substance abuse.

Similarly, an individual may be responsible for serious offending without being legally implicated, or implicable, in such offending. High-level drug offenders may operate high-volume and violent networks without ever touching drugs or a weapon with their own hands. Particularly violent individuals may go long periods without committing a violent crime; their history and reputation bear fruit without needing to be demonstrated.

Authorities routinely act on the basis of such knowledge. Much of the discretion exercised by police, prosecutors, and probation and parole authorities is so driven. Police direct investigations and make decisions about arrests, prosecutors make judgments about charging and pleading, and probation and parole gauge levels of supervision and decisions about revocation on the basis of this sort of information. At one pole of such discretion is the creation of special initiatives to target selected offenders. Such initiatives generally draw on a range of sources of information in the targeting process and may rely on indirect means to bring enforcement to bear: A violent drug-house robber may be taken off the street on an unrelated parole violation such as a failed drug test. Indianapolis' VIPER (Violent Impact Program Enhance Response) program is an example aimed at violent street, especially gang, offenders.[10] This is the everyday version of using the tax law to reach Capone. Whether such initiatives generate deterrence may turn on whether those subject to them understand what is going on—again, a question to which we will return.

This familiar framework rests on identifying the "worst" offenders. A less familiar framework involves identifying those who are worst *right now*. Some offenders are serious all the time. Many more offenders, however, are serious some of the time. Particular circumstances may give rise to periods of greatly heightened risk. A chronic domestic batterer may be a consistently abusive, but only inclined toward lethality during the ending of a relationship. A gang member may routinely offend on a variety of fronts but become quite predictably dangerous when the shooting of a friend revitalizes a historic beef with another gang. Subordinate members of a stable mob hierarchy may become unstable when a prison sentence takes their leader out of play. A relatively quiet drug group may become violent when another group encroaches on their turf. A feature of such moments is that they frequently both come and go: The period of heightened risk passes, for a variety of reasons. Such moments are often well known to authorities. Those who work with domestic violence, for example, will often say that it is impossible to predict on the basis of criminal histories, restraining orders, and the like which batterers are particularly dangerous, much less when they will become so. Asked, however, whether they generally know which batterers in their jurisdiction are particularly dangerous, and to which women, *at the moment*, they will answer that they do.[11] This kind of information can be the basis for action.

Another basis for stratifying offenders can be that they or their actions are particularly *influential*. The leaders of gangs, groups, and other such collectivities may exercise considerable control over their followers or peers. Shaping their behavior can mean shaping the behavior of many. In Lowell, Massachusetts, authorities working with Harvard researcher Anthony Braga addressed street shootings by young Asian gang members by raiding the gambling enterprises of their elders—and telling the elders that the shootings were bringing the unwanted attention. The shootings stopped entirely.[12]

Offenders may also be quite influential without being either leaders or inherently particularly serious. One suspects that those who first sold crack on street corners tended to be young, sad, and desperate, a portrait borne out by what little ethnography is available.[13] But the "keynote" behavior they modeled was critically important behavior, and the failure of authorities to address it was a critically important failure. The same might be said of the first purveyor of Ecstasy in a high school, the first chemist to set up a methamphetamine laboratory in a given rural area, the first suburban spree shooter, the first inside trader in a financial market. They, or their actions, or the failure to address their actions, have predictably large consequences.

Finally, it may make sense to single out offenders simply because they are doing what they are doing at a particular *place and time*, or in a particular *concentration*. A few public drinkers are one thing; a few public drinkers at night are another; a great number of public drinkers at night yet another; and a great number of public drinkers at night on a street with all the streetlights shot out something else again. The criminological and crime-control literature having to do with place suggests three distinct, if related, reasons for respecting such dimensions. One is that there may be quite powerful criminogenic dynamics, such as "broken windows," that are driven or precipitated by such concentrations, or by such concentrations in particular contexts. Another is that the concentration itself, set against a given level of formal or informal social control, can represent a problem. The enforcement swamping model suggests that there are tipping points in such relationships: Keeping or bringing offending below that tipping point will help keep it under control or return it to control. Finally, concentrations are just that: concentrations. Offending is far from evenly distributed in space and time. If there are strategies that can address disproportionate concentrations, they will have disproportionate results.

The range of sanctions

Shifting, or expanding, from a legalistic, case-processing framework for the imposition of sanctions to a more customized, discretion-based framework can dramatically alter the sanctions available to create deterrence. In the conventional framework, sanctions may be considered limited only to what may follow from arrest for a particular offense, including formal costs, such as those incurred by case processing and sentencing, and informal costs, such as damage to employment prospects. Both actual sanctions and sanctions that appear to offenders as prospective may serve to create deterrence. In the expanded framework, sanctions may be considered *any costs that may be imposed or follow from deliberate action by authorities, and that attach in the eyes of offenders to proscribed offenses or other actions.* This is a very different environment. The core insights of traditional deterrence theory remain useful. Sanctions may be formal (arrest) or informal (job loss). Informal sanctions may be internal (guilt and shame) or external (losing a girlfriend). Different combinations of certainty, severity, and swiftness apply. Different sanctions are viewed differently by different offenders; it is the weight of the sanction from the offender's perspective that determines impact. How these various factors can be brought to bear in actual practice, however, changes quite substantially.

The most obvious change is the creation of an extremely large and varied menu of sanctions available as responses to given offenses or behaviors. Formal sanctions include any and all formal costs deployable by authorities given the particulars of any given situation. In the ordinary course of events, a domestic assault can result only in arrest and prosecution for that assault, with formal sanctions including the costs of those processes and any attached penalties such as probation or incarceration. In the expanded framework, those sanctions are still available. So, however, is an enormous range of other possibilities. If the offender in question also offends in other ways, as is typical of domestic abusers, he may experience exposure on a number of different fronts.[14] He may be on probation or parole. He may drive drunk. He may traffic in and use drugs. He may possess and carry an illegal firearm, commit other, more "public" assaults, have outstanding warrants, face old cases that have been disregarded by police and prosecutors, or have current cases they have yet to be resolved. He may simply like to drink on his front porch. Authorities can choose to act in distinctive ways on any of these fronts *because of the domestic violence.* If the offender understands, and if other, potential offenders understand, what is being done and why, any costs thus created attach to the domestic violence, and become part of any deterrence dynamic that may be operating.[15]

The principle operating here is simple, but profound. As with Al Capone, many sanctions can be brought to bear at the discretion of authorities. In Winston-Salem, the Drug Enforcement Administration is part of the coalition of authorities working to prevent juvenile offending. It is thus possible, in theory, that a drug trafficker's use of juveniles as lookouts could be met with a federal drug investigation and federal prosecution for any actionable drug offenses. Or, to take another avenue, authorities could choose to act on a technical parole violation by the trafficker—failure to pay child support, for example—and return him to prison for the balance of a sentence for a previous crime. Or his name may be flagged at the prosecutor's office so that the next time he crosses a desk for any offense whatsoever—drunk driving, a weapons charge, a domestic complaint—the case will get special and maximal attention. The possibilities will vary enormously, given the facts obtaining in particular situations. But the possibilities will frequently expand dramatically from those that obtain for ordinary enforcement.

In addition to formal sanctions, informal sanctions may also be brought to bear. These are generally thought of as outside the direct influence of authorities. Internal informal sanctions, such as feelings of guilt and shame, and external informal sanctions, such as community and peer disapproval, may be triggered by official action, such as arrest, but only if the predicate norms already exist in the offender and in a given social setting and only if subsequent processes bring those norms into play. However, several kinds of deliberate action may lead to the creation of new norms; the emergence of existing norms; and heightened impact from the violation of those norms.

Internal norms—it's wrong to be violent, it's wrong to steal, it's wrong to sell drugs—may be established or enhanced through individual contacts such as mentoring and broad-based initiatives such as "social marketing" campaigns, examples of which include the "friends don't let friends drive drunk" and "squash it" youth violence programs.[16] These sorts of mechanisms are usually seen as "prevention" initiatives, with prevention defined in conscious opposition to, and excluding, authority-based interventions, but even where they fail in their core aspiration to be independently effective, they may create internal standards for behavior which when violated impose internal costs.[17]

Internal norms may also be created in a two (or more) stage process set in motion by enforcement actions and policies. This is a classic aspect of traditional deterrence theory, in which legal prohibitions and effective enforcement thereof, as for homicide, create internalized rules for behavior. The same can happen in a more proximate and localized, and discretion-based, fashion. Effective official action against street drug-dealing, for example, may result more or less directly in internal norms defining street drug-dealing as inappropriate. Such mechanisms as cognitive dissonance may operate in the same direction, as justificatory rationales are brought into alignment with actual behavior.[18] Finally, internal norms may be created through the influence of, and observation of, others whose behavior is being influenced by enforcement action and policies. If, as in Winston-Salem, local drug figures know that they will face trouble if their networks employ juveniles, they may instruct others in those networks that employing juveniles is inadvisable, and, perhaps, wrong. Other drug figures rising in the business may simply learn by example that employing juveniles is something one does not do.

External informal sanctions may also be created and mobilized through deliberate action. A classic example of this process is community organizing around local crime concerns. A street drug market, for example, can be seriously disrupted by neighborhood patrols, picketing, confrontation of dealers by residents, and the like.[19] Drive-through buyers from out of the neighborhood can be deterred by sending notices to the address of registration for their cars; some, perhaps most, of that deterrence will come through the subsequent actions of the buyers' parents and spouses. In some instances, making information available may be all that is necessary; this is the rationale behind publishing the names of "johns" arrested in prostitution sweeps, and facilitating access to the criminal histories of domestic abusers.[20]

All of these possibilities—formal sanctions for the target behavior, formal sanctions on other dimensions that become attached to the target behavior, internal informal sanctions, and external informal sanctions—may, and frequently will, greatly change the *certainty* and *swiftness* with which penalties may be delivered. An individual known to have committed a gang homicide, for example, will normally not be sanctioned unless the case is cleared, and not until the prosecution is successful. The first can happen quite quickly, but not uncommonly takes weeks or months; not uncommonly it will not happen at all, even when the killer and the circumstances of the killing are well-known. The latter routinely takes years from the time of arrest. At the moment the individual is identified as the murderer, however, probation or parole supervision can be enhanced; an existing cold case reopened; an existing case on another front—for example, a drug arrest—given maximal prosecutorial attention; the gang's drug markets disrupted; and the like. Authorities may not be able to do very much about threatening behavior by a chronic domestic abuser, particularly absent assistance from the victim, which the abuser may be well able to prevent. They may, however, be able to arrest him on the spot on an outstanding bench warrant for failure to appear with regard to an old drunk driving arrest.

The *severity* of penalties may also change greatly. This is true both when viewed in conventional terms and, more significantly, when viewed through the eyes of their recipients. The statutory penalty for a misdemeanor domestic assault may be limited to a few months in jail. If authorities turn their attention instead to the offender's drug trafficking, the result may be a long federal prison sentence. It is important, however, to keep in mind that that conventional reckoning of severity may or may not be how offenders see things. To turn things around, a serious young drug trafficker may be convinced he will not live into adulthood. To him, the prospect of a long federal drug sentence may carry little deterrent weight, particularly if there is little likelihood that it will be imposed until several years have passed, when he no longer expects to be around. He may, on the other hand, care deeply about his grandmother's disapproval; more deeply about the prospect of a probation supervision regime that will genuinely require him to be in his mother's home in the evening, stay away from his friends and the clubs they frequent, and abstain from smoking marijuana; and more deeply still if he is spurned by his friends themselves. Creating the prospect, and when necessary the fact, of these consequences may be far more effective than the most draconian formal penalties.

As is the case in the conventional deterrence framework, certainty, severity, and swiftness matter together as well as alone. An armed robber may be little influenced by the long-term prospect that a severe penalty will attach at some point to his offending; while that prospect may approach unity, unpredictability with regard to discovery and sanction for *any particular offense* vitiates its impact. He may, however, be influenced by knowledge that the police are soliciting information about armed robbers from confidential informants; influenced further by formal notice that he is open to a three-strikes prosecution for his next violent felony; influenced further by formal notice from prosecutors that he not only *might* but *will* be so prosecuted if the opportunity presents itself; influenced still more by a promise from his parole officer that information from the police that he is committing robberies not only *might* but *will* result in his parole being revoked; and influenced most of all by the knowledge that if any sort of proceedings are initiated, his new girlfriend will leave him. Given a full range of formal and informal sanctions, it will often be able to construct deterrence regimes that matter, or at least that matter more than the conventional workings of case-processing.

Groups, networks, and collectivities

Much offending involves various sorts of groups and networks, and many processes that influence offending do likewise. These groups and networks rarely exist in law, at least relative to their actual prevalence. They are still more rarely subject, as such, to official attention, and more rarely still to official sanction. Where they do face official attention and sanction, that fact may be obscure both to them and to other groups and networks, vitiating any deterrent impact that might otherwise obtain. A street gang, for example, may be the object of focused police attention because one of its number committed a homicide. But because the gang does not exist as a matter of law, that attention presents itself as a series of arrests and prosecutions of individuals. The gang *itself* may not understand what has happened to it; still less will other gangs understand.[21]

There are two powerful and related reasons to want to address these facts. One is that groups and networks are high-crime settings, perhaps particularly so for serious and violent crime. Another is that groups and networks are settings within which, and between which, powerful criminogenic dynamics are at work. In each case, they are frequently more than aggregations of individuals, and more important than the individuals who make them up would suggest. Authorities more often than not respond even to crimes with a very strong and evident network setting, such as a vendetta shooting between street gangs, by attempting to address the shooter alone. Such approaches have clear problems. In a gang-on-gang vendetta, for example, successfully prosecuting the shooter may do nothing to interrupt the vendetta. In a more robust deterrence framework, at least four ways of addressing networks (following Waring, we will henceforth frame gangs, groups, and similar collectivities as networks) and network dynamics suggest themselves. Deterrence strategies can address the network as such; key actions by and between networks; key figures within and between networks; and key processes and norms within and between networks.

Discretion-based strategies can readily attend to networks, even where case-processing strategies cannot. Enforcement can easily be directed to the members and the offenses of a street gang; a fence and the thieves he works with; an interstate gun-running ring; and the like. In the simplest form of such attention, discretionary action can be used to the same end that a RICO, continuing criminal enterprise, or conspiracy prosecution is generally used: to "dismantle," as the law enforcement community likes to say, the network in question. Individuals are identified, their individual legal exposures identified, investigations and prosecutions undertaken, and so on. In the end, the network is eliminated or crippled. Such actions are not uncommon in law enforcement, though by no means the norm.

A second approach is to address certain kinds of behavior by the network or its members. To continue the example, a vendetta shooting may be seen as particularly significant both in and of itself and because it will provoke further violence. Because the basic dynamic is one between networks rather than between individuals, the networks are sanctioned. Individual members are identified, their legal exposures identified and addressed, and so on. Actions may be taken that impose costs more or less on the network as a whole, such as disrupting the street drug markets where members do business. Sanctions may be delivered—that is, costs imposed—without eliminating the group, just as an individual may be punished without being permanently incapacitated. For any deterrence to result, it is, again, crucial that the networks, and any networks observing this process, understand what is being done and why. It is easy to imagine variations on this theme. As in Winston-Salem, networks could be sanctioned for recruiting juveniles. Drug-dealing networks could be sanctioned for selling to new users or for selling new drugs, as a way of inhibiting drug epidemics, or for selling in public, as a way of controlling the community harms associated with street markets.[22] Stolen-goods networks could be sanctioned for trafficking in product taken in residential burglaries.[23] The deterrence logic is simple, though its application is largely unfamiliar.

A third approach is to address key figures within networks. "Key" can take on a number of meanings. Networks rarely, though sometimes, have individuals who are "leaders" or who "run things" in the ordinary sense of there being more or less formal roles or very much in the way of structure and discipline. Eminence, as has been noted previously, tends to be more about informal standing and modeled behavior. Such eminence, however, is still eminence. Such figures and their influence can frequently be readily identified by close observers. Networks frequently—invariably, perhaps— have individuals who are considerably more active, or more dangerous, than the rest; authorities who work closely with street drug networks, for example, will often identify one or two individuals out of ten or twenty who are the only, or the main, shooters in the network. Such individuals also often model and reinforce certain norms within the group, and may also "instigate" cooffenders into particular acts and patterns of acts, their behavior acting to amplify and multiply the network's criminogenic tendencies.[24] Networks frequently include individuals who play key roles. These individuals may occupy positions of standing and influence; the literature on fencing, for example, is replete with accounts of figures who promoted and facilitated the activity of substantial numbers of thieves and burglars. The fence studied by Klockars stood at the nexus of a network that may have been national in scope.[25] They may also play no such "leadership" role, but a crucial one nonetheless. The San Diego Police Department, for example, shut down a street drug market by using deterrence techniques to hobble the activities of the "steerers" who connected buyers with sellers. The steerers were essentially street people of next to no standing, but their function was essential, and without it the market collapsed.[26] These same roles may be identified in relationships *between* networks. A gang beef, for example, may involve networks on both sides but be sustained primarily by the heightened feelings of only a few figures in each network. Shaping the behavior of the individuals in any of these roles can have disproportionate impact on the rest of the network, and sometimes on multiple networks and relationships between them.

Finally, it is possible to frame deterrence interventions that focus on *key processes and norms* within and between networks. Much urban violence, for example, currently presents itself as interactions within and between small networks of chronic offenders.[27] The violence is driven by a number of factors, which include "scripts" and "codes" that define the—frequent—situations in which violence is indicated, and more or less standing hostile relationships between different networks.[28] Deliberate interventions focused on members of networks and the norms they hold might influence their behavior. Simply deterring back-and-forth violence between groups might be enough to undercut vendettas and, beyond that, the group cohesion they foster. Other processes readily suggest themselves. Groups might be deterred from incorporating new juvenile members, or at least from deploying such members as shooters (who, because of their legal status, face little prospect of meaningful sanction). The police officers and judges who openly did business with Klockars' fence might themselves be deterred from doing so, and thus from signaling that the practice was safe and acceptable.[29] Norms might also be addressed directly, a matter we will return to in a moment.

Messages

Deterrence rests centrally on the implicit or explicit sending and receiving of messages. As has been noted, deterrence theory has not given this area much systematic thought, nor have deterrence operations, with rare exceptions, developed it practically. In this section, we will address the *content* of possible messages, while in the next we will address their *form*. In what follows the boundaries between categories is frequently blurry. A basic taxonomy, however, emerges fairly clearly from the core logic of deterrence and the deterrence process.

Risks

The most basic messages will clearly be ones about *risks*. These may take several forms.

Statutory risks

As has been seen, offenders frequently understand even *existing* statutory risks poorly. Conveying those risks—at least when the reality exceeds the current perception—might therefore be useful. This is an extremely simple, but profoundly significant, point. Offenders regularly face exposure to legal sanctions of which they are unaware. What is not known cannot, in theory or in practice, deter. Informing them satisfies the theoretical need and may make a difference in practice. It is not hard to imagine, for example, notifying each eligible firearm offender in a jurisdiction that he faces federal mandatory minimum sentencing for his next illegal possession arrest: or each newly ordained priest that any credible evidence of sexual misconduct will result in defrocking and criminal referral to the local prosecutor.

Beyond that, there is normally little reason to think that offenders will be aware of *new* statutory risks. It is not impossible, of course, that offenders would be cognizant of new law; they can read the papers and watch television news reporting on legislative developments, they may be informed by defense attorneys, probation and parole officers, and the like; or hear about such developments from peers. Some of this no doubt occurs. More often, it seems likely that knowledge of new sanctions develops only through the usually slow working of law enforcement practice, and then often in an incomplete and confused fashion. At least until practice leads to knowledge, the deterrence value of the new sanction is nil or diminished; to the extent that incomplete and confused perceptions understate risks, this will remain so. Deliberate communication of new risks may, again, matter. If offenders whose next crime was likely to win them a prosecution under California's new three-strikes law had been explicitly notified, the law might have worked better than it seems to have.

Finally, even offenders fully cognizant of statutory risks may not understand their own *exposure* to those risks. Offenders frequently have mistaken ideas about the broader legal environment; during Operation Ceasefire in Boston, we witnessed surreal conversations in which probationers lectured probation officers that the officers had no right to conduct at-will home visits: the probation officers were right, and the probationers wrong, but it was an uphill fight to counter street wisdom and prior official practice. Offenders frequently do not fully understand their own criminal histories or current legal status; they may not realize, for example, that in a string of convictions is included the three predicate felonies qualifying them for a federal armed career criminal prosecution, or that they currently have an outstanding bench warrant for failure to appear at a court proceeding. They may not understand how their histories or current behavior open them to sanction: that, for example, an old misdemeanor domestic violence conviction now makes the possession of a firearm a federal crime, or that carrying drugs with that firearm dramatically increases penalties. In practice, even authorities frequently have difficulty sorting these issues out; the application of the federal sentencing guidelines, for example, has become so involved and technical that even those who do it routinely are often confused.[30] Where offenders' misunderstanding of their exposure leads them to underestimate sanction risk, informing them of the facts may therefore matter. It is not hard to imagine, for example, expanding on local notifications of eligibility for federal firearms prosecutions by telling particular offenders that their records have been reviewed by the US Attorney and that they should presume that any such case will in fact be vigorously pursued.

Risks heightened through exercise of official discretion

The sanction risks offenders face are heavily governed by the discretionary actions of authorities. These discretionary actions can dramatically alter those risks without any change whatsoever in the applicable law. Messages about various aspects of such practices could considerably influence the views and actions of offenders.

One key area would be *general standing policies* of various agencies or groups of agencies. Different agencies at different time have often widely varying enforcement priorities within the conduct of what is still generally considered business as usual. Police departments and prosecutors, for example, may emphasize (or deemphasize) drug crime, gun crime, domestic violence, or other kinds of offending. Prosecutors may choose to minimize plea bargaining in pursuit of obtaining the highest possible statutory sanction.[31] Probation and parole departments may deemphasize office contacts with supervisees in favor of unannounced home visits and other "street" contacts. Such discretionary policies can dramatically alter, in very short order, the risks faced by particular offenders and attached to particular offenses. Such policies are virtually never promulgated in any form even in principle available to offenders. The only way they can be learned is through being subject to or observing official practice, or by word of mouth from others who have been subject to or have observed official practice. Even then what is "learned" may be quite substantially wrong. Lack of knowledge, again, can generate no deterrence, while misunderstandings may vitiate deterrence.

Another key area is what might be considered *special initiatives*. These, too, are routine. Official focus on particular offenses, particular areas, and the like can greatly heighten the risks attaches to those crimes, particular offenses in particular areas, all crimes in particular areas, and the like. Police may, for instance, choose to crack down on "quality of life" offenses in a business district, gun carrying in a dangerous neighborhood, or accounting fraud. Such initiatives, again, can dramatically and suddenly alter sanction risks. And, again, the usual factors apply: unless known, and known correctly, those risks will not translate properly into deterrence.

A special case of discretionary initiatives is the *deliberate attachment of other sanctions to specific offenses or behaviors*: the Al Capone story. These initiatives are likely to be particularly opaque from the viewpoint of offenders. It seems likely that Capone, other gangsters, and the public all understood exactly what had transpired: Capone was a known target, the previous failings of authorities well known, and the reasons for and significance of the tax prosecution needed little explanation. This will quite often not be the case. Even where the specific behavior targeted is a crime, cause and effect may well be obscure: authorities may choose to take a repeat violence domestic offender off the street using the first available opportunity, which may turn out to be a drunk-driving offense, but there may be no way for either the offender in question or other domestic violence offenders to understand the logic behind the action unless it is deliberately explained. That problem is heightened when the target behavior is *not* itself a crime, for instance the recruitment of juveniles by adult offenders. In both cases, deterrence requires two kinds of knowledge to be promulgated and understood: first, *the actual policy being followed*—action x will be sanctioned using penalties attached to other actions—and second, *cause and effect*: a particular penalty was in fact imposed because of an example of action x, and constitutes an instance of the policy being applied

Another special case of discretionary initiatives is the *deliberate focus on particular individuals or networks*. Given offenders, groups, gangs, cooffenders, rings, and the like can be singled out by authorities, and the risks that attach to their offending or other behavior greatly increased. Again, and by now familiarly, there will be no deterrence impact from that focus unless it is understood by those offenders. Authorities can choose, for example, to identify the fifty worst violent offenders in their jurisdiction and fully prosecute the next crime, of any kind, that they commit; they can choose to bring RICO cases against the ten worst drug groups in their jurisdiction. Only if those individuals and groups, and those like offenders observing the process, understand it will deterrence, or the full deterrence in principle available, be created. The difference can be stark. If, in the case of the fifty violent offenders, the sanction threat is meaningful (in the eyes of each of the fifty), credible, and *known*, all fifty may seek to avoid a next crime. If the same threat is *unknown*, none of the fifty may alter his behavior in any way. If the sanction threat is carried out, or carried out against those of the fifty who do not comply, and the logic of the process is known to the larger population of violent offenders in the jurisdiction, that population may strive to avoid being "promoted" by the authorities such that it receives like attention. If the logic of the process is not known, they will not.

A final special case of discretionary initiatives is the decision by authorities to give special attention to the first, or the next, instance of a given offense, or to put instances of offending on a shifting or other strategic schedule. The deterrence logic of these strategies has been addressed previously: to keep a given kind of offending, for instance street sales of Ecstasy, from taking hold, authorities may wish to send the message that the first such instance will get sure and heightened attention. In a situation in which offending is already established, they may wish to send the message that the next such instance, or random instances, will get special attention. In such instances deterrence will depend on the message being transmitted to and understood by a sufficient proportion of prospective offenders, and the cause and effect of any actual enforcement action being similarly explained and understood.

Malcolm Sparrow considered how federal regulators might adapt this logic to health care fraud:

> The message of Operation Ceasefire, applied to fraudulent or abusive Medicare billings by hospitals, might come out something like this.
>
> Good morning, friends. We know, and you know, that certain abusive billing practices have become systemic within this industry. We are here to name five of them and to announce that all five of them will cease by the end of this month. This gives you three weeks to examine your own billing practices and systems and correct them if necessary. In the first weeks of next month, having only limited audit and claims review resources, we will monitor incoming claims particularly for any signs that these billing practices persist, and the first ten hospitals that we find will be subjected to a rigorous and comprehensive audit of *all* their billings. In the course of those audits we will pursue enforcement and recoveries of amounts due, to the full extent permitted by law. To find yourself on that list of ten, all you need to do is carry on as you are now. We advise you to correct these problems.
>
> By the way, next month we will identify five further billing practices and advise you of the dates by which they too should be eliminated.
>
> Then one might sit back and watch the billing practices change across the industry.[32]

The context of official action

Another set of messages could be framed to enhance deterrence by influencing offenders' and others' views of authorities and of the actions of authorities. As has been discussed, where authorities and their actions are viewed as legitimate, deterrence will be enhanced, and where it is not, deterrence will be undercut. Several key areas suggest themselves.

Authorities rarely try to explain to offenders or other interested parties *why they are doing what they are doing.* Offenders and others are thus free to come to their own unfettered conclusions, and to share and build upon those conclusions through peer, network, and community processes. The same action can be, and very frequently is, viewed in deeply opposing ways by the two parties. Street drug enforcement may be viewed by authorities as their only, if not a particularly satisfactory, avenue to protect the community from drug harms. It may be viewed by offenders and the community as a purposeful attack on young black men, further evidenced by a lack of attention to upper-level traffickers and white drive-through consumers. The handling of a particular firearms case may depend on a set of issues, such as prosecutorial priorities, state and federal statutes, and the offender's criminal history, that is complex even to career enforcement officials; it may look entirely capricious and illegitimate to the offender and his peers. It is possible to address these gaps between official action and the perception of official action, and to identify and respond to existing and destructive views of authorities and their behavior.

One possibility is to articulate the *rationale for particular initiatives.* It may matter, for example, to make explicit that a focus on gang crime has come about because of concern about the loss of young black men to homicide, and the recognition that gang offending is the primary cause of such homicides. It may matter further to explain that a deterrence strategy focusing on special attention to the next instance of gang homicide is designed to minimize the number of arrests of young black men, rather than representing capricious and opportunistic enforcement. It may matter, in addressing a targeted dangerous-offender strategy, to articulate the decision process behind the targeting, the criminal histories of those targeted, and the much larger number of offenders who might have been, but were not, exposed to the strategy's special sanctions.

Another possibility is to articulate *the reasons behind practices commonly viewed as unreasonable*—or worse. Police departments, for example, may know that—to take a common example—ordinary uniformed officers do not make street drug arrests because they have been enjoined from doing so as a corruption-control measure, while the community in question sees police ignoring flagrant dealing and reads it as corruption. A single felony conviction in an offender's record may open him to a federal prosecution for illegal firearm possession, while an otherwise identical offender without one will not be so open. The resulting widely varying dispositions will seem unexceptionable to officials, but may well be read by offenders and other observers as unfair, capricious, and motivated by various kinds of ill-will. In many instances, authorities and their critics in fact share very similar views, which neither may have articulated to the other. In many jurisdictions, for example, police and prosecutors could honestly say to angry communities that they too wish to go after upper-level drug traffickers: but have largely been unable to do so, and certainly not to a degree that inhibits street trafficking in the community.

There is no certainty that any such steps would bring authorities, offenders, and other parties into accord. Nor is entire agreement necessary; degrees of enhanced understanding, or of diminished opposition, might be salutary. A process of communication and mutual learning is clearly implied here, a matter to which we will return. But the principle—that perceptions matter and can be addressed—remains.

Norms

Norms may be deliberately communicated to offenders; undesirable existing norms may be countered; desirable existing norms may be encouraged and mobilized. These, too, overlap, and their boundaries are often unclear. Again, several key categories suggest themselves.

Key standards and "rules of thumb"

Some deterrence theorists suggest that offenders' bounded rationality generates in practice "rules of thumb" and the like that then serve as persistent guides to behavior. These may arise through calculations of risks and benefits, through the observation of the behavior of others, through communications from others, or in a number of other ways. Authorities frequently—consciously and unconsciously, by word or by deed or by both—establish such rules. A small example is the police practice in many jurisdictions of requiring that alcohol consumed in public be drunk from brown-bagged containers.[33] This standard is nowhere written in law—and in fact such open containers are still statutorily forbidden—but is quite well understood by all parties. A larger—much larger—example is the standard that law enforcement officials and their families should not be the target of retributive violence. While such violence would of course be illegal, the informal standard stands apart from and is in practice more powerful than the statutes that provide penalties for, say, assault. In the other direction, the actual practice of authorities—the general failure of prosecutors to pursue cases involving the street sale of marijuana—may result in informal standards promoting such offending. Whether such standards are prudential guidelines, rules of thumb, or norms is hard to say; they may be some or all of these, or move over time from one to another. In any case, such standards play similar, and important, roles.

They may be deliberately framed and communicated. They sometimes are: campaigns to reshape public opinion around drinking and driving are efforts of this kind, as are more particular announcements by authorities announcing drunk-driving crackdowns around holidays. Many more, and less conventional, efforts of these kinds are possible. Authorities concerned about street drug-dealing may tell known offenders that such activity will be regarded with special displeasure. Violent offenders may be told that carrying and using firearms is to be particularly avoided (as was in fact done in Project Exile, if apparently without the consistency of follow-through necessary to convince the streets). Older offenders may be told to keep their distance from young people, as has occurred in Winston-Salem. Thieves and fences may be told to stay away from homes and from stolen goods taken from homes. The intimidation of witnesses may be proscribed. To be effective, such rules must be credible, which is another matter; the point here is that such rules can in fact be articulated.

Individual, peer and network, and community norms

Individual, peer and network, and community norms may be extremely influential in shaping offenders' behavior. If an offender feels positive, or does not feel negative, about a given act, he is more likely to perform it. If family and friends believe, or the offender believes them to believe, that a given act is positive, he is also more likely; if they do not, or he believes that they do not, he is less likely. The same is true around broad community norms. These norms may also be deliberately framed and/or mobilized.

It is a feature of many close studies of offenders that prosocial and anti-offending norms are visible, and that offenders have conflicting feelings about their own offending. Matza shows how offenders mobilize, and modify, mainstream norms to justify misbehavior.[34] Wright notes that armed robbers frequently feel guilty about what they do, and shows how they frame new norms to accommodate offending.[35] Bourgois found strong guilt, shame, and regret on the part of the serial rapists he came to know in New York.[36] Behavior that appears from a distance as the product of unalloyed sentiment and intent is often not that, or less so than it seems.

Such existing prosocial norms may be encouraged, and their competition discouraged. At the individual level, this is frequently one aspiration of such things as in-school drug- and violence-prevention curricula, mentoring, and the like. These interventions are rarely viewed in deterrence terms; the common definition of "prevention" as "not having to do with authority" rules out such connections. To the extent that such interventions increase the likelihood or the weight of internal and external informal sanctions such as guilt, shame, and social disapproval, however, they may in fact have deterrence impacts.

Internal norms may also be established or enhanced in such settings as "family conferences," group interventions around particular offenders and offenses which are expressly designed to, and have shown effectiveness in, both inculcating and mobilizing prosocial norms. The framework is expressly designed to provoke "pangs of conscience" in offenders, and to create a setting in which they are exposed to "social disapproval" for their actions.[37] Offenders are, in a controlled setting, put in contact with their own family and friends, and with victims and their family and friends. The aim is a "ritual of collective moral or civic education"[38] through what Braithwaite calls "reintegrative shaming."[39] The explicit intent is to help positive norms surface, challenge negative norms, and establish the offender in a web of relationships that will sustain and foster such movement. Family conferencing has generally been restricted to juveniles who have committed relatively minor offenses, but the themes may carry over to older and more serious offenders. Strang and Braithwaite and Mills have proposed similar processes for domestic violence offenders.[40]

The restorative justice literature and practices from which these interventions have emerged are not framed in deterrence terms; far from it, they generally operate in conscious opposition to traditional criminal justice processes and the idea of sanction.[41] Restorative justice practices can be viewed, however, as ways to shift the burden of deterrence entirely onto informal social control, making the operation of internal and external norms so effective that formal social control is no longer necessary. Family conferences and similar mechanisms operate by making clear to offenders the cost of their actions to victims and communities; reaching out to existing internal norms that produce guilt, shame, and embarrassment; reinforcing those norms—in the moment, and potentially afterward—through mobilizing family, friends, and other respected others; and challenging individual and community norms that support offending. All of this can easily be viewed through the lens of mobilizing deterrence through both internal and external informal sanctions.

Restorative justice interventions are generally conceived of as alternative case processing systems designed to divert usually low-level offenders from traditional criminal-justice mechanisms. They need not be, however. There is no need to wait for an arrest and a criminal case to invoke these or similar processes. If a key figure in a drug network is promoting violence, there is in principal no reason that those close to him and those he respects in his community cannot sit down with him, express disapproval, count the costs of his actions, and articulate higher expectations and aspirations; in principal, there is no reason that such intervention cannot be deliberately arranged by the authorities. If key offenders can be identified, if those who matter to them can be identified, if interventions can be framed that elevate positive norms and suppress negative ones, then in principal the same processes might work for offenders either, or both, not under arrest and not low-level. Much of what goes on in the offender call-ins central to Boston-style gang interventions can be viewed as restorative justice practices operating with very serious offenders reached in ways other than through arrest (and combined with other mechanisms, such as explicit promises of formal sanctions, not usually part of restorative justice practices).

A version of attention to individual, peer, and community norms that may hold particular promise is the deliberate undoing of pluralistic ignorance. Individuals may hold greatly erroneous views of what others regard as normative, and shape their own norms and behavior as a result. These misperceptions can be identified and systematically addressed. Even very serious offending may be open to such interventions. Anderson's "code of the street" and Fagan and Wilkinson's "scripts" are both descriptions of sets of norms that produce serious, sometimes lethal, violence. If, for example, the individual attachment of offenders to norms such as "I have to hurt someone who disrespects me" is more rooted in the felt beliefs of others than in personal belief and conviction, then steps to clarify what is really going on may matter.

Measures to identify these errors, ascertain more deeply rooted and authentic norms, and communicate and embed those norms may be powerful both as independent interventions and as part of larger interventions. Perkins, for example, reports that information campaigns based on research into actual, rather than perceived, student attitudes toward drinking and aimed at correcting misapprehensions about norms and behavior have resulted in substantial reductions in drinking.[42] The author's work with urban gang members suggests that many fear and disapprove of behavior collectively regarded as normative, such as "respect" shootings. In some gang circles there is a strong belief that leaving the gang requires extreme acts such as killing a parent; the belief is mostly myth, but that does not make it inconsequential. In many urban communities, individual residents' fervent disapproval of drug-dealing and violence goes unexpressed; those who disapprove and offenders alike may read that silence as approval. Measures that correct those misapprehensions and highlight the more desirable norms actually held might be quite powerful. In a recent Boston-style gang violence intervention in Cincinnati, ex-offenders have made this something of an art form in the gang call-ins that are a central part of the strategy.

> We say we have thug love for each other. Well, who visited you the last time you were locked up? (Nobody.) Who paid your mother's bills? (Nobody.) How long did it take one of your boys to sleep with your girlfriend? (Two days.) We say we have to hurt someone if we're disrespected, but who thinks it's OK for little girls to get shot off their porches? (Nobody does.) Do you think your boys won't flip on you if the feds get them? (No.)

So might marketing back to offenders ways in which codes taken as inviolate are often violated, as in fact they invariably are. Garot found that the young urban men he interviewed both presented the street code as inexorable and frequently failed to adhere to it:

> In the course of my interviews, I could count on every young man to tell me that anyone who walked away from a fight would be punked for life. I could also count on most young man to tell me of a time when he walked away from a fight.[43]

Garot was able to unpack a number of reasons that in practice justified walking away—one was outnumbered, the matter was trivial, one was with family, because the consequences might not be worth it. Articulating that governing "codes" are a myth, and providing offenders with a logic and encouragement to avoid adhering to them, can matter.

Another approach would be to influence the norms and the behavior of "keynotes" or "models" who influence the norms of others. As collective behavior theory underscores, the emergence of norms is a complicated, iterative process in which particular individuals and actions may have disproportionate effects. If such a figure in a "code of the street" setting visibly chooses not to follow the code, for example, others may feel safer doing so themselves. These dynamics may be within the control of authorities. If police approach a prominent gang involved in a highly visible violent beef with another gang, tell key figures within the first gang that further violence will bring strong consequences and that the second gang will be controlled, observers may see both that the violence has been abandoned and that it is acceptable to let the police intervene. Authorities may also be able to restrict and even reverse the criminogenic influence of such models; this is what Lowell, Massachusetts did in holding older Asian gang members accountable for the shootings of younger gang members.

Finally, it may be possible to work deliberately and directly on community norms. This could involve articulating existing antioffending norms, framing new ones, or some combination of the two. As Sampson and Bartusch show, "tolerance of deviance" can be quite low even in high-crime communities, and may in fact be lower than in lower-crime neighborhoods.[44] They distinguish between tolerance of deviance—support for offending, and subscription to prooffending norms—and "legal cynicism," a lack of support for authorities and their actions.[45] Communities may thus dislike *both* crime *and* what the authorities do in their attempts to control crime. If the dislike of authorities and their actions prevents, as it often does, expressions of disapproval for offending, informal control will not be exercised. Further, offenders may read that silence, or expressions of disapproval of authorities, as approval for them and their actions. This raises the possibility that if community disapproval for the authorities could be addressed, these strong, but suppressed, norms against offending could surface.

Such a process could involve—as has already been suggested—correcting frank misconceptions about official practices; addressing patterns of official actions that both sides would regard as abusive, such as police brutality and corruption; addressing enforcement practices that are not inherently illegal or abusive but that the community does not in fact support; and framing new enforcement practices that the community would support. There seem to be few examples of such processes in practice. Given the depth of animosity in many troubled neighborhoods toward the police and other authorities, the very real history of official abuse in many such neighborhoods, and the frequent community identification of official practice with long histories of racism and oppression, this is perhaps no great surprise. The best guidance toward how to frame such undertakings may lie in the quite different, but soberingly parallel, examples of such bodies as the South African Truth and Reconciliation Commission. These institutions and practices have sought means to face deep historical harms; address issues of legal and moral culpability; create settings in which grievous injuries can be articulated, witnessed, perhaps redressed, and perhaps forgiven; and framed shared understandings about how historically, and often still, hostile groups can move forward together.[46] If, for example, an historically troubled urban community and the police were to reach an explicit agreement on how street drug-dealing was to be addressed, something of similar depth and magnitude might be called for. We will in fact turn to this possibility in Chapter 9.

Communication

If messages concerning sanction risks, norms, and other information affecting deterrence dynamics are to have impact, they must be communicated. As has been discussed, despite both the theoretical place and practical significance of this fact, communication has only sometimes been recognized as important in deterrence theory, virtually never in deterrence practice, and very little theoretical or practical development of the idea has occurred. A framework for addressing communication might include four core dimensions: communication to *individual* offenders, *networks and other groups* of offenders, and to *nonoffenders*; *one-time* and *sustained* communication; *one-way* and *two-way* communication; and *techniques* for communication.

Communication to individual offenders

Individual offenders may present themselves as individually important for a variety of reasons, as has been discussed. They may be known to be significant on the basis of their own more or less isolated behavior, as with a violent domestic violence offender, a serial armed robber, or a drunk driver. They may be particularly influential, as with a gang leader. They may exhibit influential behavior, such as "keynote" offending (first street drug sale, first carjacking). Such offenders are frequently known, or knowable, to authorities. A review of criminal histories, for example, can identify all offenders in a jurisdiction who are statutorily open, should they be found in possession of an illegal firearm, to a federal prosecution as an armed career criminal. They may themselves not know this; they cannot know, unless somehow informed, that the US Attorney has recently decided to alter office policy and seek such prosecutions wherever possible. Unless they know these things, the deterrent power of potential sanctions will be less than it might be; it may be nil. Informing them will alter those dynamics. Similarly, authorities may inform a number of particularly active domestic abusers that their next known act of abuse will place them on a list that will ensure maximal official attention to their next crime of any kind; they may inform offenders first active in street drug sales that such offending will not be tolerated and will draw focused interagency attention; they may inform a gang leader that authorities will not tolerate the orchestration of violent retaliation to the recent injury of a gang member by another gang.

Communication to networks and other groups

Offending is often best understood in terms of networks and other collectivities, and dynamics within and between them. To continue the last example, a beef may exist between groups of offenders without any real leadership being exercised on either side; in this instance, the groups as such may be informed that violence will not be tolerated. Gun-carrying may be common among offenders in certain areas and with certain relationships to one another, and be supported both by shared norms and by concrete risks offenders pose to one another. In such instances, communicating to those groups and networks might be called for. Financial firms open to accounting and trading violations may feel driven to such offenses in part because they risk the loss of competitive advantage to other firms they suspect of such practices; in a similar fashion, it may make the most sense in such contexts to inform *all* firms that *no* firms will be allowed to offend. One feature of such moves can be that the overall level of offending can be lowered without any group losing position relative to the other. One gang that is disarmed, or one hospital prevented from bilking the government, may vigorously resist being put at competitive disadvantage; if all shift simultaneously, none may care very much.

Communication to nonoffenders

Nonoffenders can have direct influence on offenders; their views of official actions can influence how offenders view those actions. If community members view, for example, focused enforcement of street drug dealers as a continued expression of official racism, informal sanctions and community norms are unlikely to align with official intent. If, however, they are informed that the enforcement was a response to serious gang violence after direct warnings to the gang in question, support may be forthcoming. If it is street drug-dealing as such that authorities seek to prevent, they may seek to impose formal sanctions, or they could talk to known dealers' parents and urge familial control. As has been discussed, partnerships between authorities and offenders' peer networks may result in unstated and understated norms being mobilized.

One-time and sustained communication

Some messages need be delivered only once. An offender told that he has the predicate felonies for a federal gun prosecution will not, presumably, need to be told again. Subsequent communications may serve the purpose of further persuasion, however: Authorities might follow up the original notification with, for example, information that other offenders so notified had in fact been caught with firearms and in fact so prosecuted and convicted.

Some deterrence strategies may require sustained communication. In order to create the proper balance of power between authorities and offenders, a particular act may be given special attention in a limited area or with a limited population, with an initial communication establishing those terms; with initial success, those initial limits may be expanded, requiring further communication.[47] A strategy to give special attention to "first acts" and "next acts" will often require repeated communication. Authorities may tell a number of offenders that the first to commit a given act will be sanctioned. They may carry through on that promise while still evidently losing control of the environment: that is, a number of offenders may commit and continue to commit the act, the first one to do so may in fact be sanctioned, and what remains is an active offending environment. A subsequent communication, however, may build on the first one by saying, we did what we said we were going to do, we're ready to start again, once more, the first act (or, now, the next act) will be sanctioned. The second message, building on demonstrated behavior by authorities, may be more credible than the first; subsequent messages may be more credible still. Some strategies may benefit from the imparting of particular information at particular times. A population of gangs may be put on notice not to commit violence, for example. Even while that standard is being adhered to, authorities may learn that tensions are building between a particular pair of gangs, and reach out to both and reinforce the message in terms particular to each gang. It may then serve further to tell *each* gang that the *other* has been put on notice. All of these have obtained in Boston's Ceasefire and similar interventions, which typically establish initial communication with groups of offenders; update them as enforcement actions are actually taken; and conduct special outreach as required to particular groups.[48]

Some offenders may need to be told that they have been taken *off* special status. If a domestic abuser is identified by front-line practitioners as having become particularly dangerous—having begun to drink, or having recently been left by his partner—authorities may tell him that he is under special scrutiny and that any possible offense will be used to take him off the street. If he responds well, however, authorities may later wish to tell him that his status has reverted to normal, opening up his special "slot" for a more currently dangerous offender and demonstrating to him and others that there are rewards available for compliance. Something parallel may occur between authorities and communities with respect to special deterrence strategies. Communities may support such strategies as long as particular problems seem to them to warrant special attention. If those problems respond to the strategy, or if they attenuate for other reasons, it may be appropriate to suspend or terminate the strategy, and to so notify communities.

One-way and two-way communication

Messages need not only flow from authorities to other parties. It will frequently serve deterrence, and deterrence strategies, well for other parties to communicate with authorities. Offenders may inform authorities, for example, of the reasons that they are offending (they would refrain if they had work; they would refrain if their enemies or competition would refrain; they would refrain if peer norms would permit it or encourage it); they may inform authorities that they have in fact refrained from offending, and that special applications of authority are no longer required; they may inform authorities of how official actions are in fact being perceived (enforcement is seen as capricious and illegitimate, the corrupt actions of a few officials are tainting the standing of all); they may inform authorities of particular reasons for offending (real or perceived threats from armed others). Authorities may be able to act on these things. As they do so, they will affect the mix and the weight of sanctions and incentives offenders face.

The same is true with victims, communities and peers. A domestic-violence victim may seek help from authorities if she can be sure that her husband will not be incarcerated and lose his job; if she is unsure of this, her abuser may face no sanction, but if she is sure, he may face some sanction (and, if authorities can manage it, they may deploy a sanction which does not take him off the street but which still matters to him, and which may matter more than incarceration). Communities may be more openly critical of offenders and offending if authorities can reshape enforcement strategies so as to be less profligate with the exercise of authority; authorities may have to demonstrate and explain their ability to do this before community members will act. Parents may inform police of their sons' illegal firearms if police will agree to seize them—at possibly considerable trouble and cost to their possessors—without pursuing charges.[49] All these sorts of possibilities rest on the *exchange* of information between authorities and others.

The idea of relationship

Much of what is being described here rises to the level of *relationships* between authorities and offenders, networks of offenders, communities, and others. Traditional deterrence theory has no place for this notion. Where offenders were concerned, deterrence was viewed as a zero-sum game, with effective deterrence depending on making the offender a loser: he either refrained from something he did not want to refrain from, or suffered a consequence he did not want to suffer. Where communities and others were concerned, key factors such as the standing of authorities and norms were taken as givens, not as matters that might be affected by deliberate action and interaction.

These perspectives are clearly needlessly limiting. Even where the interests of offenders and authorities are utterly at odds, there may still be a place for close and continued contacts, and value for both parties in those contacts. An armed robber utterly devoted to armed robbery, and to escaping sanction for armed robbery, will still want to know what penalties he faces, where authorities are concentrating their efforts, how others like him are faring when caught, and the like. It may serve authorities well to tell him. If he sees a peer arrested with a gun and prosecuted by state authorities, he may naturally conclude that that will be his fate. Only if he is educated to understand that such cases are reviewed by both state and federal authorities; that his peer did not have the criminal history permitting federal prosecution; that he himself does; and that in addition his actions are known and the federal prosecutor has already determined to take his case should there ever be an opportunity, will he be able to make an informed decision. Having relations that permit this sort of education are in the interests of both the armed robber and of authorities.

It is likewise frequently in the interest of both offenders and authorities to know that sanctions are forthcoming. Where the point of sanctions is deterrence, and deterrence can be obtained through information rather than through their actual exercise, their actual exercise is wasteful and costly. If enforcement is in fact going to be deployed, and offenders care about that fact, not telling them harms both parties. Few offenders would commit a given offense if they know for certain there will be a meaningful (in their eyes) sanction attached to it. If they *know* they will be arrested if they sell drugs on the corner *today,* they will not do it. This is why even the chronic offenders authorities write off as incorrigible and uncaring even about their own safety and future do not play in traffic, or commit crimes when police are in full view. It is not that they don't care; it is that most of the time they do not know, as we saw Zimring and Hawkins put it about much more minor offenses, that their behavior is *really forbidden.* When it *is* really forbidden, it often serves no purpose not to simply tell them.

But in fact the interests of authorities and offenders are *not* always utterly at odds. Offenders may have enemies from whom they wish to be protected. They may do things because the collective behavior of their offender peers makes it rational to do so and irrational not to do so, while still wishing that that larger context were different. They may do things because the social norms of their peers demand it, while wishing that those norms were otherwise. They may act mistakenly, believing that the behavior and opinions of others express norms that those others do not in fact hold. They may do things because their enemies and competitors are, without much liking it. Where these and similar things are true, actions by authorities—such as interrupting a gang dispute, or preventing accounting fraud—may serve *both* offenders and authorities. Clear official standards and sanctions, such as the promise of a certain, rapid, and meaningful sanction for a shooting in a gang dispute, may even create acceptable reasons to refrain from what offenders would privately rather not do anyway: Zimring and Hawkins' conforming-conduct rationalizations.

One of the striking revelations of the original Boston intervention was that at least some gang members liked the new regime *better* than the old. In one notable instance, gang members approached authorities after street violence had largely abated and worked with gang officers to identify and address a group that was threatening the peace.[50] This is perhaps not hard to understand; their world had become a good deal safer as a result of the intervention. It is thus not at all, in fact, incompatible with the logic of deterrence that offenders and authorities should have at least a certain amount of common ground. And where ground is common, relationships are both a theoretical and a practical possibility.

Techniques for communication

Messages may be *delivered and exchanged,* of course, in all sorts of ways. They may also be *framed* in different ways, even where the same core message is concerned.

Many of the categories and techniques used by for-profit communicators turn out to be surprisingly applicable, at least in principle, to deterrence messages (Madison Avenue may not, as Cook observed, have gotten into the crime-control business, but that need not mean it cannot, or that its methods cannot). Shapiro and Wyman identify media advertising, direct mail, telephone selling, trade shows, and face-to-face selling as traditional methods of reaching consumers.[51] All these barring trade shows have evident application. Authorities may, in fact, take out television ads to advertise penalties and enforcement initiatives, as was done in practice by Project Exile and the "Click It or Ticket" seat-belt enforcement initiative. Direct mail may be used to reach, for example, those with known addresses—examples would include probationers, parolees, recipients of restraining orders, many offenders with criminal histories, drive-through drug buyers identified through automobile registrations, and others. Telephone contacts could reach many of these same persons. The habits of many offenders are well known to enforcement personnel, who can often find them and speak to them face-to-face at their homes or on the street. Probation and parole officers have the power to call in supervisees individually or in groups, and speak to them or create the opportunity for others to speak with them. All of these techniques could be used to reach rosters of persons identified for particular purposes, such as known armed robbers or, following Sparrow, hospital administrators. Authorities could list such offenders, for instance on the basis of their network affiliation, and seek them out on the street or in their offices for conversations around special enforcement practices and the progress of such practices. This was in fact done around gang violence in Minneapolis.[52]

This latter point highlights a key opportunity in communicating with offenders. The prevalence of cooffending and network relationships amongst offenders may often mean that it will be possible to communicate with a number, and often a selected population, of offenders by working through a much smaller number. This was the logic behind the "forums" piloted as part of Operation Ceasefire in Boston. Street gangs were identified, probationers in those gangs were identified, and probation utilized to call those persons into meetings, where they were addressed by authorities, service providers, and others. They were regarded as "ambassadors" back to their peers, and explicitly asked to carry information, including written handouts, back to their groups. In other aspects of Operation Ceasefire, members of particular groups were visited on the street by police officers or gang outreach workers, and even more specific deterrence messages delivered. There is good reason, in both Boston and Minneapolis, to believe that those methods were productive.

One powerful concept from commercial marketing is that of an "account," and the related idea of "account management," also sometimes called, with interesting resonances for the current discussion, "relationship management."[53] An account is simply a substantial concentration in the market capable of being attended to in special ways, including special sales attention and special attention to market needs. An electrical equipment supplier, thus, might designate a large manufacturing concern an "account," and seek both to sell it existing products and to develop new products to sell it. Both activities would result from relatively close and sustained contacts. The framework might have considerable application in deterrence. To stay with the preceding example, individual police officers might be designated "account managers" with particular street gangs. They could then stay in relatively close contact with those gangs, for instance

- informing them initially of new deterrence initiatives (that authorities were waiting for the first gang-involved homicide and would comprehensively sanction the gang in question);
- explain more welcome facets of the strategy (that rival gangs were also being so warned);
- pass on relevant information (review key members' criminal histories and spell out to them their legal exposure);
- explain developments (the sanctioning of a gang and the new status of the authorities in waiting for the next homicide);
- broker access to facilitative services such as job training and drug treatment;
- take steps that would make the gang feel safer and more prepared to withdraw from violent behavior (making sure that a rival gang is prevented from violence directed at the "account" gang);
- communicate modifications to the original deterrence initiative (not just violence but also street drug sales were now off limits).

Such relationships are anything but routine in enforcement circles, but they are not unimaginable.

Another aspect of commercial marketing of relevance is its attention to research methods to *frame* messages and then to gauge their impact and to modify them accordingly. It is a commonplace in marketing that different audiences listen and learn in different ways and that care, including formal methodology, should be used to uncover and respond to those differences. This includes, again interestingly for the present discussion, "language structured around honest straightforward communication geared to fight the audience's reaction to previous overblown claims and half-truths."[54] Research methods such as individual interviews, surveys, focus groups, test viewings of pilot art forms, and the like are used to ascertain the target audience's media habits, norms, use of language, reactions to particular ways of presenting target messages, the content that is or is not carried away from those messages, what is remembered and for how long, and the like.[55] Needless to say, nothing of the kind now occurs in the testing of deterrence messages. It easily could, however.

One tantalizing example—the only example, perhaps, to date—of how this might work in practice is an exercise conducted by the advertising firm Mullen in support of the Justice Department's initiative to replicate Project Exile in more jurisdictions. Mullen conducted research with parents and guardians of youth at risk for gun violence, incarcerated and nonincarcerated juveniles and young adults, community leaders, Bureau of Alcohol, Tobacco, and Firearms agents, and "significant others," and rode with gang officers. They found that, as is commonly perceived, juvenile and young offenders evidenced little concern for their risks of dying or going to prison. They also found, however, that those offenders were deeply concerned about the impact of their dying or being imprisoned on their *families*. Mullen therefore recommended that Exile broadcast advertising focus on those issues, rather than the original Exile advertising message that offenders would get "federal time for gun crime."[56]

There is little reason to think that offenders actually hear what is said to them, when it is said at all, as it is intended to be heard, and there is ample evidence that what they infer from official action is often mistaken. There is also ample evidence that what they infer from official action is often accurate but undesirable. Many of those dynamics could be systematically revealed using a variety of research approaches and the results used to shape both official practice and official communications. It is not, perhaps, unreasonable that we should be as systematic about public safety as we are about soap.

9 Applications I

Eliminating overt drug markets: the "High Point" strategy

How might deterrence strategies built around these ideas look in practice? In this and the following chapter, we will look at two examples, the first concrete and the second speculative. Both are aimed at core public safety problems that have proved stubbornly resistant to traditional deterrence, enforcement, and prevention approaches.

The first, the subject of this chapter, was designed to address community drug markets. Drug markets are extraordinarily toxic to communities. Street sales and drug houses create crime hot spots; take over public spaces like sidewalks, parks, and stores; attract drive-through buyers and prostitutes; drive residents out and attract transients; drive out businesses and reduce the value of housing and commercial buildings; ease entry into criminality for young people; and facilitate drug use and addiction and the personal, family, and community harms they engender.

Routine drug enforcement also creates serious community harms. Overt markets are located almost entirely in poor minority neighborhoods, housing projects, and the like. In these neighborhoods, persistent drug enforcement frequently leads to very high levels of arrest, conviction, probation, incarceration, and parole for, especially, younger men. In some neighborhoods substantial majorities of younger men end up with criminal records and histories of incarceration or court supervision. Their criminal records inhibit them from finishing school and pursuing further education and cut them off from legitimate work and career advancement. High rates of arrest and incarceration can foster an informal street culture is which drug-dealing, arrest, and prison come to be viewed as routine, status-enhancing, and even a marker of adulthood. The routine use of intrusive enforcement measures, such as street stops, vehicle stops, and search warrants, often means that even law-abiding residents have hostile encounters with police.

Perhaps worse, powerful "narratives"—accounts of and explanations for what is going on—are developed by the affected communities, by law enforcement, and by drug dealers themselves. A dominant community narrative embeds drug issues and the community's experience with drug enforcement in the historic experience of minorities, especially African Americans, in America. On this account, drug enforcement is part of an unbroken chain of deliberate oppression that began with the enforcement of slave codes and slave-catching and continued through the legal and extra-legal repression of Reconstruction; law enforcement's involvement with the Ku Klux Klan and other white racial terrorists; the use of law enforcement to enforce Jim Crow laws and the informal racist rules of the pre-civil rights era; and law enforcement's attacks on civil-rights activists. The heroin epidemic of the late 1960s and crack epidemic of the late 1980s and early 1990s—which continues in force in many neighborhoods—are viewed as deliberate government actions to damage communities finally freed by the civil-rights movement from formal legal oppression. The community believes that the drug trade could not exist without at least the acquiescence of the police and other authorities, and authorities are believed to be complicit in drug-trafficking. It is believed that the real money in the drug trade goes to high-level figures outside the community, and that there are more drugs sold and used in majority neighborhoods, but that law enforcement has no interest in those people or those crimes. High levels of enforcement, arrest, and incarceration are seen as the intended outcomes of a deliberate outside attack, designed to destabilize the community, control strong young men, and provide work for law-enforcement agencies and prison staff.

A dominant law-enforcement narrative is that the affected communities have entirely lost their fundamental social and moral standards. On this account, the community as a whole no longer stands against drugs, violence, and other crime; sets and enforces no standards for its young people; takes no responsibility for itself but seizes any opportunity to blame outsiders, especially the police; does not insist that its young people finish school, go to work, care for their own children, and the like; and lives off drug money. Drug dealers themselves are sees as irrational and often predatory and sociopathic. They are not deterred by frequent arrest and incarceration or by high levels of homicide and other serious violence; they use violence to settle trivial personal disputes; their drug-dealing destroys their own communities; they corrupt very young children into the drug trade as runners, look-outs, and the like; and they care about nobody, including themselves.

A dominant narrative among street dealers and similar offenders is that they have no choice in what they do because of the barriers created by racist outsiders; that history and current conditions have left them no options; that whites and other outsiders commit more serious crimes—as exemplified by such things as the Iran–Contra and Enron scandals—but do not pay for them as severely; that arrest, incarceration, and death are inevitable and nothing to be afraid of; that "respect" is everything and disrespect must be met with violence; that the community tolerates or supports what they do; and that the police and others in law enforcement are racist predators.

These narratives are rarely voiced in any consistent way across the groups involved—community members say to each other that the police must be conspirators in the drug trade, but do not say it to the police; the police say to each other that it is impossible to do anything about drugs because everyone in the community is living off the trade, but they do not say it to residents. These strong beliefs therefore go unexamined, unchallenged, and become even more deeply internalized. The result is a profound racial schism with impact and implications well beyond issues of crime and drugs.

The "High Point" drug market intervention—so called after the city of High Point, North Carolina, where it was worked out and first implemented—was framed around the ideas developed so far in this volume and was designed to address all these issues. Perhaps most interesting was that it explicitly recognized and addressed the "norms and narratives" around drug issues that are embedded in law enforcement, communities, and offenders. In so doing, it recognized implicit common ground among all these parties and crafted—despite wide initial polarization—a strategic response in which all parties could change their behavior for mutual benefit.

This chapter is not a formal evaluation of the intervention.[1] Some apparent impacts will be presented, and some reasons will be suggested to believe that those apparent impacts are likely to have been caused by the intervention. The main point here, however, is to show one way in which the ideas thus far presented could be applied in practice to an important public-safety problem.

High Point

High Point is a city with a population of approximately 95,000 in central North Carolina (it adjoins the much larger city of Greensboro). Shifting manufacturing patterns in its core furniture industry have led to a declining industrial base. The city is 60 percent white and 30 percent African American; some 13 percent of the population and 10 percent of families live below the poverty line. High Point started experiencing serious drug activity and gun violence in the mid-1990s, when its homicide rate climbed higher than the much larger adjoining cities of Greensboro and nearby Winston-Salem.

High Point, working with the author, became one of the first cities to replicate Boston's focused-deterrence violence prevention strategy, launching the interagency Violent Crime Task Force (VCTF) in 1997. The VCTF grew to include the High Point Police Department (HPPD); the US Attorney; the Guilford County District Attorney; probation; parole; the Bureau of Alcohol, Tobacco, Firearms, and Explosives; the Drug Enforcement Administration; the Federal Bureau of Investigation; numerous city agencies, service providers, churches, and community groups; and research partners from Harvard, Winston-Salem State University and the University of North Carolina, Greensboro. Violent crime in the city seemed to respond to that intervention. More than that, the focused deterrence/direct engagement approach became part of the way HPPD and its partners thought about and did its work.

In 2002, James Fealy, a career police officer in the Austin, Texas police department, was named chief in High Point and immediately decided to focus on overt drug markets. Fealy's first tour of the city was enough to observe chronic street-corner dealing, crack houses, prostitution, and drive-through drug buyers. These markets were exclusively in poor minority neighborhoods, though drug and sex buyers often came from outside. The markets drove a wide range of crime; community complaints were chronic. HPPD and its partners did a great deal of street drug enforcement, warrant service, and investigation of mid-level dealers, but to no effect; some of High Point's open-air markets, such as that in the heavily hit West End neighborhood, had been active for more than twenty years. All of this was familiar to Fealy, who had the same experiences and frustrations from Austin.

In the fall of 2003, Fealy and HPPD Majors Marty Sumner and Randy Tysinger, Narcotics Unit Lieutenant Larry Casterline, and Assistant US Attorney Rob Lang began discussions with the author about framing a different approach to the problem. High Point's goal was to eliminate overt drug markets citywide and to address the key problems associated with them: homicide, gun assault, robberies and other serious violence; sexual assault; prostitution; drive-through drug buyers; and broad community quality of life concerns. To these goals, the author added an additional set of issues: addressing racial conflict between communities and law enforcement, and the individual and community harm produced by traditional drug enforcement. The "High Point" strategy was developed by that team in the following fashion.[2]

Key themes in the strategy

Strategic problem definition: not a "drug problem"— a "drug market" problem

The strategy began with the idea that what had to be dealt with was not "the drug problem"—as it is usually framed—but a *drug market* problem. Many of the crime and community problems associated with "the drug problem" are a function of overt, disorderly drug markets, rather than with drugs as such. Street-dealing and crack houses create dynamics in communities that discreet drug markets do not. There are forms of drug markets that do not bring with them public dealing, drive-through buyers, or street prostitutes, and associated issues of violence, other crime, and disorder.[3] Those problems are associated with particular forms of the drug market—with "overt markets"—rather than with drug-dealing and use as such. There is a clear parallel here to various forms of other illicit markets, such as that for prostitution. A street sex market creates greatly more harm, both for the affected neighborhood and for actual participants, than does an escort service. The project was thus framed not as *doing something about drugs* but as *eliminating overt drug markets*.

Contingent nonlinear dynamics: "tipping" in overt markets

Overt drug markets have strong sustaining dynamics. They are usually quite well defined geographically. Once they establish themselves in particular places, buyers know that they can buy there, and sellers know that they can sell there, so both have reason to continue in the same place even in the face of real risks. There is safety for both sides in numbers. Enforcement rarely reaches the whole market at once—for instance, addressing all sellers and buyers simultaneously—so even large numbers of drug arrests over time do not shut the market down. Buyers and sellers subject to enforcement action return to a thriving market and are easily reincorporated. The constant but unsuccessful enforcement attention such markets usually receive emboldens dealers and buyers, demoralizes and angers residents, makes law enforcement look weak and foolish, and contributes to the various harms and narratives described above.

Overt markets do not suddenly emerge full-blown in particular places, however. They develop gradually over time. Similarly, if it were possible to deliberately shut one down for a time, even if it were to reestablish itself it would not do so instantly. A few dealers would begin again, other dealers and potential dealers would observe them and follow, buyers would learn the market was back and start patronizing it. Before long the market would be back in full force, but if this process were to be interrupted at the very beginning, it would be possible to prevent the market from returning. If the process were routinely interrupted early, the market could be routinely and consistently "headed off." Over time this could mean that dealers would stop trying to sell there, buyers no longer bother to look there, and community confidence would be reestablished. The effort necessary to maintain the market in its "closed" position would then be greatly reduced.

This is a classic "tipping" dynamic—a big problem that nevertheless starts small and has two natural stable points: completely out of control, on the one hand, and almost completely quiet, on the other. The High Point strategy therefore focused on (1) deliberately shutting the market down all at once and completely, and (2) building in a maintenance strategy that had law enforcement steadily looking for the "first movers" seeking to open it again and preventing them from succeeding.

Create formal social control: Ensure predictable formal sanctions

Low-level drug dealers tend to accrue extensive criminal histories but tend to face low and almost completely unpredictable risks at any given moment. Research shows street dealers can average hundreds of transactions between arrests,[4] and most drug arrests result in low-level sanctions: the prison risk per cocaine transaction has been calculated at 1 : 15,000.[5] Even when a dealer in fact faces a real risk, he usually doesn't know it until he's been arrested and charged. The deterrence value of ordinary drug enforcement is probably, therefore, almost nil, even in the midst of very high levels of police activity. Ideally, dealers should know, when they think about going out to sell, that they face a real risk. An effective deterrence framework should thus produce a high risk of a meaningful sanction, and make that clear to offenders.

Formal sanctions should be minimized

High levels of drug enforcement do enormous damage to individuals and communities. Personal and social capital is damaged; individuals and whole cohorts have little reason to finish school and take entry-level jobs; families are disrupted; the stigma of conviction and imprisonment are reduced and even reversed; and relations between communities and law enforcement are poisoned. The actual application of formal sanctions should thus be minimized. Deterrence, rather than enforcement, should be the goal.

Community, family, and peer standards matter more than law enforcement, but local norms and narratives stand in the way

Individual morality, the views of respected family, peers, and role models, and clear community standards are the most powerful underpinnings of good behavior. These influences are not aligned against drug-dealing in troubled communities. Deeply racialized narratives identify drug enforcement with the long history of deliberate oppression of the minority community, implicate government conspiracies in the drug trade, and label law enforcement as racist. Among networks of offenders, informal norms require individuals to act as if jail and prison are nothing to fear, and violence nothing to avoid—that, indeed, they build credibility—early death is inevitable, disrespect requires violence, and the like. There are strong community feelings against drug offending, and offenders have real interests in stepping away from the street, but these "norms and narratives" keep them from being clearly expressed.

Mutual misunderstandings perpetuates these dynamics

Law enforcement, communities, and drug dealers misunderstand each other in important ways. Law enforcement and other outsiders see no clear stand from communities against drug offending and believe that the moral strength of communities has been lost. Communities see law enforcement pursuing transparently ineffective and destructive strategies and infer corruption and deliberate oppression. Drug offenders do not see clear stands against drug offending from their own communities and believe that their own actions are excused, tolerated, and even celebrated. Drug offenders see each other and believe that each is committed to deviance. Law enforcement sees offenders as irrational and even sociopathic.

None of these things is true. But systematic misunderstandings perpetuate the errors. Law enforcement does not say out loud what it says behind closed doors: Nobody in law enforcement thinks the drug war is being won, and law enforcement would love to do something that would in fact work, but they do not say so to the affected communities. Communities loathe the drug-dealing and violence and despair over the future of their young people, but they do not say so to the police. Low-level dealers are afraid, do not want to go to prison, and are not making a lot of money, but they do not say so to each other, to their own community, or to the police. These norms, narratives, and dynamics are never explicitly addressed, misunderstandings are not revealed, and common ground is not apparent.

Help matters

Drug offenders should have help to do better. Support and services—mentoring, treatment, education, employment, and the like—should be provided. If drug proceeds are in fact paying for rent, food, and the like, then families should get help making the transition to living without drug money. This is important for at least two reasons. If dealers and families in fact start leading legitimate lives, that is a good thing, and attachment to legitimate others and activities will help prevent their and the community's return to drug-dealing. If they do not, but a legitimate offer of help has been made, then they will no longer have any excuse for criminality, and the offender and community narrative that justifies drug dealing will have been undercut.

Small numbers of drug dealers

Even in communities with severe drug market problems, only a small number of offenders drive the problem. Research shows that at any given time only a few percent of (largely) young men are heavily involved. In-depth examination of particular drug "crews" and drug markets frequently shows that very small numbers—from less than ten to a few dozen—are involved. This means that if all the offenders in a given market need to be addressed, the challenge—whether from law enforcement, community engagement, or social services—need only be sufficient to those numbers.

The "High Point" drug market intervention

The operational, "High Point" plan that resulted from these considerations was designed to eliminate overt markets citywide by closing individual markets permanently one at a time. The belief was that the most powerful step that could be taken was for the community, and dealers' own families and peers, to make it very clear to dealers that selling drugs was unacceptable and must stop; in so doing awakening any latent norms and narratives within and amongst offenders that stood against drug-dealing; and establishing a consensual narrative that if law enforcement had to take enforcement steps then those steps represented the will of the community, not outside oppression.

In order to do those things, it would be necessary to address the conflict and misunderstanding between law enforcement and communities; to elevate positive norms within communities, families, peers, and offenders; and to focus those influences on dealers. It would also be necessary to provide social services and support to dealers and perhaps to their families. If those steps failed, it would be necessary back them up with immediate, meaningful and predictable criminal sanctions.

Addressing law enforcement, community, and drug dealer norms and narratives

Central to the process was a series of discussions: first, within law enforcement, and then between law enforcement and communities. These discussions were, in effect, a specification of each group's own "norms and narratives," a translation of those ideas from one group to the other, and a discussion of the impact on the core drug market problem of how each group was behaving and interacting with the other. The discussions began in small and private groups and gradually expanded to include more participants and then into open sessions (history with similar conversations has shown that open-door meetings are impossible settings in which to talk about these issues, at least initially). The emergent central themes from these discussions were very clear.

Law enforcement needed to understand that its commitment to enforcement, even when it did not solve the problem, did unintended damage to communities and was seen by the community through the lens of a powerful historic and racial narrative that painted contemporary law enforcement as oppressive and often couched drug enforcement as a deliberate means to that end. Constant arrests, street stops, and even harsher measures like going into houses on warrants was not seen by the community as well-intentioned police work that was regrettably not producing the desired effect; it was seen as a destructive and even conscious attack on the community.

For many in law enforcement, this was not at all difficult to take in; Chief Fealy, in an early conversation, told members of the West End community that one of the worst moments in his career was when, upon completing a drug sweep in his native Austin, Texas, an elderly black woman in the neighborhood told him that he and the police were almost as bad as the drug dealers. The depth of the community beliefs came as a great shock to many in law enforcement, however. Community members frequently said, for example, that the police let the drugs come into the community because otherwise they would be out of work, a perspective that had never so much as occurred to the police, who knew perfectly well that they'd have more than enough to do regardless. Chief Fealy, in turn, told community members that nobody in law enforcement, from the head of the Drug Enforcement Administration on down, thought the drug war was winnable and that he couldn't keep drugs out of the community no matter what he did: an admission that equally shocked the community. This kind of exchange—facts understood in one way by one side but understood in completely different ways by the other side—was a routine occurrence in these conversations. Fundamental attribution error was in full force. "We thought we were on good terms with the community, and that we understood each other," says High Point Major Marty Sumner. "We didn't understand each other at all." It didn't take long for many in law enforcement to see what they had been doing in substantially new ways. "Well-intended officers recognize these areas as problematic but apply tactics that alienate the community," said Lieutenant Larry Casterline, who ran the HPPD narcotics unit.

Community members, in turn, needed to understand that their silence about drug and violence issues was read by both outsiders and street offenders as tolerance, support, disinterest, or some combination thereof, that no community could flourish without setting clear standards about right and wrong, and that neither law enforcement nor anybody else could set and enforce those standards from the outside. Community members generally responded to this with frank assessments that this was true, frequently saying to each other that their own parents would never have tolerated such misbehavior and that the community today needed to return to those kinds of attitudes. Those in law enforcement who had written off the community as disintegrated, complicit, and even corrupt were in turn frequently shocked by what they heard.

Both law enforcement and communities needed to understand that low-level drug activity was frequently a product more of informal peer and "street" dynamics than of sensible economic calculation or organized criminal enterprise. Repeated arrests and returns to jail and prison may not mean that a young man is self-destructive or irrational; it may simply mean that he's running with other young men who constantly say they don't fear prison and death, whatever they actually believe privately. In both law enforcement and in the community, there were widespread myths and misunderstanding that needed to be addressed. Many on both sides, for example, believed that nonexistent "gang leadership" would not allow dealers to stop, or that low-level dealers routinely make vast sums in short times (minimum wage or less is closer to reality). As these conversations developed members of the community who were very close to the streets, such as ex-offenders and gang outreach workers, were enormously valuable, able to say from direct experience and exposure what the street drug trade and street life were really like—realities that were often quite far away from the images held by others.

These conversations were, for the most part, saying out loud what both community and law enforcement routinely said in private, dealing with the misunderstanding and mythologies, and recognizing that both sides were contributing to the terrible outcomes on the street. They went surprisingly easily. And clearly evident was important common ground: that everybody loathed the drug activity and the violence; that everybody wanted pointless heavy enforcement to stop; that everybody wanted dangerous offenders and those who would not listen to be controlled; and that everybody would rather find a way to work together than to continue in angry polarization. "The community was deeply angry at law enforcement and felt that we were incompetent or doing deliberate harm," says Chief Fealy. "We did not see community opposition to drugs and violence. We did not credit at all that dealers were rational and reachable, as events have clearly proven."

These conversations started early and continued during and beyond the development and implementation of the drug market strategy (see Exhibit 9.1).

Identifying and selecting an initial drug market

The HPPD felt that it was very important to be as objective as possible about identifying and selecting overt drug markets for attention. Police departments, particularly street level and narcotics officers, know perfectly well where their markets are without special analysis. HPPD wanted, however, to be able to show clear evidence to community members, politicians, and the media how and why they had selected particular markets and to use solid data to choose the most serious one and to justify not choosing others. "If somebody said, why are you picking on my neighborhood, or somebody else said, why didn't you come to my neighborhood, we wanted to be able to show it was objective and not prejudice or politics," says Major Sumner. HPPD mapped drug arrests, calls for service, field contacts, and Part I, weapons, sexual, and prostitution offenses. Within hot spots, serious crimes were individually reviewed for a drug connection. Information from patrol officers, vice/narcotics investigators, informants, and crime tip lines was analyzed. The West End, Daniel Brooks/Washington Drive and Southside

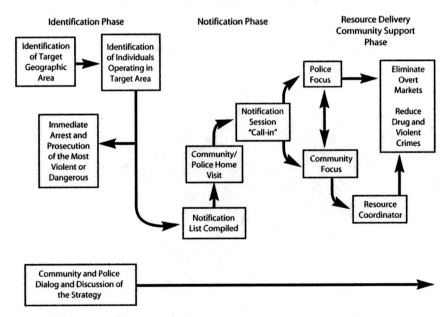

Exhibit 9.1 The High Point drug market process

neighborhoods were identified as major overt markets (see Exhibit 9.2); a fourth area, East Central, emerged later. The West End and Southside areas are largely rental housing; Daniel Brooks is entirely public housing. In the West End, which was selected for the initial operation, analysis showed that the small hot-spot area had generated roughly 10 percent of High Point's violent crime for over a decade. A recent home-invasion homicide in which three young men had gone from breaking into cars to murder in less than a year sealed the selection of the West End as the initial site. An important additional factor was the presence of a strong community network, High Point Communities Against Violence.

Careful identification of all dealers

Intervening simultaneously with all dealers in a market was seen as crucial to disrupting the market and the small-group/network dynamics supporting offending. For each market, vice/narcotics detectives surveyed patrol officers, probation officers, street narcotics officers and community members and reviewed every arrest report, incident report, and field interview associated with possible dealers. All known associates were reviewed. Suspects' current activities were checked. The relatively large initial list generated by this process was repeatedly trimmed as it turned out that dealer once active in the area no longer were, or were not actually dealing, or were in prison.

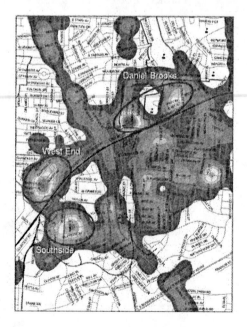

Exhibit 9.2 Drug market hot spots: from north, Daniel Brooks, the West End, and Southside

The process uncovered a very small number of active dealers. The West End turned out to have only sixteen active dealers (High Point's next site, the Daniel Brooks public-housing project, also had sixteen; its third site, the Southside neighborhood, had twenty-six; the final East Central neighborhood had thirty-two). "We'd been doing sweeps in the West End every month for years, and I thought there were hundreds of dealers there," says Major Sumner. "When it turned out to be sixteen, that's when it became manageable. I thought, we can do this." When Winston-Salem went through this process in its Cleveland Avenue neighborhood, in a public-housing project that had been an open market going back to the first heroin epidemic, they too thought they were essentially drowning in drug dealers. Careful police work identified thirty-one. "There were a lot of people hanging around, and a lot of users and just people in the mix, but not many actual dealers," says Winston-Salem chief of police Pat Norris. "The small number of dealers in any given market became quite apparent to law enforcement when we researched identified markets," says HPPD's Casterline. "This exercise helped officers realize that they may have been directing enforcement action toward individuals who lived in and around the drug market but who were not actually involved in it."

Creating certain formal sanctions: "banking" cases

It turned out to be relatively easy—if, in some quarters, somewhat controversial—to deter these dealers, to put them in a position where they knew that they would face meaningful formal consequences for any future drug-dealing. In each market, ordinary investigative techniques were used to make cases against each dealer. Undercover police officers or confidential informants got video and audio recordings of all buys. High-level and clearly dangerous dealers were arrested and, by prior arrangement with prosecutors, got careful state and sometimes federal attention. In general, if dealers had prior convictions for violent crimes or gun offenses, or there was intelligence that they were dangerous, they were arrested. The proportion of such "high level" dealers varies from market to market; in the West End, only four of the initial sixteen dealers were arrested.

For "low level" dealers without a history of violence, however, the cases were "banked": taken to the point that a warrant could be signed, and held there. This permitted law enforcement to tell dealers, at a time of their choosing, that if they continued dealing they would immediately be arrested—without further investigation—but that if they stopped nothing need happen to them. The chance that something meaningful would happen to them if they continued dealing was now not 1 : 15,000 but roughly 1 : 1—and they knew it.

Not surprisingly, this step is difficult or impossible to swallow for many in law enforcement. Well after the initial High Point intervention, the National

Urban League approached Karen Richards, county prosecutor in Fort Wayne, Indiana, in an attempt to replicate the approach there, but she wanted nothing to do with it. "Why not slam 'em from the beginning and forget this foolishness?" she said. "Drug dealers are drug dealers [...] They won't have an epiphany and end up as model citizens."[6] A participant in a workshop on the High Point strategy at the Justice Department's 2006 Project Safe Neighborhoods National Conference had similar reservations. "Can't we just arrest them all, and then do the rest of the strategy?" he asked.

For a variety of reasons, others—so far, most—in law enforcement who have considered the strategy have been have been willing to take the step. One reason is that they believe that more of the usual will not give different results. "I've been in narcotics enforcement my whole career," says Chief Fealy. "It's never worked." In the normal course of events, when these low-level dealers would be—to their surprise—arrested, they would be bonded out and returned to the streets, where they would be free to continue dealing (it is a commonplace among police that their dealing often increases at that point, as they have lost profits to make uo and legal bills to pay). Most cases would then be pled, piecemeal, over the next year or so to probation–which would keep them on the street–or to relatively minor jail or prison terms; while on the street on probation little supervision would be exercised; when their jail or prison terms were over, little or none would. The apparently tough step of arrest and prosecution was in fact next to meaningless: which was clearly understood by no one better than the dealers themselves.

"Banking" the cases, on the other hand, meant that the dealers knew to a certainty *ahead of time* that they faced whatever inconvenience, expense, and formal penalties their arrests would precipitate. Since the charge was being held over their heads, they faced those consequences not just for the single drug transaction (or few drug transactions) for which they could be arrested at the moment, but for all transactions they might contemplate while the charge was banked. They were on the street but *not* free to continue dealing, unless they wanted to risk the very high chance of activating the case. Most, as it turned out, did not, making a mockery of the street bravado that nobody cared about the police or prison: it was easy to posture thus when it was too late to do anything about it, but much harder when there was in fact a clear choice. As backward as it seemed, banking the case was greatly more onerous than pursuing it.

Banking the cases also greatly changed the underlying moral calculus: it was a graphic and concrete way to show the community, dealers, and their families that the views they had of law enforcement as conspiring to harm the community and control young black men is wrong. Steven Hairston, Head of the Winston-Salem NAACP (National Association for the Advancement of Colored People), spoke at the first open community meeting about the prospective Winston-Salem drug market intervention. "I never would have believed that the police would hold our young men in their hands, able to put them in prison, and not do it," he said. "If they can do that, we can do our part." Another is that an arrest and conviction does permanent harm to a dealer's future, should he later want to change. "We've come to see the damage it can do," says Marty Sumner. "I tell them, I don't want to turn you into a felon."

Identifying "influentials"

Following on the core idea that dealers would stop when those around them made it clear they should, a core hope was to enlist those close to offenders—parents, grandparents, guardians, elders in the communities, ministers—to create and reinforce positive norms and expectations. There was a great deal of concern in High Point about whether this would be possible, whether those close to the dealer would in fact stand for the right things, would accuse the police of setting up or profiling the dealer, were living on drug money, were in denial, or a range of other possibilities. For the most part, in practice, such fears have been unfounded: When approached, told their son or daughter or grandchild or friend was in serious trouble but could also get help, such figures have usually rallied. For each dealer, one or several "influentials" was identified—in practice, primarily mothers and grandmothers—by reviewing the dealer's contact history, booking records, probation officer contact logs, and jail-visit lists. When contacted—a process detailed below—most were willing, even grateful and eager, to step forward.

Organizing services

Services were identified and organized. The city of High Point hired a resource coordinator to work closely with dealers and their families (this was one of the few uses of new funding in the intervention). A group of ministers, service providers, healthcare workers, nonprofit organizations, educators, and elected officials worked to ensure that needs—most commonly employment, housing, transportation, and help enrolling in GED (General Equivalency Diploma: the equivalent of a high-school diploma) programs—were met. For the initial intervention in the West End, the High Point city manager even offered jobs to several offenders once they could pass a drug test.

Shutting the market down: The "call-in"

The key operational moment in the strategy was a "call-in" at which law enforcement, community members, and service providers delivered a unified message to dealers in the company of their influentials. When it was clear that a "beachhead" market could be maintained effectively, a new one would be identified and addressed. In the end, in High Point, only four operations were necessary: the West End (May 2004), Daniel Brooks (April 2005), Southside (June 2006), and East Central (August 2007).

Over the early months of 2004, the law-enforcement and community conversations took place in the West End, dealers were identified and investigated, services organized, and "influentials" identified (see Exhibit 9.1 for a flow model of the strategy). During the two weeks before the May 18 call-in, teams consisting (for the most part) of a HPPD detective and Revd. Summey, pastor of English Road Baptist Church in the West End, made home visits to the dealers and their "influentials." They were told that police had made undercover buys from the offender; that probable cause existed for an arrest; that an opportunity to avoid prosecution and an offer of assistance would be discussed at the call-in; and that family members and others were encouraged to attend. The offender received a letter from Chief Fealy inviting them to the call-in with a promise that no one would be arrested that night (see Exhibit 9.3).

For the initial West End notification, nine of the twelve dealers came to the meeting, accompanied by many "influentials" and others. They heard an uncompromising message from community speakers: "We care deeply about you, we'll help you, but you're hurting people and destroying the community and you need to stop." They heard an uncompromising message from law enforcement: "You could be in jail tonight, we don't want to do that, we want to help you succeed, but you are out of the drug business." Enlarged surveillance photos of drug locations lined the walls; the dealers' case books were on a table in front of them; and four chairs, bearing pictures of the dangerous offenders arrested as part of the operation, sat empty. Dealers' mothers and grandmothers cheered both the community and law-enforcement messages. Law enforcement's willingness *not* to act on existing cases seemed to make a profound impression on the dealers' families and other community members. Most of dealers signed up for services; the next morning the coordinator got a call from a dealer previously unknown to law enforcement asking if he too could participate. This same basic pattern has continued for subsequent call-ins in other markets (twenty of twenty invited dealers showed up at the third, Southside meeting).

The call-ins have been electrifying events, with police officers moved profoundly, drug dealers testifying to their gratitude for a second chance, community figures speaking in terms of both accountability and redemption, and family members speaking strongly and plainly to their children. "As hard as it was to believe that drug dealers would change their behavior," says Chief Fealy, "we now find it harder to understand how they would not." Larry Casterline says, "It turns out dealers *are* rational. Scratch another narrative." While not probative, there is some evidence that dealers in fact responded as the theory of the intervention hoped they might. Randy Dejournette, one of the West End dealers, told the *Wall Street Journal* that he was surprised by the community's new stand, ashamed at disappointing his mother, who continued to keep him in line after the meeting, and that "everybody's gone" now from the West End's streets. "I'm not going to go out there by myself and sit on the corner and look dumb."[7]

Jim Fealy
Chief of Police

PHONE (336) 887-7970
FAX (336) 887-7972
TDD (336) 883-8517

High Point Police Department

April 29, 2004

John William Doe:

As Chief of Police with the High Point Police Department, I am writing to let you know that your activities have come to my attention. Specifically, I know that you are involved in selling drugs on the street. You have been identified as a street level drug dealer after an extensive undercover campaign in the West End area.

I want to invite you to a meeting on May 18,2004, at 6:00 PM at the Police Department. You will **not** be arrested. This is not a trick. You may bring someone with you who is important to you, like a friend or relative. I want you to see the evidence I have of your involvement in criminal activity, and I want to give you an option to stop before my officers are forced to take action. Let me say again, you will not be arrested at this meeting.

If you choose not to attend this meeting, we will be in contact with you along with members of the community. Street level drug sales and violence have to stop in High Point. We are giving you one chance to hear our message before we are forced to take action against you.

Chief James Fealy
High Point Police Department

Exhibit 9.3 The call-in letter

Impact

Closing the markets

There are no remaining overt drug markets in High Point. The quality of life in the affected neighborhoods has improved dramatically. "Most important, these changes are almost entirely self-sustaining," says Chief Fealy. "We continue to work in these neighborhoods, but an active community consensus now stands against drug-dealing."

The West End drug market vanished literally overnight. Street-corner and drug-house activity, drive-through buyers, and prostitutes were simply not in evidence. The character of the neighborhood changed immediately, with residents going outside again, children playing, people taking care of their properties, and a multitude of other signs of transformation. Particularly satisfying was that for the first time large numbers of local children attended one church's summer program: The kids said that their mothers had told them it was now safe to walk to church. Street and narcotics officers soon picked up a clear sense from offenders across High Point that the West End had become a "no go" area for drug dealers.

The same occurred in turn in Daniel Brooks, Southside, and East Central, with the fascinating development that in Daniel Brooks the market collapsed when HPPD began public discussions with the community, and in Southside when HPPD delivered the invitations to the notification. Offenders clearly knew what was coming and complied immediately, a classic instance of the "anticipatory benefits" of effective deterrence communication strategies.

The markets are genuinely closed. In just over a month prior to the call-in, narcotics officers made multiple purchases from eleven different people at seventeen locations in West End. In Daniel Brooks, narcotics officers made multiple purchases from twelve different people at eight locations. In the Southside, fifty-one street buys were made at twenty-nine locations, multiple times at some locations. In each market, undercover officers and informants were able to make buys every time they tried. Following the call-ins, focusing on both these and other locations, HPPD was unable to make a single buy. Informants attempted to make buys in the West End and Daniel Brooks several times a week for three months, without success. Informants now spot-check these neighborhoods once a month. The West End has now been closed for over three years, Daniel Brooks for over two years, and Southside for a year. The same pattern is apparent in the recently closed East Central market.

No displacement has been evident. With the closure of the East Central market, no overt market remains anywhere in the city. HPPD investigators are aware of and continuing to pursue discreet drug dealing and higher-level traffickers, but are aware of no locations where there is public dealing or where strangers can make drug connections.

Violent and drug crime

In the West End, violent and drug crime also dropped dramatically, not just in the formal target area but also in the larger area recognized as the West End neighborhood. Small absolute numbers make for large percentage shifts, particularly for short comparison periods, but three years out the reductions in violent crime—defined as murder, rape, robbery, aggravated assault, prostitution, sex offenses, and weapons—appear to have stabilized at about 41 percent (see Exhibit 9.4). Most important, there has not been a homicide, rape, or gun assault in reported in the West End since the intervention. Gunshot calls for service have dropped by over 50 percent. Violent crime in the Southside area has followed a similar pattern (see Exhibit 9.5). Drug crime is similarly down and has shifted from dealing offenses to minor possession, paraphernalia, and the like (Exhibit 9.6). Violent crime citywide is down 20 percent over the more than three years of the initiative. In Daniel Brooks, what appears to be more realistic reporting of crime—a common phenomenon when police/community relations improve—and a serious domestic violence problem has kept numbers up; those numbers are now declining (see Exhibit 9.7). Early returns on the East Central intervention show it following the same pattern as the West End and Southside.

Some dealers doing well

The hardest part of the overall strategy has been helping dealers lead normal lives and get good jobs. Most of the dealers in the initial West End site, for example, did not make their way through to getting and keeping good jobs. The most successful approach seems to involve ex-offender mentors working with the dealers. In High Point's Daniel Brooks initiative—in addition to the regular menu of services—a church-based ex-offenders' group matched mentors with the dealers. Most of those dealers are now working regular jobs.

Maintenance

It has in fact turned out to be relatively easy to hold onto these gains and keep the markets closed. All the sites report that the areas are more or less recognized as off-limits by drug dealers and that clear community standards

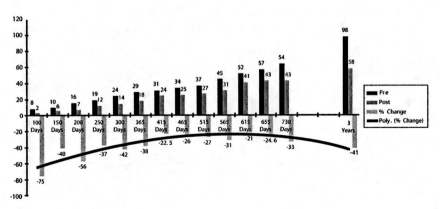

Exhibit 9.4 Serious crime in the West End

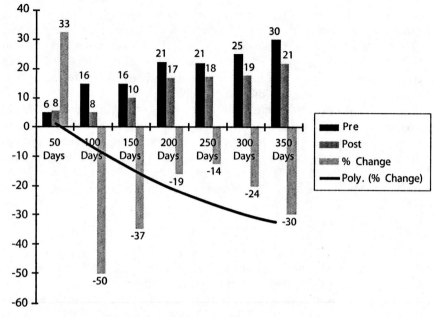

Exhibit 9.5 Violent crime in Southside

are doing a lot of the work of keeping them free of dealing. "I say, they got their outrage back," says Major Sumner.

The main lesson has been to frame any additional enforcement work in terms of *communicating deterrence*. "We realized that when we saw something, or got a complaint, we had to do something visible right away," says Major Sumner. If someone called about a drug house in one of the market areas, doing undercover work, setting up a warrant, and serving it might take a month. That process was, of necessity, secret, while residents and dealers alike watched and thought nothing was being done and that law enforcement's promises had been empty. HPPD therefore made sure that something clearly visible was done immediately upon getting information

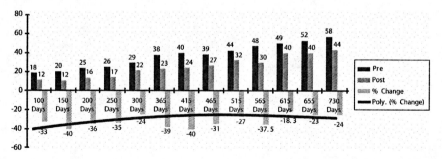

Exhibit 9.6 Drug crime in the West End

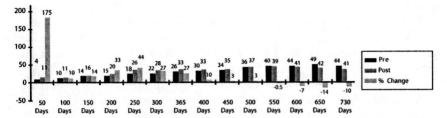

Exhibit 9.7 Serious crime in Daniel Brooks

that there was a dealing problem. Often it was relatively low-level: talking to the dealer or, if appropriate, a landlord; parking officers outside the location; and the like. Such steps were often effective, however. Drug complaints are responded to in numerous ways, which could include additional surveillance, an undercover buy, procurement of a search warrant, a consent search, personal notification of residents of the complaint location, or a visible disruption of the complaint location (i.e., posting an officer near or in front of the location). If more serious enforcement action was necessary, it was made a top priority, no matter how minor the actual dealing was. HPPD changed the way it managed informants so that instead of rewarding them for cases involving large volumes of drugs anywhere in the city, they were rewarded for cases of any kind involving dealers in the target areas. The overall intent was to make it clear on the streets that these were, and would remain, no-go areas.

It has also turned out to be critical to make sure that community members and other dealers are informed of any enforcement actions. The intended deterrent effect will not occur if steps are taken, but nobody outside law enforcement and those actually arrested knows about it. HPPD thus undertook repeated communication with notified drug dealers, their families, and the neighborhood, using home visits, telephone calls, newsletters, and community meetings.

Early replications

A number of other jurisdictions have applied the basic High Point approach since the initial West End intervention. At the time of this writing, Winston-Salem, North Carolina, shut down a market in the Cleveland Homes housing project;[8] Rockford, Illinois has shut down two areas; and Raleigh, North Carolina, Newburgh and Hempstead, New York, Providence, Rhode Island,[9] Nashville, Tennessee, and Milwaukee, Wisconsin have all shut down single markets. All of them report broadly equivalent outcomes, with abrupt and dramatic changes in drug activity and violent crime (in Winston-Salem, departmental dissatisfaction with its maintenance activity is leading it to revisit the market several years after the initial shutdown). In Providence, a year after that market was closed, overall calls for service in the drug market area have dropped 58 percent, reported drug crime has dropped 70 percent, and residents' calls to police about drug crime have dropped 81 percent.[10] Police–community relations have improved dramatically. "One of the things that's so important is the relationship the police have created with the neighbors," says resident Ken Cabral. "They're recognizing the difference between the kids that are doing bad and those kids just trying to have fun in their neighborhood. I've never seen this in any community in the city of Providence."[11]

Raleigh rolled out its own version of the strategy on February 8, 2007. Fourteen drug dealers—twelve men and two women, aged from seventeen to seventy-one years—from one of Raleigh's most dangerous neighborhoods were invited to the call-in; all fourteen walked in the door. The police department played a DVD, edited down from hours of investigative surveillance, showing each dealer making a drug sale: The fourteen dealers watched in apparent shock. They then heard, in turn, from Kent Sholar, Deputy Chief of the Raleigh Police Department; District Captain Tom Earnhardt; Wake County District Attorney Ned Mangum; Sheriff Donnie Harrison; North Carolina Department of Community Corrections District Manager Doug Pardue; Assistant US Attorney Jane Jackson, Bureau of Alcohol, Tobacco, and Firearms agent James Avant; CCBI (City-County Bureau of Identification, which provides forensic and identification services to law enforcement) Director Sam Pennica; Wake County Public Defender Bryan Collins; Christian Faith Baptist Church Pastor and Chair of The Triangle Lost Generation Taskforce Revd. Dr. David Forbes; residents Betty Burrell and Siddiq Abdallah; Shaloam Community Church Reverend Lola Fuller; City Councilor James West; and the "My Brother's Keeper" social-services team: in the company of 150 neighborhood residents.

The message was clear and consistent: Your involvement in drug-dealing harms the community, and it must stop today; there are serious consequences if you choose to continue your involvement in drug-dealing or commit a violent act; we believe you can succeed by making better choices with support from the community; we hope you accept our offer of assistance to turn around your lives. Dr. Forbes stood before the dealers and said to them that they hailed from the cradle of civilization, that the blood of kings and mathematicians ran in their veins, and that the community needed them to live up to that and would help them to do so. Police officers watched approvingly and lent their own voices of support. The meeting ended with the entire room sharing a buffet dinner; police officers served the dealers pizza, and the meeting broke into small conversational groups of dealers, residents, law enforcement, ministers, and others. Two hundred days later, violent crime in the area was down 42 percent, fourteen of the sixteen dealers were in a recovery program and doing well; a number of them were working; and more than 100 additional people from the neighborhood had come forward voluntarily and joined the fourteen in their quest to leave the streets.[12]

One of the original fourteen, Burlee Kersey, spoke publicly at a North Carolina event in December of 2007. He gave eloquent testimony to the common ground on which effective deterrence can be built:

> My name is Burlee Kersey. I am seventy-two years old and I have been on drugs for forty years. I was given a second chance when I was chosen to be in the CHOICE project. I was given hope when I thought there was no hope for me.
>
> I am forever thankful to the Raleigh Police Department for choosing me. The right name was given to the program. The police department called it CHOICE, because you have a CHOICE to either turn your life around or go to jail. When God asked Cain, "Where is thy brother?" and Cain replied, "Am I my Brother's keeper?" I believe God probably answered him back and said, "Yes, you are your brother's keeper." The CHOICE program showed all of us that they really are their brother's keeper.
>
> When I was first asked to be part of the project, I was asked "Do you want to be on drugs all of your life?" I made it up in my mind I didn't want to be, so I am struggling to stay clean every day, every minute. But today I have support. I know I have people who don't look down on me.
>
> I had been on drugs for so long until I had lost everybody that cared about me. I didn't think no one else cared so I got to the point where I didn't care. I was living on the streets. I sold everything I could get my hands on. My family and nobody else had trust in me. My daughter and I had not spoken in twenty years. Today all of that has changed. My family cares and looks out for me. I have a nice place to live and I'm not out on the streets. I am kicking my drug habit one day at a time. But I thank God today that I am clean.
>
> The people in the program treat you with dignity and respect. They let you see the good in them. So tonight I want to thank the people that were a part of My Brother's Keeper because a name doesn't make a program. It's the people who carry out the intent of the program.[13]

At a Justice Department conference on the High Point strategy held in October of 2007, Kersey also gave testimony—pithier, but no less eloquent— to the idea that direct communication with offenders can work. Asked what he told his friends in the target neighborhood after the February call-in, he said, "I was Paul Revere. 'The British are coming! The British are coming!'"

Conclusion

As noted above, this chapter does not purport to be a formal evaluation of these drug-market interventions. It seems reasonable to conclude, however, that something real happened in High Point and the other sites. To believe otherwise is to suppose that in all these places drug markets that had been in place for years, often decades, spontaneously collapsed at just the moment these interventions were put in place— something altogether unlikely.

The participants are convinced. A little over a month after the strategy was put in place in Nashville, Tennessee, a resident in the neighborhood sent the following e-mail to Nashville Police Department Chief Ronal Serpas:

> Let me give you a bit of a picture of what this area was like a year ago. On Hancock St. between Dickerson Rd. and N 2nd (a two block strip), it was not unusual for there to be a dozen or more people milling the streets. This went on 24/7. No attempt was made to hide the drug deals or prostitution. A decent uninterrupted nights sleep was impossible due to people yelling up and down the streets all night long. Men and women alike used the alleyways and peoples yards for restrooms. I live on a corner, and there were times I would have to water down the side yard of my house just to cut through the stench of urine. There were *bags* of trash to be picked up daily from my yard. The litter consisted not only of fast food wrappers and beer cans and liquor bottles, but crack pipes, debit cards, condoms and other personal hygiene items of which I will spare you the details. Pretty disgusting. It was not unusual to find people hanging out in my yard. (Upon the advice of the officers patrolling the area, I posted a "No Trespassing" sign and was able to have a couple of them arrested.) It was not unusual to leave for work at 6 a.m. and be approached by a panhandler. When I would work in my yard, constant interruptions were the norm by people bumming money, a glass of iced tea, anything they thought they could get out of you, or just plain talking smack. Anything left outside was inviting theft. I had to have my trash can replaced three times last year due to theft. Now it is like a whole new neighborhood. The drug dealers and prostitutes are gone. There aren't people hanging out in the streets all of the time. The volume of litter is down. The nights are quiet. I see the residents coming out of their homes again, the children are beginning to play outside. I can work in my yard without having to fend off bums and without feeling like I have to "watch my back" constantly.[14]

"In a thirty-year law enforcement career, I have never seen an effort like this," says High Point Chief of Police James Fealy.

> It produces results that are so dramatic it's almost incredible. It is sustainable. It does not produce the community harms that our traditional street-sweeping, unfocused efforts of the past have. The most important benefit of this work by the people of High Point is the reconciliation that emerges from the dialogue between the minority community and the police. It's nothing short of miraculous.

"We confronted these people who had been a terror in the community," says James Summey, pastor of English Road Baptist Church in the West End.

> But at the same time we embraced them, by saying at the same time, you're worth something. It's redemptive. So many times the police and the community don't see eye to eye, but on this we could. We're working together like we never have in our lives. This is the most fantastic thing I have ever seen.

For the purposes of this discussion, the central point is that it appears to be possible to apply in practice the ideas previously developed in theory. It is possible to approach a knotty crime issue like "drugs" and parse it into a more manageable key problem such as "overt community drug markets." It is possible to apply a deterrence framework to that problem: to create strategies, using mostly existing capacities deployed in new ways, to ensure predictable formal sanctions; to greatly minimize the use of those sanctions; to address and even alter law enforcement, community, and offender norms and narratives; to mobilize informal social control; to focus both formal and informal social control on identified offenders; to identify nonlinear "tipping" dynamics and to make lasting changes in those dynamics. It is possible to enter into relationships with offenders that are legitimate and mutually beneficial. Authorities, communities, and offenders do in fact share common ground. The "High Point" strategy suggests that we really can make deterrence operate in these ways.[15]

10 Applications II

A thought experiment: the framework of a deterrence approach to domestic violence

How might these ideas be applied to a very different crime problem? The drug-market problem just described, like the gang-violence problem from which this whole line of thought originated, is public, obvious, more or less collective, and at least to some degree economic. Domestic violence stands out for its contrasts: It is private, concealed, more or less individual, and deeply personal. Do these ideas offer anything to our thinking about how we might address domestic violence? Let us see.

Enhancing informal sanctions: providing information to women

It is well known that many domestic-violence offenders are serial abusers within and across relationships. Many of them come to the attention of criminal-justice authorities: They are arrested; they are sometimes convicted; and they are subject to restraining orders. It could be very useful to women to have access to such information, for instance when considering entering a relationship, or when trouble first arises within a relationship. As a practical matter, this information is not very available—while it is often a matter of public record, obtaining it is difficult procedurally, requires a specialist knowledge of what questions to ask, can require consulting multiple databases in multiple jurisdictions, and the like. Many women would not enter a relationship if they knew the man had a history of domestic abuse; many would exit troubled relationships earlier if possessed of the same knowledge. Information systems that made such information easy to obtain would impose new costs to abusers for their previous behavior.[1] Laws aimed at sex offenders, such as New Jersey's "Megan's Law," have created an affirmative obligation that offenders supply the authorities with information, such as places of residence, that facilitate the implementation of such systems. There is no reason in principal that such structures could not be brought to bear on domestic abusers.[2]

Communicating existing enforcement actions to potential offenders

Law-enforcement authorities currently do a great deal to address domestic violence and domestic-violence offenders. Unless *other* offenders and potential offenders know what is going on, however, the deterrent power of these actions is nil. For example, the US Attorney for the District of Maine indicted thirteen men and women on federal domestic violence-related fire-arms charges, either because they had a previous misdemeanor domestic-violence conviction, which recent changes in federal law made prohibitive of firearms possession, or because they lied about such convictions in attempt-ing to purchase firearms.[3] The deterrent value of this action as such is likely to be small, bordering on zero: While the US Attorney's office issued a press release, it seems unlikely that the information it contained reached very far into even the target population of the moment, far less that of the future. It could be greatly increased, however, through simple steps: by explaining it, and the potential for more such enforcement, in mailings to individuals with the relevant prior convictions; by in-person briefings by law enforcement per-sonnel to men involved in treatment programs and on probation for domes-tic violence offenses; as part of judicial statements to men sentenced for new domestic violence offenses, through posters in gun stores, and the like.

Similar steps could be taken in connection with other routine enforcement actions. Police arrest, prosecutors charge, and judges sentence domestic-vio-lence offenders constantly in every jurisdiction. Probation and parole officers supervise and sometimes violate domestic-violence offenders. Men are sanc-tioned for violating restraining orders. None of this is visible, for the most part, to other active and potential offenders unless they know those sanc-tioned personally. Nor, when such actions occur side by side with other actions in which opportunities for enforcement are forgone, is the reasoning of authorities very evident; if there is logic to those choices, it is obscure, and unlikely to shape offenders' behavior in any useful way. Deliberate commu-nication of these actions, in the manner suggested above or in other ways, could significantly raise the preventive power of such routine enforcement activities. Communication could be "retail" or "narrowcast" to men who have already identified themselves as problems (meetings with or mailings to, for example, those under probation supervision and with current or prior restraining orders), and "wholesale" or "broadcast" to a wider population (television spots and billboards).

Enhancing the likelihood of formal sanctions: An "A Group" dangerous offender program

In any given jurisdiction, particular domestic-violence offenders single themselves out as especially dangerous; especially chronic; or otherwise deserving of removal from the streets. These "A Group" offenders can be identified and, with the correct actions from various enforcement agencies, various tools can lead to their sanctioning. This should not be an innovative operation, and most not experienced with the actual workings of criminal justice agencies no doubt assume that this is already standard practice. In fact, in most jurisdictions it is not.

Even a moderately sophisticated such enterprise would entail communication and coordination amongst police, prosecutors, probation, and parole; it would be better if others with knowledge of offenders and victims, such as shelter operators, treatment providers, advocates, healthcare workers, and the like were included. The first is very rare, and the second almost unheard of. In most jurisdictions units within police departments operate in isolation (so that patrol officers responding to a domestic disturbance and detectives investigating a prior assault at the same address would have no contact); prosecutors make isolated decisions on the basis of particular police incident reports and criminal histories (so that a prosecutor considering the foregoing assault would have no knowledge that the man's behavior was continuing and escalating); and probation and parole officers have little contact with other law enforcement agencies (so neither police nor prosecutors would know that the man had recently lost his job and recommenced drinking, circumstances that had triggered previous assaults, and there is likely to be no mechanism in place so that a domestic violence complaint that does not lead to an arrest is made known to probation or parole authorities).

Constructing such partnerships is entirely possible but requires substantial and unusual commitments from the participating agencies. When they exist, they should be able substantially to increase the sanctioning of dangerous offenders. This can be true whether the offender is question is first-time—prosecutors have considerable discretion to take such cases very seriously, if they have reason to do so—or serial. Even simple examples of such operations can be quite effective. One such in Westminster, California combines special training of patrol officers with a co-housed team of prosecutors and victim advocates. An evaluation showed that the program increased the rate of successful prosecution by 47 percent and the average length of sentence by 37 percent.[4]

Where such offenders are also chronic offenders in a broader sense—that is, frequent violators of a variety of laws—such programs will have other tools to draw upon. It is often believed that domestic-violence offenders are different from other violent offenders in that their domestic violence presents itself without the pattern of varied chronic offending typical of those most likely to commit "stranger" violence. Domestic violence advocates, researchers, and theorists have tended to argue that domestic violence is fundamentally unlike other kinds of violence—and that domestic-violence offenders are similarly distinctive. Students of domestic violence argued, in the words of Hotaling, Straus, and Lincoln, that "[domestic violence] is a special and unique kind of violence and should not be approached as a subset of general violent behavior."[5] This conception of the "'batterer as anyone'"[6] led to a clear distinction between these men and other violent offenders.

Violent criminals are portrayed as inhabiting a different socio-demographic space than violent family members. While a profile of the street criminal begins to emerge through the discovery of risk factors, the violent family member remains invisible. He is depicted as being anyone. He could possess some of the characteristics of the street criminal, but that is not seen in the research literature as setting him apart. His distinctiveness resides in his ability to avoid sociological labels. If those who assault other family members are depicted as otherwise law-abiding citizens, there is no compelling reason to apply notions of criminality to explain their behavior.[7]

The conclusion here does not follow logically from the predicate: Even if domestic-violence offenders *are* otherwise completely law-abiding, there is no reason to believe that criminal-justice interventions might not be able to provide rehabilitation, incapacitation, or deterrence. Pedophile priests, to take one parallel example, are likely notably law-abiding in other aspects of their lives; this should not and does not prevent us from seeking criminal sanctions against them. Where domestic violence was concerned, however, it followed in practice that the tools of criminal justice were generally considered inappropriate.

This may not be true, and is clearly less true than is often believed. Hotaling, Straus, and Lincoln, in a 1989 review of the literature on domestic vs. nondomestic offending, conclude that:

The findings support the notion that assault is a generalized pattern in interpersonal relations that crosses settings and is used across targets. Men in families in which children and wives are assaulted are five times more likely to have also assaulted a nonfamily person than are men in nonassaultive families. These same men are also more severely violent toward fellow citizens, being eight times more likely to have assaulted and injured someone outside the family. Men from multi-assaultive families also come to the attention of police more often than others, having an arrest rate that is 3.6 times higher than their less violent counterparts. The link between family and nonfamily assault also holds across social class although blue-collar persons report higher rates, especially of more severe assaults outside the family. [8]

This is a finding that tends to hold across studies of domestic violence. In a review of eight studies of nondomestic offenses by wife batterers, the authors found the lowest proportion of batterers with records for other offenses to be 12 percent (previous criminal assault); all other studies showed considerably higher proportions, including some truly striking findings, such as that 80 percent of batterers had prior nondomestic criminal histories, 92 percent had previous arrests (for batterers killed by their wives), and 46 percent had previous arrests for nondomestic violence.[9]

Other sources present similar pictures. In a review of individuals arrested for assault in Lowell, Massachusetts, Solomon and Thomson found that

Domestic offenders are commonly thought to be "specialists" who do not pose a threat to the community at large. Our data indicate that this is not the case. The domestic offenders [studied] were just as likely as the non-domestic offenders to have committed non-domestic offenses in the five years prior (46 percent of each group had been arraigned for non-domestic offenses). Additionally, the two groups had statistically equal proportions of high-rate offenders.[10]

Similarly, a study of more than 18,000 Massachusetts men with restraining orders found that three-quarters had some sort of prior criminal history; nearly half had an arraignment or conviction for a violent crime; more than 40 percent for a property crime; more than 20 percent for a drug offense; a quarter for driving under the influence; and nearly half for other offenses.[11]

Looking at the problem from the other direction tends to paint a similar picture: that those most likely to be killed and seriously hurt are drawn from groups and places quite traditionally at the highest risk for serious victimization. In a study of female victims of domestic homicide in New York City between 1990 and 1997, Frye, Wilt and Schomberg found that victims were quite disproportionately black—half of all victims were black, relative to about a quarter of the population—and somewhat disproportionately Latina, and that victims came primarily from the poor boroughs of Brooklyn, the Bronx, and Queens.[12] Several studies have found that women living in distressed neighborhoods are more likely to suffer domestic victimization.[13] Rhagavan et al. report that women living in public housing report *annual* domestic violence incidence rates of from 19 percent to 35 percent; general population studies report *lifetime* rates of 1.5 percent to 16 percent.[14]

Qualitative work gives similar results. Buzawa and Buzawa describe Klein's unpublished research on the Quincy, Massachusetts Probation Project; from victim interviews, Klein found that 55 percent of batterers had prior criminal records of which the victim was aware.[15] Fagan et al. examined reports from 270 women in intervention programs and found that nearly half of spouse abusers had previously been arrested for violent crimes and that those who had been arrested for violence against strangers were more frequently and severely violent at home.[16]

Thus, many dangerous domestic-violence offenders need not be addressed solely through domestic violence and related offending, such as violations of restraining orders. In principle, *any* actionable offense will do. If an individual passes a relevant dangerousness threshold, authorities dealing with chronic offenders will often have multiple opportunities. A drug trafficking or possession offense, a violation of probation or parole (for instance, for drug use, noncompliance with reporting requirements, or address and association violations), a drunk driving offense, a weapons charge, a nondomestic assault: any of these, and other, offenses could serve. It could well be that the sort of focused enforcement regimes previously described for other chronic offenders could be adapted to particular domestic offenders.

Such strategies are apparently rare in the domestic violence context. However, Brockton, Massachusetts has a program designed to do just this; key partners include the Brockton Police Department, the District Attorney, the US Attorney, probation, victim advocates, and shelter providers.[17] It seeks to identify repeat and high-risk offenders through data analysis (records indicating, for instance, three or more domestic violence incidents/year or two or more victims/year) and qualitative review (guidance from law-enforcement personnel, advocates, and shelter providers[18]). Once identified, such offenders get special attention: for example, heightened probation scrutiny (including home visits, drug tests, and the like) or, if deemed necessary, the use of any available nondomestic offense to take them off the streets. Targeted offenders then get special attention while incarcerated (heightened monitoring while in treatment programs, for instance), and the group is notified when their release is imminent.

A similar program operates in Lowell, Massachusetts. In Lowell, the main trigger for special attention is repeat calls for police service in connection with a domestic disturbance: Two or more within thirty days is considered "high priority," two or more within ninety days is considered "repeat."[19] Such addresses get unannounced visits from police officers and (where the offender is under supervision) probation officers; a warrant search is conducted and where outstanding warrants are found they are served; criminal histories are obtained and reviewed for past domestic offending and other signs of dangerousness such as weapons offenses and a history of alcohol and drug abuse; if children are present, an assessment is performed (if there is current Department of Social Services (DSS) involvement, DSS is notified; if there is none and it is deemed warranted, DSS is mobilized); victims are introduced to advocates, offered priority at shelters, informed about available services, and the like; and offenders are warned that they are under enhanced scrutiny.

An "A Group/B Group" communication strategy

If it is possible to create enforcement regimes that raise the likelihood of sanctions for particular offenders, it might then be possible to greatly enhance their deterrence value by explaining them to selected other offenders. Here, the existence of the operation aimed at the A Group, and the consequences of being so targeted, would be directly communicated to a larger B Group of less serious offenders, as would be the criteria that will result in their "promotion" to the A Group. Continued communication with "B group" offenders—these guys have done well, they're still on the street; these guys didn't, here's what happened to them—would keep the message fresh and drive home its seriousness. Marketing research—for example, focus groups and surveys with "B group" offenders—could track the impact of communications and shape the message and its delivery.

Tailored formal sanctions: Custom domestic violence probation/parole structures

Incarceration is not the only, or necessarily the preferable, enforcement action. Meaningful probation and parole supervision can be as or more desirable. An effective structure might include high levels of field (rather than office) contacts; frequent contacts with those close to victims (see below) to gather information about misbehavior by supervised offenders; and compliance conditions that required complete abstinence from drugs and alcohol;[20] and frequent and meaningful testing, with immediate sanctions for failure. Here, again, research with offenders and with their partners and peers might shed important light on what really matters to offenders, and how such sanctions should be designed and structured.

Increasing certainty

The more information is available regarding offenders' behavior and threats to victims, the better these strategies will work. The more such information as seen by offenders as coming from sources other than their targets, and as being comprehensive and impersonal, the lower the risk to victims will be and the more effective the strategies will be. This clearly implies that there should be routine and high-quality information gathering from a variety of sources other than offenders' victims. This would resemble the "behavioral supervision" approach used in some strategies to monitor and treat sex offenders.[21]

This process will never be perfect, but it can easily be much better than it usually is now. Useful information is clearly available through these means. For example, in a study of stalking and homicide, McFarlane *et al.* surveyed close relatives of victims and found that in 67 percent of cases those sources were aware of stalking prior to the homicide.[22] Friends, neighbors, advocates, shelter operators, medical personnel, and the like will all frequently have useful information. To do this properly would clearly be immensely labor-intensive. It could be practical, however, in the A Group/B Group setting described above, with the more dangerous A Group getting this treatment and that fact advertised to the B Group. Random assignment of B Group offenders to this sort of comprehensive scrutiny for limited periods would then be desirable in order to guard against those offenders coercing their targets from contacting authorities in order to prevent their "promotion." Both the Brockton and Lowell programs report that victims' friends and family are often utilized, on a case-by-case basis, as sources of information about offenders.

This process has been formalized in the *Construyendo Circulos de Paz* (CCP, or Constructing Circles of Peace) domestic-violence intervention program in Nogales, Arizona. Each domestic-violence offender in CCP is assigned a "safety monitor" drawn from his personal social network. Grauwiler *et al.* write that:

Safety monitors must: 1) maintain close contact with the parties involved; 2) have direct or indirect experience with the parties and their history of violence; 3) be able to judge changes in the behavior of the applicant and victim/participant in order to interrupt potential violence; 4) have the trust of the parties involved; and 5) show a capacity to share sensitive safety information with the appropriate parties, including the authorities, if threats are made.[23]

Another particularly important step would be to convene working groups of front-line domestic-violence practitioners (advocates, shelter providers, prosecutors, police investigators and first responders, medical personnel, probation and parole officers, and the like) on a regular basis and gather core information. Basic questions—Who's particularly at risk right now? Who's particularly dangerous right now? Are previously identified cases being properly managed?—can be addressed and acted upon in this setting. The author has conducted these exercises, with very good results. In one such setting in Boston, the question, Do you in the room usually know who's most at risk at any given time, and from whom?, was asked. The answers were initially negative, and revolved around questions of *prediction*—on the basis of restraining orders, the criminal histories of offenders, and the like. When the question was reemphasized as being about *knowledge*—that is, do you, today, on the basis of your work and experience, know who's at great risk, and from whom—the answers were overwhelmingly in the affirmative. In this, at least, domestic violence is potentially much like gang and street violence: The professionals close to the scene do in fact know a great deal about what's going on. That knowledge is usually wasted, to a great extent, but it need not be. One way in which this process might be particularly useful is in identifying times, perhaps quite limited ones, in which offenders are particularly dangerous and during which they and their targets should be accorded special attention and protection. These groups will often know, for example, when a woman has left her abuser or when an offender has started drinking. This kind of more or less real-time situational knowledge can be immensely valuable if the larger structure is capable of acting upon it. This, too, is part of operations in the Brockton and Lowell programs.

Influencing "norms and narratives"

Could the "norms and narratives" of offenders, "influentials," and even communities be mobilized, and perhaps altered, to discourage offending? There is reason to believe they could be. Existing restorative justice practices aimed at domestic violence feature steps to do so in the context of particular domestic-violence offenses. Coker describes how restorative justice circles in Navajo communities work to hold offenders accountable, remove their excuses, and undercut support for offending by those around them:

Peacemakers and participants confront the abuser's denials, including that he committed the violence, that it was harmful and that it was a moral choice not compelled by the victim's 'provocation' or life's circumstances. Peacemakers also confront denials by the abuser's family or friends, thus diminishing social supports for his abuse.[24]

In the CCP program, coordinators work with offenders to identify an individualized "care community" incorporating "family, the victim/participant, or friends who seek to help this applicant address his/her violence in constructive ways."[25] These steps are designed to reinforce offenders' existing, if weak, prosocial norms and to create or reinforce relationships with others who will both communicate prosocial norms, impose informal sanctions and, if necessary, trigger the imposition of formal sanctions.

These interventions take place within alternative case-processing systems: They are triggered by particular offenses which then are then handled by diverting the case from normal criminal justice channels. There is no reason, however, that such measures need be restricted to either formal or informal case processing mechanisms. As occurred in High Point, such "influentials" could be mobilized for any population of identified offenders. A program in Arizona prisons is doing just that with incarcerated offenders:

Beth Hendrickson tapes the last photo she has of her daughter onto a white board. In the picture, Tanya Ramsdell's eyes are closed and soot from a bullet fired point-blank colors her forehead black. "This is what I have to live with," Hendrickson tells a group of 22 inmates at the Arizona State Prison Complex-Florence. "When I close my eyes, this is what I see." The men gasp at the photo. [...] Afterward, inmate Larry Severns said the class helps put inmates in others' shoes. "Usually, as an inmate, it's always been about instant gratification, doing this right at the moment to satisfy ourselves," said Severns, who is serving six years for burglary. "You never look at the consequences down the line. It's hard to see."[26]

Again, as High Point shows, there is no reason such interventions cannot also be made more or less at will in the community.

Another step around "norms and narratives" would be to influence *victims'* norms. To take what one hopes is an extreme example, Lieutenant Gary French, as commander of the Boston Police Department's sexual-assault unit, found that many victims of sexual assault were so accustomed to such behavior that they did not realize that it was either criminal or unacceptable.[27] Similar patterns may be inferred from such accounts as Bourgois's ethnography. French therefore worked directly with high-risk populations of young women to articulate to them the law around sexual assault, their legal position with respect to sexual assault, and beyond that what they ought to expect and demand from their partners and peers.

Domestic-violence researchers have noted that poor women at high risk for domestic violence are likely to be in social relationships with women who are also at high risk of domestic violence, and that in such networks domestic violence may come to be seen as "neither abusive nor unusual."[28] Intervening in those network norms could influence both individual behavior and collective dynamics.

Finally, it might be possible to take specific steps to address community norms, overall or in particular settings such as high-risk neighborhoods. It is striking, for example, that there appears to be no parallel for domestic violence to public campaigns around drunk-driving and firearms violence. We are told that friends don't let friends drive drunk, and in some settings that getting caught with a gun will bring federal penalties; we are not told that friends don't let friends hit women, or that doing so will bring certain sanction. Such campaigns are of course possible. Any impact on norms from any of these interventions would alter, to some extent, the internal and external informal sanctions experienced by offenders.

Attention to offending networks

A variation on this theme would be bringing a range of sanctions to bear on offending *networks* for domestic violence. Qualitative research consistently shows very high levels of domestic violence associated with street gangs, drug groups, and the like, whose members tend to be high-rate chronic offenders. Fagan and Wilkinson, in an ethnographic study of such offenders in New York City, write that

> When conducted in front of an audience (i.e., in public), the stakes become high if the female behaves without respect for the male. Male violence is perceived as a necessary response to control one's girlfriend, a necessary step in maintaining not just control over "your woman," but in being a "man." [...] It is an assault on respect, and in many cases mandates a violent response.[29]

A study of homicide in several high-risk neighborhoods in Washington, DC found the usual connection of homicide to high-rate offending groups—gangs, drug crews, and the like. Interestingly, in this context, this was true for domestic homicide as well. Of 108 homicides in which motives could be ascertained, seventeen were domestic. Of these, six—or 35 percent—were committed by a group-involved offender.[30] Given that in such neighborhoods only about 5 percent of young men, and a much smaller proportion of men overall, are generally involved in such groups, this is a greatly disproportionate connection to domestic homicide. Bourgois found, as has been discussed, very high rates of sexual assault, much of it directed against friends and relatives of the offenders, and domestic violence in his work with Dominican drug-dealing networks in New York. He also found what might be taken as evidence of pluralistic ignorance: As is often the case, participants in that violence expressed—in private—deep reservations about their own and others' behavior.[31] Intervening in group and network processes might thus disrupt the dynamics producing such violence.

Such concentrations of domestic violence could be addressed by making it clear to such groups that domestic violence by a *member* of the network would result in sanctions being delivered on any available front to the network *as such*: To take, again, an extreme example, a DEA investigation could be triggered by an assault on a spouse or a girlfriend.[32] The aim, as usual in such interventions, would be to create self-policing in the group, undercut norms and narratives supportive of domestic violence, and give those who wished it a justification for not committing domestic violence. Such groups could also be the focus of the sort of direct "norms and narratives" interventions contemplated above.

An intervention: a preliminary sketch

What might, based on these thoughts, an intervention look like? One can imagine a room full of "B list" domestic-violence offenders hearing the following message from law enforcement:

> We have people here from the police, the local prosecutor, the US Attorney, probation and parole. We will not put up with domestic violence any longer. We will stop it any way we can. We want you to know this, so you can avoid what can happen to you. Right now, you're under scrutiny; you've already crossed the line. We have a program for people who cross it again. We put their name on a list. When you're on that list, you're gone, as far as we're concerned; it's just a matter of time. We put your names out to patrol officers and detectives; they'll be watching for you. They'll arrest you for anything they can. There's a file with your name on it at the DA's office. Any case they see, they'll take to the wall: high bail, no pleas, maximum charges, special handling, nobody skates. We'll meet with the feds and see if they can take you: drugs, weapons, anything, and with the feds you go out of state and serve all your time. We're going to talk to the people you're involved with pretty regularly and make sure that they're OK; if they're not, we're going to act. If you're on probation or parole, we have officers who will come to you, on your street, where you live: no more showing up in the office and saying everything's OK. We'll check your addresses, we'll search your house, we'll drug test you, we'll check to see if you're going to work or going to school or paying your fines or going to bars or hanging with felons, everything. If you slip up we'll hand-carry the violation to the judge. We're not playing any more. And we mean it: here's what's happened to the guys we used to have on the A list. They're gone, which means there's room for you. This doesn't have to happen to you, and we'd rather it didn't. But it's up to you now.

They could hear the following message from social-service providers:

> We want to help you. If there's something you need, we'll do our best to make sure you get it. If you need work, we'll help. If you're having trouble at work, we have people to work with you and your employer. If you're having trouble with drugs or alcohol, we have programs and groups for that. If there are family issues that are driving you crazy, we have programs and groups that can work with you. If you're having money problems, or need basics at home, we have programs and churches that might be able to help. If we've missed something, tell us what it is and we'll do our best.

They could hear the following message from the community:

> We care about you and your families. We want this to be a community where people are safe and secure. That includes you; if you're up against something, we want to help you. But there's no excuse for hurting or scaring or abusing our wives and girlfriends and partners. I lost my daughter and I've never been the same. I'm worried that her daughter could go the same way; I'm worried that her son might imitate his father and end up in prison, like he is. He wasn't a bad guy, but he did a bad thing: His father abused his mother, and then he did it too. His mother aches for him, just like I do for my daughter. We have to stop this. You can stop it, here, today. We need you do this: For yourselves, for your families, for all of us.

They could hear the following message from ex-offenders:

> I've been you. I'm not special. I'm ashamed of what I did. I terrorized my wife and my kids. It's not manly, it's not strong, it's something to be ashamed of. I told myself that it was her fault, but it wasn't, it was my fault. I told myself I couldn't help it, but I could: I didn't hit her in public, I waited until I could get away with it. I told myself she was disrespecting me, but respect is something you earn, that you carry inside you, and I didn't earn it, and if I had respected myself nothing anybody else did should have mattered. My friends and I all told each other that we deserved to do what we did, that it was OK, but really we knew better. You can't put your wife in the hospital, see them have fear in their eyes, and have that be OK. It's not OK. My dad hurt my mom, and I hated him for it. I don't want my son to hate me, and I don't want him to do this to his wife and his son. Here's my phone number. You feel it coming on, you call me. I'll meet you, and we'll deal with it.

Killingbeck

Would it work? There is tantalizing evidence that it might. In 1997, the West Yorkshire Police Force in England crafted a strategy to address domestic violence in its Killingbeck Division, comprising almost 152,000 people.[33]

The Killingbeck intervention, while not grounded in the ideas proposed here, in fact had a great deal in common with them.

The Killingbeck project began with the observation that domestic violence involved high levels of both repeat offending and repeat victimization. During 1997, as the strategy played out, Killingbeck police attended 2,163 incidents of domestic violence; 914, or 42 percent, involved men who were repeat domestic-violence offenders. Three hundred eight-seven men were responsible for a total of 1,301 incidents; 31 percent of men were responsible for nearly 60 percent of all incidents.

The strategy was based on several simple ideas. Every domestic-violence incident would get a response: Neither offenders nor victims would be allowed to think that domestic violence did not matter to the police. In each case, the police would have contact with both the victim and the offender and make it clear to each that domestic violence was not to be tolerated and that action was being and would be taken. Repeat offending—defined as any known instances in which an offender had previously victimized any woman—would get escalating responses.

The strategy defined three levels:

1. For a first offense, police would gather information from the victim and give her a written document underscoring the force's commitment to respond to domestic violence; advising on how to contact the police if the abuse continued; advising on how to get supportive services; and ensuring her that as a result of the complaint police would be patrolling more heavily and otherwise paying additional attention to her home, coordinated if possible to any pattern of behavior by the offender. Some officers stopped to ask the woman and her family if all was well. Police would directly inform offenders that they were making domestic violence a priority; bring any appropriate civil and criminal charges, and put prosecutors on notice to review any applications by offenders to receive bail; explain to offenders that future offenses would bring a heightened response; and provide a written document memorializing these facts and informing that the victim would be getting heightened police attention. Prosecutors and probation authorities agreed to give domestic-violence cases heightened attention, faster processing, and to go outside their usual procedures when police requested it in specific cases.
2. For any instance of a first repeat offense, victims received a home visit from a community officer trained in domestic-violence prevention. The victim's home was examined and "target hardening" measures, such as enhancing locks, were taken. Routine police attention was increased, and the victim was offered the option of having the police organize "cocoon watch": surveillance by her neighbors or police contact with family and friends, and relevant agencies, so that they could inform authorities of any trouble. The offender was again talked to by police, and the protective actions being taken by police were explained verbally and in writing;

any appropriate civil and criminal charges were brought, and magistrates put on notice to oppose bail; a special file on the offender was opened by prosecutors such that further criminal contacts would trigger a special response; and offenders were informed that any further offending would bring heightened attention. All this was again conveyed in writing to both victims and offenders.

3. For any second or subsequent repeat offense, an interagency meeting was convened to assess how to assist and protect the victim; the victim received a home visit from a specialist domestic-violence officer; routine police attention was again increased; the victim was given a "panic button" allowing emergency notification of police. Prosecutors were put on notice to take any legal opportunities to take action against the offender. All this was again conveyed in writing to both victims and offenders.

As simple as it was, the intervention seems to have substantially reduced repeat offending over the course of just a year. In the calendar quarter preceding the introduction of the scheme, 66 percent of offenders were judged to be Level 1, meaning that the instance offense was their first domestic violence offense; by the end of the year, that proportion had grown to 85 percent. In that preceding quarter, 21 percent of offenders were Level 2, and 13 percent were Level 3; by the end of the year, both Level 2 and Level 3 had fallen to 1 percent. There was strong apparent impact of consistent action by the authorities. Of the 852 men who entered the project as first offenders, 25 percent (210) required a second police attendance, 9 percent (75) required a third, and only 1 percent (11) went on to require five or more. In stark contrast, of the thirty-three men who entered the project as Level 3 offenders, 64 percent (twenty-one) required a second attendance, 39 percent (thirteen) required a third, and 18 percent (six) required five or more. This was, in all likelihood, the "experiential effect" at work: Men who were seasoned offenders when the project began had learned from their prior experience that the police would not take action and continued to act accordingly—even when their objective environment had changed.

We do not have data on death, injury or other harms to women. However, qualitative research with the victims involved suggested that this commonsense deterrence structure worked as intended. Even as simple a device as enhanced police patrol in the wake of an incident—properly framed and explained to offenders—seemed to make a difference:

Police Watch was highlighted as an intervention that increased the women's sense of safety, both for the women themselves and for their children. One woman who received Police Watch said, "the bit that helped me most was the letter about surveillance. I really believe that had a big impact on him. He doesn't like to be locked up." The sight of a police car was often attributed to the project and served to further the women's confidence in the police. On occasions the men were reported to have observed police cars and to have been shocked at their presence.[34]

Women's reactions also bore out the power of directly communicating existing risks and the commonsense importance of accuracy and consistency in communication and subsequent official behavior:

> The realisation that domestic violence could result in arrest, even without a court appearance, was said to shock a number of men, particularly when the men were employed or concerned about their wider families becoming aware of their violence. Women at Levels 2 and 3 added that a strong verbal warning of arrest could be a disincentive. The power of these warnings was diminished, however, if they were not implemented on subsequent police attendances.[35]

Women, the evaluation reported, valued "support for the victim through giving a verbal warning to the man. This may be the first time anyone has said his behaviour is unacceptable."[36] Here, too, perhaps, the lesson is how little it takes to make a difference. One wonders what the more robust "norms and narratives" component envisioned above might accomplish.

Conclusion

This is, as noted, speculative. We do not know that an effective deterrence regime could be constructed around domestic-violence offenders. If it could, we do not know that it would look much like what has been described. We do not know how many domestic-violence offenders we know about, or could take new steps to identify; how many could be reached with creative sanctioning strategies; what difference it would make to spell those strategies out to them; who could be enlisted to support standards against domestic violence, and what difference that would make; or what kind of help domestic-violence offenders might need, want, and take, and what difference it would make if they got it.

This speculation, still, tells us something. Even with a problem as spectacularly thorny as domestic violence, there may well be ways to craft better deterrence. We do not know all domestic offenders, but we know a lot of them, and it may be that the more dangerous they are the more likely we are to know them. We can imagine ways to know more about offenders and make better use of that information. The overall conduct of many domestic-violence offenders, and perhaps particularly of those who put the most vulnerable women at the most risk, may give us a range of new opportunities to attach penalties to domestic violence. We can imagine communicating those new risks to those offenders. We can imagine finding allies who will help set standards and insist on compliance. We can imagine ways to awaken in offenders latent unease about their own conduct, and to interfere in the social dynamics that suppress such unease. We know that some domestic-violence offenders operate in networks and other collective settings that might well offer even greater opportunity for impact.

The Killingbeck intervention suggests that—like, perhaps, Boston and High Point—it may be possible to rearrange our existing tools, add some new ones, and produce substantially different results. If that is true, then—again, perhaps like Boston and High Point—it may be that it is not so much that domestic violence is immune to deterrence as that the mechanisms we are currently using to produce deterrence are simply not doing so: or, even worse, that they are inadvertently undercutting deterrence. And if all that is true for as nonconducive a problem as domestic violence, then it seems likely to be true for a wide range of problems indeed.

11 Listening to Lysistrata

We began with the commonsense notion that costs attached to actions ought to reduce those actions. We also end there. Deterrence is at root a simple idea. Much of the work here has been to reclaim that simple, commonsense idea from a rather highly stylized and bounded set of conventions that has over time come to characterize both theoretical treatments and practical applications of deterrence. That reclamation is both liberating and intriguing.

We can see, from these explorations, that it is *what matters to offenders*—not what matters to those designing deterrence regimes, and not what those designers think matters to offenders—that matters in deterrence. This core fact is universally acknowledged in deterrence theory, and then almost always promptly forgotten in practice. Once we remember it and take it seriously, it has a number of simple, self-evident, but profound implications.

It means that if offenders do not know about the sanctions they face, those sanctions cannot matter. We know beyond question that offenders very often do not know the sanctions they face. It can be a remarkably simple matter to tell them. This alone could transform the way we practice deterrence.

It means that we should strive to provide the sanctions that matter to offenders. Even within the range of formal sanctions, there is no reason to think that our ordering of seriousness matches those of offenders. A week of curfew imposed today may mean more than life in prison imposed next year. A ten-year prison sentence may mean no more than a one-year sentence. This ordering is very likely different for different sorts of offenders and in different sorts of settings. These things are not only true but entirely researchable. We can, and should—both as scholars and as practitioners—figure this out and apply it.

It means that it is not only formal sanctions that matter to offenders. Everything we know tells us, in fact, that it is formal sanctions that matter least to offenders. Their own ideas about right and wrong matter most; the ideas of those they care about and respect matter more. We can explore both of those domains, and we demonstrably have tools with which to intervene in them. Nearly all of us grew up more afraid of our mothers than of the police. If the police cannot get the attention of the streets, it would make sense to organize the mothers to do it. As we have seen, this is in no way implausible.

For both formal and informal sanctions, it means that what matters is what offenders will care about and whether that can be arranged, rather than what traditional legal procedures would dictate. We very often know what offenders are doing and can deploy consequences that they will care about. Those consequences, as we have seen, need in no way be limited to the formal sanctions for defined criminal acts or to the routine and traditional workings of criminal-justice agencies.

It means that we need to take seriously the way offenders and those close to them regard authorities. If authorities are seen as unpredictable, capricious, dishonest, corrupt, racist, or predatory, their actions will lose the meaning we want them to have. Their actions may take on meaning that actually exacerbates offending. Those interpretations can be investigated and addressed.

It means that we need to pay attention to the ways in which our attempts to produce deterrence, and other actions of authorities in the name of crime control, alter the objective circumstances of offenders and the networks and communities in which the live. If an arrest at age eighteen—in the name of deterrence, incapacitation, and justice—means that when that offender decides ten years later that he want to be honest and productive he cannot be, because it prevents him from working, we had better think about the arrest, the ways in which it cripples him later, or both. If a volume of such arrests mean that whole communities are stripped of adults and those remaining are filled with anger and suspicion, then we had best think about that and try to do things differently.

It means that we should think of helping offenders not just as a moral obligation, or as good works, but as a concrete step to enhance deterrence. Those with more to lose are less likely to put it at risk. Those enmeshed in relationships with people who model and encourage positive norms and narratives, and counter negative ones, are less likely to act wrongly.

It means that we should take offenders as we find them, and not as narrow legal categories define them. If it is a group, a network, or some other real presentation that is driving a problem, we need to attend to the group, regardless of whether the law recognizes that presentation. As we have seen, this too is clearly possible.

It means that we need to pay attention to the dynamics within groups, networks, communities, and other settings that have special influence on the perceptions and behavior of offenders. It may be particular people, particular relationships, or particular ideas that influence offender behavior. We can often intervene with those people, in those relationships, and around those ideas.

These steps, or some of them, may be taken as routine aspects of criminal justice (or other) processes. We can inform all those whose offending history makes them vulnerable to a newly passed law or a newly decided discretionary enforcement policy. They can also be constructed as special strategies to address particular problems: We can take on gang violence, or child sexual abuse, or insider trading. Here deterrence becomes a particular tool whose strengths may suggest it as an appropriate remedy for a given problem, or as an asset to be worked into existing problem-focused frameworks like problem-oriented policing, situational crime prevention, or public health.

When thinking about crime problems, we should accustom ourselves to thinking not just about our usual stratifications of people, places, and legal categories. We should also think about crime *dynamics*, and particularly about contingent dynamics like tipping, enforcement swamping, and the like. These dynamics are real, common, and particularly ripe for intervention. Deterrence will often be a very useful tool for intervening in them.

We should think about deterrence as a *process*, not only as a static array of forces. As we work to address crime problems, we can use deterrence to reset a dynamic, communication to particular offenders to prevent them from tipping it back, communication to others to let them know the first have in fact been prevented. We can use deterrence to address problems in sequence when we would be overwhelmed—are overwhelmed—by their totality. Deterrence can be fluid and flexible, not just a monolithic and grinding tug-of-war.

And we should realize the possibility of common ground between authorities, offenders, and influential third parties. Closely related, we should realize that in what is in fact a set of relationships, authorities, offenders, and third parties can push each other to places that none of them like. Even gang members want to be safe, and even law enforcement wants to do something beside stuff the prisons. Communities angry at both gang members and law enforcement may be willing to meet both in a different place. In that new place, the objective dynamics around crime problems may be different; offender, community, and official norms and narratives may be different; the meaning—and therefore the impact—that attaches to formal sanctions may be different; informal sanction may come to carry some of the weight that formal sanction was being made, however unsuccessfully, to carry.

The wellspring of the thoughts that have led us here was in the gang work that began in Boston. From here, the possibility that Ceasefire might in fact work no longer seems remarkable. A city full of gangs produces conditions that nobody, including gang members, likes very much. The dynamic between gangs can be dire and self-sustaining in a way that none of the gangs either likes or can see a way out of. Authorities can know full well what is going on without being able, in ordinary legal frameworks, to take effective action. Their attempts to do what they can do at ever-higher levels does not work, but does objective harm to gang members and communities and plays into awful and mostly unspoken stereotypes. That gangs continue to do what they do, even if at some level they would rather not, plays into awful and mostly unspoken stereotypes. A strategic deterrence intervention customized to that situation can be framed and implemented. A dynamic that has tipped in one direction can tip in the other. It seems reasonable to think that many other dynamics we care about a good deal might do likewise.

These are not new ideas. If we let loose of the complicated conventions that we have become accustomed to attaching to deterrence, the sophistications of rational choice theory and the analysis of the workings of the criminal justice system, we might remember just how simple a business this really is. We might remember, for example, the lessons of Aristophanes on how the women of Athens and Sparta brought the Peloponnesian War to an end: They announced to both sides that they would withhold themselves until the men stopped fighting; which the men promptly did.

We have here a dynamic ripe for deterrence: Two groups of easily identified chronic offenders locked in a symmetrical hostile relationship which, undoubtedly, neither side liked but from which neither could extricate themselves. The direct communication of a credible threat of an immediately deployable informal social sanction—one of considerable salience to the target population—tipped the dynamic from one natural pole—sustained hostilities—to the other: peace. We can easily imagine the pluralistic ignorance operating within the armies on both sides (soldiers will profess the martial virtues to one another, but none wish to die), the release contagion when key figures on both sides began to lay down their arms, the conforming conduct rationalization used by the rest (I'd love to keep on fighting, but really I'm not strong enough to stand up to this, and anyway look at Cineseas, he's shed his armor already). We should, perhaps, listen more closely to Lysistrata.

The women of Pereira, Colombia did. In 2006, they launched what they called the "crossed legs" strike to convince their gangster husbands and boyfriends to disarm. They were backed by the mayor: formal authority lining up behind the exercise of informal social control.[1] The strategy, if not informed by sophisticated social-science analysis, was congruent with it: studies had found that "local gang members were drawn to criminality by the desire for status, power, and sexual attractiveness, not economic necessity."[2]

And there were some early indications of impact:

> One gang member's girlfriend said withholding sex was proving a powerful incentive. "The boys listen to us. When we close ourselves off a bit they listen to us. If they don't give up their weapons, then we won't be with them," Margarita told AP Television [...] "They say that if we don't drop our weapons, they won't be with us anymore," said a local gang member, who called himself Caleno. "We need our women, and you'll change for your woman.[3]

This was, perhaps, what Aristophanes meant when he had Lysistrata say, "What we want here is not bolts and bars and locks, but common sense." In deterrence theory, as in many things, it may be that what was old could be new again.

Notes

Introduction

1 See Herman Goldstein (1990) *Problem-Oriented Policing*, Philadelphia, Pa.: Temple University Press.
2 Anthony A. Braga, David M. Kennedy, Elin J. Waring, and Anne M. Piehl (2001) "Problem-Oriented Policing, Deterrence, and Youth Violence: an Evaluation of Boston's Operation Ceasefire," *Journal of Research in Crime and Delinquency*, 38: 195–225.
3 Anne M. Piehl, S. J. Cooper and A. A. Braga (2003) "Testing for Structural Breaks in the Evaluation of Programs," *Review of Economics and Statistics*, 85 (3): 550–8.
4 Piehl *et al.* "Testing for Structural Breaks."
5 Piehl *et al.* "Testing for Structural Breaks."
6 Richard Rosenfeld, Robert Fornango, and Eric Baumer (2005) "Did Ceasefire, Compstat, and Exile Reduce Homicide?" *Criminology and Public Policy*, 4 (3): 419–50. See also Jens Ludwig (2005) "Better Gun Enforcement, Less Crime," *Criminology and Public Policy*, 4 (4): 677–716.
7 Charles F. Wellford, John V. Pepper, and Carol V. Petrie (eds) (2004) *Firearms and Violence: A Critical Review Committee to Improve Research Information and Data on Firearms*, National Research Council, Washington, DC: National Academies Press, p. 238.
8 Wellford *et al.*, *Firearms and Violence*, p. 241.
9 Edmund F. McGarrell, Steven Chermak, Jeremy M. Wilson, and Nicholas Corsaro (2006) "Reducing Homicide through a Lever-Pulling Strategy" *Justice Quarterly*, 23 (2): 214–31.
10 Andrew Papachristos, Tracey Meares, and Jeffrey Fagan (2007) "Attention Felons: Evaluating Project Safe Neighborhood in Chicago," University of Chicago, Department of Law and Economics, online working paper, No. 269. Available at http://ssrn.com/abstract = 860685.
11 David M. Kennedy and Anthony A. Braga (1998) "Homicide in Minneapolis: Research for Problem Solving," *Homicide Studies*, 2 (3): 263–90.
12 Stewart Wakeling (2003) "Ending Gang Homicide: Deterrence Can Work," *Perspectives on Violence Prevention*, 1–7. California Attorney General's Office, California Health and Human Services Agency, No. 1, February.
13 Erin Dalton (2003) "Lessons in Preventing Homicide," Project Safe Neighborhoods Report, Michigan State University, December, pp. 1–60. The author was involved in SACSI and, independently, in High Point.
14 Anthony A. Braga, Jack McDevitt, and Glenn Piece (2006) "Understanding and Preventing Gang Violence: Problem Analysis and Response Development in Lowell, Massachusetts," *Police Quarterly*, 9 (1): 20–46.

15 Anthony A. Braga, David M. Kennedy, and George E. Tita (2002) "New Approaches to the Strategic Prevention of Gang and Group-Involved Violence," in C. Ronald Huff (ed.), *Gangs in America III*, Thousand Oaks, Calif.: Sage Publications, pp. 271–86.
16 George Tita, K. Jack Riley, Greg Ridgeway, Clifford Grammich, Allan F. Abrahamse, and Peter W. Greenwood (2003) "Reducing Gun Violence: Results from an Intervention in East Los Angeles," Los Angeles, Calif.: Rand Corporation.
17 Jack McDevitt, Scott H. Decker, Natalie Kroovand Hipple, and Edmund McGarrell, with John Klofas and Tim Bynum (2006) "Offender Notifications: Case Study 2" Project Safe Neighborhoods: Strategic Interventions, US Department of Justice, May.
18 Desmond Enrique Arias (2004) "Faith in Our Neighbors: Networks and Social Order in Three Brazilian Favelas," *Latin American Politics and Society*, 46 (1): 1–38; Claudio Estadio de Caso Beato (2005) *"Fica Vivo" Proyecto para el Control de Homicides en Belo Horizonte*, Washington, DC: The World Bank; Andrew Downie (2000) "Taking Boston's Lead, Police in Rio Lighten Up," *Christian Science Monitor*, November 8.
19 BBC News, "Police to Hold Talks with Gangs," London, November 16, 2007.
20 Monsignor David Cappo (2007) "To Break the Cycle: Prevention and Rehabilitation Responses to Serious Repeat Offending by Young People," Social Inclusion Board, Adelaide, South Australia.
21 David M. Kennedy (1997) "Pulling Levers: Chronic Offenders, High-Crime Settings, and a Theory of Prevention" Valparaiso University Law Review; David M. Kennedy (1998) "Pulling Levers: Getting Deterrence Right," *National Institute of Justice Journal*, 236 (July): 2–8.
22 Anthony Braga and I prepared that flyer on our office computer the morning of the first Ceasefire forum on May 18, 2006.
23 Narrowing one's focus is central to problem-oriented policing. See Goldstein, *Problem-Oriented Policing*.
24 Judge Sydney Hanlon, personal communication.
25 Vernon Clark and Martha Woodall (2004) "Young Lives, Violent Deaths," *The Philadelphia Inquirer*, April 4.
26 Quoted in Al Baker (2007) "City Homicide Rate Still Dropping, to Under 500," *New York Times*, November 23.
27 Wellford *et al.*, *Firearms and Violence*, p. 239.

1 Does deterrence work?

1 Home Office (1990) *Crime, Justice, and Protecting the Public*, London: HM Stationery Office, para. 2.8. Quoted in Michael Tonry and D. Farrington (eds), *Building a Safer Society: Strategic Approaches to Crime Prevention*, Chicago, Ill.: University of Chicago Press, p. 7.
2 The author has observed this phenomenon in Baltimore, San Francisco, Washington, and elsewhere.
4 Philip J. Cook, Jens Ludwig, Sudhir Venketesh and Anthony A. Braga (2007) "Underground Gun Markets" *The Economic Journal*, 117 (November): F558–F618.
5 Personal communication with Joe Vince, who saw this phenomenon in several cities as an agent with the Bureau of Alcohol, Tobacco and Firearms.
6 For an account of a police strike in Montreal, Canada see Ralph H. Turner and Lewis M. Killian (1987) *Collective Behavior*, Englewood Cliffs, N.J.: Prentice-Hall, p. 45.
7 Philip J. Cook (1980) "Research in Criminal Deterrence: Laying the Groundwork for the Second Decade," *Crime and Justice*, 2: 213.

8 Christopher Maxwell, Joel H. Garner, and Jeffrey Fagan (2002) "The Preventive Effects of Arrest on Intimate Partner Violence: Research, Policy, and Theory," *Criminology and Public Policy*, 2 (1): 51–80.
9 Lawrence Sherman and D. Weisburd (1995) "General Deterrent Effects of Police Patrol in Crime Hot Spots: A Randomized Controlled Trial," *Justice Quarterly*, 12 (4): 625–48.
10 David Weisburd and Lorraine Green (1995) "Policing Drug Hot Spots: The Jersey City DMA Experiment," *Justice Quarterly*, 12 (3): 711–36.
11 Jan M. Chaiken, Michael W. Lawless, and Keith A. Stevenson (1974) "The Impact of Police Activity on Subway Crime," *Urban Analysis*, 3: 173–205.
12 H. Laurence Ross (1973) "Law, Science, and Accidents: The British Road Safety Act of 1967," *Journal of Legal Studies*, 2 (1): 1–78; H. Laurence Ross (1977) "Deterrence Regained: The Cheshire Constabulary's 'Breathalyzer Blitz,'" *Journal of Legal Studies*, 6 (1): 241–9.
13 William M. Landes (1978) "An Economic Study of US Aircraft Hijacking, 1961–76," *Journal of Law and Economics* 21 (1): 1–31.
14 James A. Beha II (1977) "And *Nobody* Can Get You Out: The Impact of a Mandatory Prison Sentence for the Illegal Carrying of a Firearm on the Use of Firearms and On the Administration of Criminal Justice in Boston—1," *Boston University Law Review*, 57: 96–146.
15 The cities were Detroit, Jacksonville, Tampa, Miami, Philadelphia, and Pittsburgh. David McDowell, Colin Loftin, and Brian Wiersema (1992) "A Comparative Study of the Preventive Effects of Mandatory Sentencing Laws for Gun Crimes," *Journal of Criminal Law and Criminology*, 83 (2): 378–394.
16 Robert J. Sampson and Jacqueline Cohen (1988) "Deterrent Effects of Police on Crime: A Replication and Theoretical Expansion," *Law and Society Review*, 22: 163–89.
17 Mark A. R. Kleiman (1988) "Crackdowns: The Effects of Intensive Enforcement on Retail Heroin Dealing," in Marcia Chaiken (ed.), *Street-Level Drug Enforcement: Examining the Issues*, Washington, DC: US National Institute of Justice.
18 David M. Kennedy (1990) "Fighting the Drug Trade in Link Valley," Kennedy School of Government, case C16-90-935.0, Cambridge, Mass.: Harvard University.
19 Edmund F. McGarrell, Steven Chermak, and Alexander Weiss (2002) "Reducing Gun Violence: Evaluation of the Indianapolis Police Department's Directed Patrol Project," National Institute of Justice, Washington, DC.
20 See Gary F. Jensen (1969) "'Crime Doesn't Pay': Correlates of a Shared Misunderstanding," *Social Problems*, 17 (2): 189–201; William W. Minor and Joseph Harry (1982) "Deterrent and Experiential Effects in Perceptual Deterrence Research: A Replication and Extension," *Journal of Research in Crime and Delinquency*, 19 (2): 190–203; Harold G. Grasmick and Robert J. Bryjak (1980) "The Deterrent Effect of Perceived Severity of Punishment," *Social Forces*, 59 (2): 471–91; Harold G. Grasmick and Robert J. Bursik, Jr. (1990) "Conscience, Significant Others, and Rational Choice: Extending the Deterrence Model," *Law and Society Review*, 24 (3): 837–61; Ronet Bachman, Raymond Paternoster and Sally Ward (1992) "The Rationality of Sexual Offending: Testing a Deterrence/ Rational Choice Conception of Sexual Assault," *Law and Society Review*, 26 (2): 343–72; Raymond Paternoster and Sally Simpson (1996) "Sanction Threats and Appeals to Morality: Testing a Rational Choice Model of Corporate Crime," *Law and Society Review*, 30 (3): 549–83. For reviews of this research, see Daniel S. Nagin (1998) "Criminal Deterrence Research at the Outset of the Twenty-First Century," *Crime and Justice*, 23: 1–42; and Irving Pilavian, Rosemary Gartner, Craig Thornton, and Ross L. Matsueda (1986), "Crime, Deterrence, and Rational Choice," *American Sociological Review*, 51 (1): 101–19.

21 Gordon P. Waldo and Theodore G. Chiricos (1972) "Perceived Penal Sanction and Self-Reported Criminality: a Neglected Approach to Deterrence Research," *Social Problems,* 19 (4): 522–40.

22 Daniel S. Claster (1967) "Comparison of Risk Perception Between Delinquents and Non-Delinquents," *Journal of Criminal Law, Criminology, and Police Science,* 58 (1): 80–6.

23 Raymond Paternoster (1987) "The Deterrent Effect of the Perceived Certainty and Severity of Punishment: A Review of the Evidence and Issues," *Justice Quarterly,* 4 (2): 180.

24 Charles R. Tittle (1980) *Sanctions and Social Deviance: The Question of Deterrence,* New York: Praeger. Cited in Nagin, "Criminal Deterrence Research," p. 15.

25 Daniel Nagin and Raymond Paternoster (1993) "Enduring Individual Differences and Rational Choice Theories of Crime," *Law and Society Review,* 27 (3): 467–96. See also Nagin, "Criminal Deterrence Research," p. 15.

26 Julie Horney and Ineke Haen Marshall (1992) "Risk Perceptions Among Serious Offenders," *Criminology,* 30 (4): 575–94.

27 L. Lochner (2003) "Individual Perceptions of the Criminal Justice System," National Bureau of Economic Research, Working Paper 9474.

28 National Research Council (2004) *Fairness and Effectiveness in Policing: The Evidence. Committee to Review Research on Police Policy and Practices,* edited by Wesley Skogan and Kathleen Frydl, Committee on Law and Justice, Division of Behavioral and Social Sciences and Education, Washington, DC: The National Academies Press, p. 296.

29 Patrick A. Langan and David J. Levin (2004) "Recidivism of Prisoners Released in 1994," Bureau of Justice Statistics, Office of Justice Programs, Department of Justice, Washington, DC, pp. 1–16.

30 Steven Raphael and Jens Ludwig (2003) "Prison Sentence Enhancements: The Case of Project Exile," in Jens Ludwig and Philip J. Cook (eds), *Evaluating Gun Policy: Effects on Crime and Violence,* Washington, DC: Brookings Institution Press, pp. 251–86; Klofas, John (2001) "Guns, Disputes, and Drug Sales: Focus Groups at Monroe Correctional Facility." Rochester SACSI Research Working Paper No. 12, Rochester Insitute of Technology, August 21, p. 6.

31 Anthony N. Doob and Cheryl Marie Webster (2003) "Sentence Severity and Crime: Accepting the Null Hypothesis," in Michael Tonry (ed.) *Crime and Justice: A Review of Research,* Chicago, Ill.: University of Chicago Press, pp. 143–95; p. 30, citing Kenneth D. Tunnell (1996) "Choosing Crime: Close Your Eyes and Take Your Chances," in Barry W. Hancock and Paul M. Sharp (eds), *Criminal Justice in America: Theory, Practice, and Policy,* Upper Saddle River, N.J.: Prentice-Hall, pp. 38–50; p. 24.

32 Robin Engel, S. Gregory Baker, Marie Skubak Tillyer, John Eck, and Jessica Dunham (2000) "Implementation of the Cincinnati Initiative to Reduce Violence (CIRV): Interim Report," issued by the University of Cincinnati Policing Institute, report update dated March 20, 2008.

33 George Kelling, Tony Pate, Duane Dieckman, Charles E. Brown (1974) *The Kansas City Preventive Patrol Experiment: A Summary Report,* Washington, DC: The Police Foundation.

34 Police Foundation (1981) *The Newark Foot Patrol Experiment,* Washington DC: The Police Foundation.

35 Colin Loftin and David McDowall (1984) "The Deterrent Effects of the Florida Firearm Law," *Journal of Criminal Law and Criminology,* 75 (1): 250–9; Colin Loftin and David McDowall (1981) "'One with a Gun Gets You Two': Mandatory Sentencing and Firearms Violence in Detroit," *Annals of the American Academy of Political and Social Science,* 455 (1): 150–67; Colin Loftin, Milton Heumann and David McDowall (1983) "Mandatory Sentencing and

Firearms Violence: Evaluating an Alternative to Gun Control," *Law and Society Review*, 17 (2): 287–318.

36 Jeffrey A. Fagan (1994) "Do Criminal Sanctions Deter Drug Crimes?" in Doris Layton MacKenzie and Craig D. Uchida (eds), *Drugs and Crime: Evaluating Policy Initiatives*, Thousand Oaks, Calif.: Sage Publications, pp. 188–214.

37 Franklin E. Zimring, Gordon Hawkins, and Sam Kamin (2001) *Punishment and Democracy: Three Strikes and You're Out in California*, Oxford: Oxford University Press.

38 See, for example, Ross, "Deterrence Regained."

39 See, for example, Raymond Paternoster, L. E. Saltzman, T. G. Chiricos, and G. P. Waldo (1982) "Perceived Risk and Deterrence: Methodological Artifacts in Perceptual Deterrence Research," *Journal of Criminal Law and Criminology*, 73 (3): 1238–58; Raymond Paternoster, L. E. Saltzman, T. G. Chiricos, and G. P. Waldo (1983) "Perceived Risk and Social Control: Do Sanctions Really Deter?" *Law and Society Review*, 17 (3): 457–80; L. E. Saltzman, Raymond Patnernoster, G. P. Waldo, and T. G. Chiricos (1982) "Deterrence and Experiential Effects: The Problem of Causal Order in Perceptual Deterrence Research," *Journal of Research in Crime and Delinquency*, 19 (2): 172–89.

40 Alex R. Piquero and Greg Pogarsky (2002) "Beyond Stafford and Warr's Reconceptualization of Deterrence: Personal and Vicarious Experiences, Impulsivity, and Offending Behavior," *Journal of Research in Crime and Delinquency*, 39 (2): 167.

41 Cook, *Research in Criminal Deterrence*, p. 214.

2 How, and do, criminals think?

1 Franklin Zimring and Gordon Hawkins (1973) *Deterrence: The Legal Threat in Crime Control*, Chicago, Ill.: University of Chicago Press, p. 5.

2 M. Geerken and W. Grove (1975) "Deterrence: Some Theoretical Considerations," *Law and Society Review*, 9 (spring): 497; quoted in Harold G. Grasmick and George J. Bryjak (1980) "The Deterrent Effect of Perceived Severity of Punishment," *Social Forces*, 59 (2): 471.

3 Irving Piliavin, Craig Thornton, Rosemary Gartner, and Ross L. Matsueda (1986) "Crime, Deterrence, and Rational Choice," *American Sociological Review*, 51 (February): 101.

4 Richard T. Wright and Scott H. Decker (1997) *Armed Robbers in Action: Stickups and Street Culture*, Boston, Mass.: Northeastern University Press, p. 120.

5 Julie L. Ozanne, Ronald Paul Hill, and Newell D. Wright (1998) "Juvenile Delinquents' Use of Consumption as Cultural Resistance: Implications for Juvenile Reform Programs and Public Policy," *Journal of Public Policy and Marketing*, 17 (2): 189.

6 Wright and Decker, *Armed Robbers in Action*, p. 30.

7 Jerome Michael and Herbert Wechsler (1937) "A Rationale of the Law of Homicide II," *Columbia Law Review*, 37 (8): 1261–325; Colum. L. Rev. 759 in Zimring and Hawkins, *Deterrence*, p. 107.

8 Edwin H. Sutherland and Donald R. Cressey (1958) *Criminology*, Philadelphia, Pa.: J. B. Lippincott Company, p. 156.

9 Scott H. Decker and Carol W. Kohfeld (1985) "Crime, Crime Rates, Arrests, and Arrest Ratios: Implications for Deterrence Theory," *Criminology*, 23 (3): 443.

10 D. Abramson, quoted in John S. Carroll (1978) "A Psychological Approach to Deterrence: The Evaluation of Crime Opportunities," *Journal of Personality and Social Psychology*, 36 (12): 1513.

11 Herbert Jacob (1978) "Rationality and Criminality," *Social Science Quarterly*, 59 (3): 584–5. References omitted.

12 Jacob, "Rationality and Criminality."
13 Don W. Brown and Stephen L. McDougal (1978) "A Reply to Professor Jacob," *Social Science Quarterly*, 59 (3): 586–7; p. 587.
14 R. V. Stover and D. W. Brown (1977) "Understanding Compliance and Noncompliance with Law: The Contribution of Utility Theory," *Social Science Quarterly*, 56 (3): 363–75; quoted in Brown and McDougal, "A Reply to Professor Jacob," p. 587.
15 Quoted in Richard L. Henshel and Robert A. Silverman (1975) *Perceptions in Criminology*, New York: Columbia University Press, p. 4, n. 7.
16 Franz Gabriel Alexander and Hugo Staub (1956) *The Criminal, the Judge, and the Public: A Psychological Analysis*, Glencoe, Ill.: Free Press, p. 107; quoted in Zimring and Hawkins, *Deterrence*, p. 110.
17 Gordon Tullock (1974) "Does Punishment Control Crime?" *The Public Interest*, 36 (summer): 108.
18 Jens Ludwig, personal communication.
19 Phillip J. Cook (1980) "Research in Criminal Deterrence: Laying the Groundwork for the Second Decade," in Norval Morris and Michael Tonry (eds), *Crime and Justice: An Annual Review of Research*, Chicago, Ill.: University of Chicago Press, Vol. II, p. 119.
20 John S. Carroll (1978) "A Psychological Approach to Deterrence: The Evaluation of Crime Opportunities," *Journal of Personality and Social Psychology*, 36 (12): 1513.
21 Carroll, "A Psychological Approach to Deterrence."
22 John S. Carroll (1982) "Committing a Crime: The Offender's Decision," in Vladimir J. Konecni and Ebbe B. Ebbesen (eds), *The Criminal Justice System: A Social-Psychological Analysis*, San Francisco, Calif.: W. H. Freeman & Co., p. 60.
23 R. V. Clarke and D. B. Cornish (1985) "Modeling Offenders' Decisions: a Framework for Research and Policy," in M. Tonry and N. Morris (eds), *Crime and Justice: A Review of Research*, No. 6, Chicago, Ill.: University of Chicago Press, pp. 147–85.
24 Cook, "Research in Criminal Deterrence," p. 220.
25 Cook, "Research in Criminal Deterrence," p. 220.
26 Christopher Jencks and Susan E. Mayer (1990) "The Social Consequences of Growing Up in a Poor Neighborhood," in Lawrence Lynn and Michael McGeary (eds), *Inner-City Poverty in the United States*, Washington, DC: National Academy Press, p. 117.

3 Some implications of the subjectivity of deterrence

1 Isaac Ehrlich (1979) "The Economic Approach to Crime," in Sheldon Messinger and Egon Bittner (eds), *Criminology Review Yearbook*, Beverly Hills, Calif.: Sage Publications, pp. 25–60; p. 35.
2 Social Psychiatry Research Associates (1968) *Public Knowledge of Criminal Penalties: A Research Report;* untitled poll conducted in 1968–9 by the Center for Studies in Criminal Justice, University of Chicago; both cited in Franklin Zimring and Gordon Hawkins (1973) *Deterrence: The Legal Threat in Crime Control*, Chicago, Ill.: University of Chicago Press, p. 143, notes 155–7.
3 Daniel S. Nagin (1998) "Criminal Deterrence Research at the Outset of the Twenty-First Century," *Crime and Justice: A Review of Research*, No. 23, Chicago, Ill.: University of Chicago Press, p. 17.
4 Nagin, "Criminal Deterrence Research," p. 19.
5 Gary Kleck, Brion Sever, Spencer Li, and Marc Gertz (2005) "The Missing Link in General Deterrence Research," *Criminology*, 43 (3): 623–59; p. 644.
6 Kleck *et al.*, "The Missing Link," p. 648.
7 California Senate Commission on Public Safety "Sentencing Commission: History" 2007–2008 Regular Session.

8 California Senate Commission on Public Safety "Sentencing Commission: History" 2007-2008 Regular Session, Note 9, citing *Community Release Bd.* v. *Superior Court* (1979) 91 Cal.App.3d 814, 815, fn. 1 (154 Cal.Rptr. 383).

9 "Protecting America: The Effectiveness of the Federal Armed Career Criminal Statute," 1992 Bureau of Alcohol, Tobacco, and Firearms, US Department of the Treasury, p. 13.

10 Toni Makkai and John Braithwaite (1994) "The Dialectics of Corporate Deterrence," *Journal of Research in Crime and Delinquency*, 31 (4): 347–73; p. 362.

11 Fox Butterfield (1995) "In for Life: The Three-Strikes Law—A Special Report: First Federal 3-Strikes Conviction Ends a Criminal's 25-Year Career," *New York Times*, September 11.

12 Julie Bykowicz (2007) "A 'Back Door' into Prison," *Baltimore Sun*, December 2.

13 Zimring and Hawkins, *Deterrence*, p. 142.

14 Philip J. Cook (1980) "Research in Criminal Deterrene: Laying the Groudwork for the Second Decade," *Crime and Justice*, Vol. II, Chicago, Ill.: University of Chicago Press, pp. 211–68.

15 United States Government Accountability Office (2006) "ONDCP Media Campaign: Contractor's National Evaluation Did Not Find That the Youth Anti-Media Campaign Was Effective in Reducing Youth Drug Use," Report to the Subcommittee on Transportation, Treasury, the Judiciary, Housing and Urban Development, and Related Agencies, Committee on Appropriations, US Senate.

16 D. Riley, and P. Mayhew (1980) *Crime Prevention Publicity: An Assessment*, Home Office Research Study, London: Her Majesty's Stationery Office London, p. 63.

17 Margot Kuttschreuter and Oene Wiegman (1998) "Crime Prevention and the Attitude Toward the Criminal Justice System: The Effects of a Multimedia Campaign," *Journal of Criminal Justice*, 26 (6): 441–52; p. 1.

18 Cook, *Research in Criminal Deterrence*, pp. 222–4.

19 R. Van Houton and P. A. Nau (1983) "Feedback Interventions and Driving Speed: a Parametric and Comparative Analysis," *Journal of Applied Behavior Analysis*, 16 (3): 253–81; R. Van Houton, P. A. Nau, R. Friedman, M. Becker, I. Chalodovsky, and M. Scherer (1983) "Large-Scale Reductions in Speeding and Accidents in Canada and Israel: a Behavioral Ecological Perspective," *Journal of Applied Behavior Analysis*, 18 (1): 87–93. Quoted in Terry Connolly and Lars Aberg (1993) "Some Contagion Models of Speeding," *Accident Analysis and Prevention*, 25 (1): 57–66; p. 58.

20 Lawrence W. Sherman (1990) "Police Crackdowns: Initial and Residual Deterrence," in Michael Tonry and Norval Morris (eds), *Crime and Justice: A Review of Research*, No. 12, Chicago, Ill.: University of Chicago Press, pp. 1–48; p. 25.

21 H. Laurence Ross (1973) "Law, Science, and Accidents: The British Road Safety Act of 1967," *Journal of Legal Studies*, 2 (1): 1-78; H. Laurence Ross (1981) *Deterring the Drinking Driver: Legal Policy and Social Control*, Lexington, Mass.: Heath. Quoted in Sherman, "Police Crackdowns," p. 26; H. Laurence Ross (1977) "Deterrence Regained: The Cheshire Constabulary's 'Breathalyzer Blitz'" *Journal of Legal Studies*, 6 (1): 241–9; H. Laurence Ross, R. McCleary, and T. Epperlein (1982) "Deterrence of Drinking and Driving in France: An Evaluation of the Law of July 12 1978," *Law and Society Review*, 16 (3): 345–74. Quoted in Sherman, "Police Crackdowns," p. 26.

22 Shane D. Johnson and Kate J. Bowers (2003) "Opportunity Is in the Eye of the Beholder: The Role of Publicity in Crime Prevention," *Criminology and Public Policy*, 2 (3): 497–524.

23 Gary S. Green (1985) "General Deterrence and Television Cable Crime: A Field Experiment in Social Control," *Criminology*, 23 (4): 629–45. Quoted in Sherman, "Police Crackdowns," p. 31.

24 James A. Beha, II (1977) "And *Nobody* Can Get You Out: The Impact of a Mandatory Prison Sentence for the Illegal Carrying of a Firearm on the Use of Firearms and on the Administration of Criminal Justice in Boston—Part II," *Boston University Law Review*, 57: 289–333; pp. 314–15.

25 William J. Chambliss (1966) "The Deterrent Influence of Punishment," *Crime and Delinquency*, 12: 70–5, cited in Zimring and Hawkins, *Deterrence*, p. 159, n. 195.

26 Zimring and Hawkins, *Deterrence*, p. 159.

27 Jeremy Travis, personal communication.

28 Martha J. Smith, Ron V. Clarke, and Ken Pease (2002) "Anticipatory Benefits in Crime Prevention," in Nick Tilley (ed.), *Analysis for Crime Prevention*, Monsey, NY: Criminal Justice Press, pp. 71–88.

29 Smith *et al.* "Anticipatory Benefits," p. 79.

30 Smith *et al.* "Anticipatory Benefits," p. 72.

31 Cook, *Research in Criminal Deterrence*, p. 224.

32 Robert M. Fisher and Daniel Nagin (1978) "On the Feasibility of Identifying the Crime Function in a Simultaneous Model of Crime Rates and Sanction Levels," in Alfred Blumstein, Jacqueline Cohen, and Daniel Nagin (eds), *Deterrence and Incapacitation: Estimating the Effects of Criminal Sanctions on Crime Rates*, Washington, DC: National Academy of Sciences, pp. 361–99; cited in Scott H. Decker and Carol W. Kohfeld (eds) (1985) "Crimes, Crime Rates, Arrests, and Arrest Rations: Implication for Deterrence Theory," *Criminology*, 23 (3): 437–50; p. 440.

33 Sherman, "Police Crackdowns," p. 3.

34 Decker and Kohfeld, *Crime, Crime Rates, Arrests, and Arrest Ratios*, p. 442.

35 Nagin, "Criminal Deterrence Research," p. 17.

36 Campaign for an Effective Crime Policy, "The Impact of Three Strikes and You're Out Laws: What Have We Learned?" Executive Summary, September 1996.

37 Zimring and Hawkins, *Deterrence*, p. 173.

38 Zimring and Hawkins, *Deterrence*, p. 190.

39 Zimring and Hawkins, *Deterrence*, pp. 175–90.

40 Travis Hirshi (1969) *Causes of Delinquency*, Berkeley, Calif.: University of California Press.

41 Raymond Paternoster, Linda E. Saltzman, Gordon P. Waldo, and Theodore G. Chiricos (1983) "Perceived Risk and Social Control: Do Sanctions Really Deter?" *Law and Society Review*, 17 (3): 457–80; p. 462.

42 Daniel S. Nagin and Raymond Paternoster (1994) "Personal Capital and Social Control: The Deterrence Implications of a Theory of Individual Differences in Criminal Offending," *Criminology* 32 (4): 581–606; p. 586.

43 Nagin and Paternoster, "Personal Capital and Social Control," p. 584.

44 See, for example, Irving Pilavian, Craig Thornton, Rosemary Gartner, and Ross L. Matsueda (1986) "Crime, Deterrence, and Rational Choice," *American Sociological Review*, 51 (1): 101–19; p. 104.

45 Kirk R. Williams and Richard Hawkins (1986) "Perceptual Research on General Deterrence: A Critical Review," *Law and Society Review*, 20 (4): 545–72; p. 564.

46 See also, for example, William H. Minor (1977) "A Deterrence-Control Theory of Crime," in Robert F. Meier (ed.), *Theory in Criminology*, Beverly Hills, Calif.: Sage Publications, pp. 117–37; p. 123.

47 R. F. Meier and W. T. Johnson (1977) "Deterrence As Social Control: the Legal and Extralegal Production of Conformity," *American Sociological Review*, 42 (2): 292–304.

48 Cook, *Research in Criminal Deterrence*, p. 233.

49 Philip Cook (2006) "The Deterrent Effects of California's Proposition 8," *Criminology and Public Policy*, 5 (3): 413–16; p. 415.

50 Kent A. McClelland and Geoffrey P. Alpert (1985) "Factor Analysis Applied to Magnitude Estimates of Punishment Seriousness: Patterns of Individual Differences," *Journal of Quantitative Criminology*, 1 (3): 307–18.

51 Eleni Apospori and Geoffrey Alpert (1993) "Research Note: The Role of Differential Experience With the Criminal Justice System in Changes in Perceptions of Severity of Legal Sanctions Over Time," *Crime and Delinquency*, 39 (2): 184–94. Ratios calculated from data presented on p. 189.
52 Anthony N. Doob and Cheryl Marie Webster (2003) "Sentence Severity and Crime: Accepting the Null Hypothesis," in Michael Tonry (ed.), *Crime and Justice: a Review of Research*, No. 30. Chicago, Ill.: University of Chicago Press, pp. 143–95; p. 28.
53 Lisa Stolzenberg and Stewart J. D'Alessio (1997) "'Three Strikes and You're Out': The Impact of California's New Mandatory Sentencing Law on Serious Crime Rates," *Crime and Delinquency*, 43: 457–69, discussed in Doob and Webster, *Sentence and Severity*, p. 21.
54 James Austin, John Clark, Patricia Hardyman, and D. Alan Henry (1999) "The Impact of 'Three Strikes and You're Out,'" *Punishment and Society*, 1 (2): 131–62, discussed in Doob and Webster, *Sentence and Severity*, p. 21.
55 Tamasak Wicharaya (1995) *Simple Theory, Hard Reality: The Impact of Sentencing Reforms on Courts, Prisons, and Crime*, Albany, N.Y.: State University of New York Press, discussed in Doob and Webster, *Sentence and Severity*, p. 22.
56 Michael Tonry and David P. Farrington (1995) "Strategic Approaches to Crime Prevention," in Michael Tonry and David P. Farrington (eds), *Building a Safer Society: Strategic Approaches to Crime Prevention*, Chicago, Ill.: University of Chicago Press, pp. 6, 7.
57 Tonry and Farrington, "Strategic Approaches to Crime Prevention," p. 6.
58 Dale O. Cloninger and Roberto Marchesini (2001) "Execution and Deterrence: A Quasi-Controlled Group Experiment," *Applied Economics*, 33: 569–76.
59 H. Naci Mocan and R. Kaj Gittings (2001) "Pardons, Executions and Homicides," Cambridge, Mass.: National Bureau of Economic Research, p. 4.
60 See, for example, Richard Berk (2005) "New Claims about Executions and General Deterrence: Déjà Vu All Over Again?" *Journal of Empirical Legal Studies*, 2 (2): 303–30.
61 Mocan and Gittings, "Pardons, Executions and Homicides," p. 4. See also H. Naci Mocan and R. Kaj Gittings (2003) "Getting Off Death Row: Commuted Sentences and the Deterrent Effect of Capital Punishment," *Journal of Law and Economics*, 46 (2): 453–78.
62 Doob and Webster, *Sentence and Severity*, p. 28.
63 Harold G. Grasmick and George J. Bryjak (1980) "The Deterrent Effect of Perceived Severity of Punishment," *Social Forces*, 59: 471–91.
64 W. Buikhuisen (1975) "General Deterrence: Research and Theory," in *General Deterrence*, Stockholm: National Swedish Council for Crime Prevention, p. 82; cited in Grasmick and Bryjack, "The Deterrent Effect of Perceived Severity of Punishment," p. 476.
65 Richard T. Wright and Scott H. Decker (1997) *Armed Robbers in Action: Stickups and Street Culture*, Boston, Mass.: Notheastern University Press, p. 123.
66 See, for example, Anne M. Piehl (2002) *From Cell to Street: A Plan to Supervise Inmates After Release*, Boston, Mass.: Massachusetts Institute for a New Commonwealth, p. 8.
67 Ben M. Crouch (1993) "Is Incarceration Really Worse? Analysis of Offenders' Preferences for Prison Over Probation," *Justice Quarterly*, 10 (1): 67–88. See also Petersilia, Joan and Deschenes, Elizabeth (1994) "Perceptions of Punishment: Inmates and Staff Rank the Severity of Prison Versus Intermediate Sanctions," *Prison Journal*, 74 (3): 306–28.
68 William Spelman (1995) "The Severity of Intermediate Sanctions," *Journal of Research in Crime and Delinquency*, 32 (2): 107–35.

69 David C. May, Peter B. Wood, Jennifer L. Mooney, and Kevin I. Minor (2005) "Predicting Offender-Generated Exchange Rates: Implications for a Theory of Sentence Severity," *Crime and Delinquency*, 51 (3): 373–99.
70 David Weisburd, Elin Waring, and Ellen Chayet (1995) "Specific Deterrence in a Sample of Offenders Convicted of White-Collar Crimes," *Criminology*, 33 (4): 587–607; p. 599.
71 Weisburd *et al.*, "Specific Deterrence," p. 599.
72 Harold G. Grasmick and Robert J. Bursik (1990) "Conscience, Significant Others, and Rational Choice: Extending the Deterrence Model," *Law and Society Review*, 24 (3): 837–61.
73 Raymond Paternoster, Linda E. Saltzman, Gordon P. Waldo, and Theodore Choricos (1983) "Estimating Perceptual Stability and Deterrent Effects: The Role of Perceived Legal Punishment in the Inhibition of Criminal Involvement," *Journal of Criminal Law and Criminology*, 74 (1): 270–97; p. 295.
74 Raymond Paternoster and Sally Simpson (1996)" Sancation Threats and Appeals to Morality: Testing a Rational Choice Model of Corporate Crime," *Law and Society Review*, 30 (3): 549–83; p. 571.
75 Makkai and Braithwaite, "The Dialectice of Corporate Deterrence," p. 360.
76 Minor, "A Deterrence-Control Theory of Crime," p. 129.
77 Pamela Richards and Charles R. Tittle (1981) "Gender and Perceived Chances of Arrest," *Social Forces* 59 (4): 1182–99; p. 1192.
78 Charles R. Tittle (1977) "Sanction Fear and the Maintenance of Social Order," *Social Forces*, 53 (3): 579–96; p. 592.
79 Ronet Bachman, Raymond Paternoster, and Sally Ward (1992) "The Rationality of Sexual Offending: Testing a Deterrence/Rational Choice Conception of Sexual Assault," *Law and Society Review*, 26 (2): 343–72; pp. 364–5.
80 Williams and Hawkins, "Perceptual Research on General Deterrence," p. 564.
81 Daniel S. Nagin and Raymond Paternoster, "Enduring Individual Differences and Rational Choice Theories of Crime," *Law and Society Review*, 27 (3): 467–96; p. 490; see also Nagin and Paternoster, "Personal Capital and Social Control."
82 Scott H. Decker and Janet L. Lauritsen (2002) "Leaving the Gang," in C. Ronald Huff (ed.), *Gangs in America III*, Thousand Oaks, Calif.: Sage Publications, p. 51.
83 Daniel Romer (1994) "Using Mass Media to Reduce Adolescent Involvement in Drug Trafficking," *Pediatrics*, 93 (6) Supplement, Part 2 of 2.

4 Initial reflections

1 Philip J. Cook (1980) "Research in Criminal Deterrence: Laying the Groundwork for the Second Decade," *Crime and Justice*, 2: 211–68.
2 My thanks to Sandy Jencks for this, a deterrence-theory version of the McNaughton Rule.
3 Frank Zimring and Gordon Hawkins (1973) *Deterrence: The Legal Threat in Crime Control*, Chicago, Ill.: University of Chicago Press.

5 Crime and criminal-justice practice

1 Richard B. Freeman (1991) "Crime and the Employment of Disadvantaged Youths," NBER Working Paper No. 3875, National Bureau of Economic Research, Cambridge, Mass., pp. 4–5.
2 Freeman, "Crime and the Employment of Disadvantaged Youths," p. 8.
3 Finn-Aage Esbensen, Dana Peterson, Adrienne Freng, and Terrance J. Taylor (2002) "Initiation of Drug Use, Drug Sales, and Violent Offending Among a

Sample of Gang and Nongang Youth" in C. Ronald Huff (ed.), *Gangs in America III*, Thousand Oaks, Calif.: Sage Publications, pp. 37–50; p. 45.

4 Bonita Stanton and Jennifer Galbraith (1994) "Drug Trafficking Among African-American Early Adolescents: Prevalence, Consequences, and Associated Behaviors and Beliefs," *Pediatrics*, 93 (6) Supplement, Part 2 of 2.

5 Irene Hanson Frieze and Angela Browne (1989) "Violence in Marriage" in Lloyd Ohlin and Michael Tonry (eds), *Family Violence Crime and Justice: A Review of Research*, Chicago, Ill.: University of Chicago Press, pp. 179–80.

6 For a review of these literatures, see Anthony A. Braga (2002) *Problem-Oriented Policing and Crime Prevention*, Monsey, NY: Criminal Justice Press.

7 David M. Kennedy, Anthony A. Braga, and Gillian Thomson (2000) "Problem Solving for Homicide Prevention in Baltimore," paper presented at the annual meeting of the American Society of Criminology, San Francisco.

8 See, for example, David M. Kennedy (1997) "Pulling Levers: Chronic Offenders, High-Crime Settings, and a Theory of Prevention," *Valparaiso University Law Review*, 31: 449–84.

9 See, for example, Elijah Anderson (1999) *Code of the Streets: Decency, Violence, and the Moral Life of the Inner City*, New York: W. W. Norton & Co; Philippe Bourgois (1995) *In Search of Respect: Selling Crack in El Barrio*, Cambridge: Cambridge University Press; David Simon and Edward Burns (1997) *The Corner: A Year in the Life of an Inner-City Neighborhood*, New York: Broadway Books; Alex Kotlowitz (1992) *There Are No Children Here*, New York: Doubleday.

10 R. Dembo, P. Hughes, L. Jackson, and T. Mieczowski (1993) "Crack Cocaine Dealing by Adolescents in Two Public Housing Projects: A Pilot Study," *Human Organization*, 52 (1): 89–96; cited in Li Xiaoming and Susan Feigelmann (1994) "Recent and Intended Drug Trafficking Among Male and Female Urban African-American Early Adolescents," *Pediatrics*, 93 (6) Supplement, Part 2 of 2.

11 Stan Grossfeld (2003) "Rallying Cry for a Fallen Teammate," *Boston Globe*, November 9, p. C22.

12 Commission to Investigate Allegations of Police Corruption and the City's Anti-Corruption Procedures (1972) *Commission Report*, New York: Knapp Commission.

13 Commission to Investigate Allegations of Police Corruption and the Anti-Corruption Procedures of the New York City Police Department, "Interim Report and Principal Recommendations," December 27, 1993.

14 Boston Globe (2002) *Betrayal: The Crisis in the Catholic Church*, New York: Little, Brown & Co.

15 Mark H. Moore, Carol V. Petrie, Anthony A. Braga, and Brenda L. McLaughlin (eds), *Deadly Lessons: Understanding Lethal School Violence*, Washington, DC: National Academies Press, p. 317.

16 Diana Jean Schemo (2003) "Rate of Rape at Academy Is Found High," *New York Times*, August 29, A16.

17 Franklin E. Zimring and Gordon Hawkins (1993) "Crime, Justice, and the Savings and Loan Crisis," in Michael Tonry and Albert J. Reiss, Jr. (eds), *Crime and Justice: A Review of Research*, No. 18, *Beyond the Law: Crime in Complex Organizations*, Chicago, Ill.: University of Chicago Press, pp. 247–92; p. 265.

18 Martin Mayer (1990) *The Greatest-Ever Bank Robbery: The Collapse of the Savings and Loan Industry*, New York: Scribner's, cited in Zimring and Hawkins, "The Savings and Loan Crisis," p. 265.

19 Zimring and Hawkins, "The Savings and Loan Crisis," p. 253, Figure 2.

20 Peter Reuter (1993) "The Cartage Industry in New York," in Michael Tonry and Albert J. Reiss, Jr. (eds), *Beyond the Law: Crime in Complex Organizations Crime and Justice: A Review of Research*, No. 18, Chicago, Ill.: University of Chicago Press, pp. 149–201.

21 Gilbert Geis (1977) "The Heavy Electrical Equipment Antitrust Cases of 1961," in Gilbert Geis and Robert F. Meier (eds), *White-Collar Crime: Offenses in Business, Politics, and the Professions*, New York: The Free Press, pp. 118–19.

22 James A. Inciardi (1975) *Careers in Crime*, Chicago, Ill.: Rand McNally, p. 30.

23 Malcom K. Sparrow (1994) *Imposing Duties: Government's Changing Approach to Compliance*, Westport, Conn.: Praeger, p. 39.

24 Gary F. Jensen (1969) "'Crime Doesn't Pay': Correlates of a Shared Misunderstanding," *Social Problems*, 17 (2): 189–201.

25 Edwin H. Sutherland and Donald R. Cressey (1958) *Criminology*, Philadelphia, Pa.: J. B. Lippincott Company.

26 Dean G. Kilpatrick, Benjamin E. Saunders, and Daniel W. Smith (2003) "Youth Victimization: Prevalence and Implications" National Institute of Justice, Research in Brief, US Department of Justice, p. 10.

27 Nancy Loving (1980) *Responding to Spouse Abuse and Wife Beating: A Guide for Police*, Washington, DC: Police Executive Research Forum; cited in Delbert S. Elliot (1989) "Criminal Justice in Procedures in Family Violence Crimes," in Lloyd Ohlin and Michael Tonry (eds), *Family Violence Crime and Justice: A Review of Research*, Chicago, Ill.: University of Chicago Press, pp. 427–80; p. 437.

28 William Spelman and D. Brown (1984) *Calling the Police: Citizen Reporting of Serious Crime*, Washington, DC: US Government Printing Office.

29 Daniel G. Saunders and Sandra T. Asar (1989) "Treatment Programs for Family Violence" in Lloyd Ohlin and Michael Tonry (eds), *Family Violence Crime and Justice: A Review of Research*, Chicago, Ill.: University of Chicago Press, pp. 481–546; p. 485.

30 J. Hoover, R. Oliver and R. Hazler (1992) "Bullying: Perceptions of Adolescent Victims in the Midwestern USA," *Social Psychology International*, 13 (1): 5–16; cited in Rana Sampson (n.d.) "Bullying in Schools," Problem-Oriented Guides for Police Series, No. 12, US Department of Justice, Office of Community Oriented Policing Services, p. 5.

31 Terrence Real (1997) *I Don't Want to Talk About It: Overcoming the Secret Legacy of Male Depression*, New York: Simon and Schuster, p. 115.

32 One of my current graduate students at John Jay College of Criminal Justice, waitressing at a chic Manhattan lounge, found management procuring cocaine for customers and encouraging staff to prostitute themselves. "I know where white people commit crimes," she says. "Hotels."

33 Braga, *Problem-Oriented Policing*, p. 8.

34 Peter W. Greenwood, Jan M. Chaiken, and Joan Petersilia (1977) *The Criminal Investigative Process*, Lexington, Mass.: D. C. Heath.

35 Matthew Miranda, Office of the United States Attorney, personal communication, June 16, 2003. These numbers may be expected to increase slightly as open investigation proceed.

36 Bernstein, David (2005) "The Worst Homicide Squad in the Country," *Boston Phoenix*, August 19.

37 Bruce A. Jacobs (1999) *Dealing Crack: The Social World of Streetcorner Selling*, Boston, Mass.: Northeastern University Press, p. 100.

38 Tom Mieczkowski (1990) "Crack Distribution in Detroit," *Contemporary Drug Problems*, 17 (1): 9–30; citation to Bruce Johnson, Ansley Hamid, Edmundo Morales, Harry Sanabria (1987) "Critical Dimensions of Crack Distribution," Paper presented at the 1987 American Society of Criminology annual meeting, Montreal, Quebec.

39 Richard T. Wright and Scott H. Decker (1997) *Armed Robbers in Action*, Boston, Mass.: Northeastern University Press.

40 Bruce A. Jacobs (2000) *Robbing Drug Dealers*, New York: Aldine de Gruyter, p. 76.

41 Elliot, "Criminal Justice in Procedures," p. 438.

42 Peter Letkemann (1973) *Crime As Work*, New York: Prentice-Hall, p. 30.
43 See, for example, Jacobs, *Dealing Crack* and *Robbing Drug Dealers;* Tom Mieczowski (1990) "Crack Distribution in Detroit," *Contemporary Drug Problems*, 19: 9–30; Tom Mieczowski (1992) "Crack Dealing on the Street: The Crew System and the Crack House," *Justice Quarterly*, 9 (1): 151–63; Bruce D. Johnson and Mangal Natarajan (1995) "Strategies to Avoid Arrest: Crack Sellers' Response to Intensified Policing," *American Journal of Police*, 14 (3/4): 49–69; Jerome H. Skolnick, Theodore Correl, Elizabeth Navarro, and Roger Rabb (1990) "The Social Structure of Street Drug Dealing," *American Journal of Police*, 9 (1): 1–41.
44 Lawrence W. Sherman (1990) "Police Crackdowns: Intitial and Residual Deterrence," *Crime and Justice*, 12: 1–48.
45 Simon and Burns, *The Corner*, p. 187.
46 Jacobs, *Dealing Crack*, p. 48.
47 Knapp Commission Report.
48 "Warranting Improvement: Reforming the Arrest Warrant Management System," A Report of the Senate Committee on Post Audit and Oversight, Massachusetts State Legislature, January 1999.
49 Interview, confidential informant "B," July 21, 2003.
50 Joan Petersilia (ed.) (1997) *Community Corrections*, New York: Oxford University Press.
51 Petersilia, *Community Corrections*, p. 489.
52 Mark Kleiman (2001) "Controlling Drug Use and Crime Among Drug-Involved Offenders: Testing, Sanctions, and Treatment," in Phillip Heymann and Will Brownsberger (eds), *Drug Addiction and Drug Policy: The Struggle to Control Dependence*, Cambridge, Mass.: Harvard University Press, pp. 168–92.
53 William Stewart, personal communication.
54 Adele Harrell, Shannon Cavanaugh, and John Roman (1998) "Findings from the Evaluation of the DC Superior Court Drug Intervention Program," The Urban Institute, Washington, DC, p. 33.
55 Petersilia, *Community Corrections*, p. 490.
56 Joan Petersilia and Susan Turner (1991) "An Evaluation of Intensive Probation in California," *Journal of Criminal Law and Criminology*, 82 (3): 610–58.
57 Amy Solomon, Vera Kachnowski, and Avinash Bhati (2005) "Does Parole Work? Analyzing the Impact of Postprison Supervision on Rearrest Outcomes," The Urban Institute, Washington, DC, p. 8.
58 Frank Remington (1993) "The Decision to Charge, the Decision to Convict on a Plea of Guilty and the Impact of Sentence Structure on Prosecution Practices," in Lloyd E. Ohlin and Frank J. Remington (eds), *Discretion in Criminal Justice*, Albany, N.Y.: SUNY Press, pp. 73–109.
59 Steven Raphael and Jens Ludwig (2003) "Prison Sentence Enhancements: The Case of Project Exile," in Jens Ludwig and Philip J. Cook (eds), *Evaluating Gun Policy*, Washington, DC: Brookings Institution Press, pp. 251–86; p. 258.
61 "SFPD Dead Last in Solving Violent Crime," *San Francisco Chronicle*, Sunday, May 19, 2002.
62 Elliot, "Criminal Justice in Procedures," p. 460.
63 Wright and Decker, *Armed Robbers in Action*, p. 15.
64 Rebecca Hollander-Blumoff (1997) "Getting to 'Guilty': Plea Bargaining as Negotiation," *Harvard Negotiation Law Review*, 2: 115–46.
65 Wright and Decker, *Armed Robbers in Action*, p. 123.
66 Simon and Burns, *The Corner*, p. 162.
67 Jack P. Gibbs (1968) "Crime, Punishment, and Deterrence," *Social Science Quarterly*, 48: 515–30; cited in Maynard L. Erickson and Jack P. Gibbs, "Specific Versus General Properties of Legal Punishments and Deterrence," *Social Science Quarterly*, 56 (3): 390–97; p. 391.

68 David Boyum and Peter Reuter (2005) *An Analytic Assessment of US Drug Policy*, Washington, DC: AEI Press, p. 57.

70 Matthew Miranda, Office of the US Attorney, personal communication.

71 J. Fagan (1974) "Do Criminal Sacntions Deter Drug Crimes?" in Doris L. MacKenzie, and Craig Uchida (eds), *Drugs and the Criminal Justice System: Evaluating Public Policy Alternatives*, Newbury Park, Calif.: Sage, pp. 188–214.

72 Joan Petersilia and Susan Turner (1993) "Intensive Probation and Parole" in Michael Tonry (ed.), *Crime and Justice: An Annual Review of Research*, No. 17, Chicago, Ill.: University of Chicago Press, pp. 281–335.

73 Brooks Egerton and Reese Dunklin (2007) "Unequal Justice: Murderers on Probation," *Dallas Morning News*, November 11.

74 Patrick Langan and Mark Cuniff (1992) "Recidivism of Felons on Probation 1986–89," Washington, DC: Bureau of Justice Statistics.

75 David M. Kennedy, Anne M. Piehl, and Anthony A. Braga (1999) "Youth Violence in Boston: Gun Markets, Serious Youth Offenders, and a Use-Reduction Strategy," *Law and Contemporary Problems*, 59 (1): 147–97.

76 Stephen J. Schulhofer and Ilene H. Nagel (1997) "Plea Negotiations under the Federal Sentencing Guidelines: Guideline Circumvention and Its Dynamics in the Post-Mistretta Period," *Northwestern University Law Review*, 91: 1284–1317.

77 Sharon Bunzel (1995) "The Probation Officer and the Federal Sentencing Guidelines: Strange Philosophical Bed Fellows," *Yale Law Journal*, 104 (5): 933–66.

78 H. Laurence Ross (1976) "The Neutralization of Severe Penalties: Some Traffic Law Studies," *Law and Society*, 10 (spring): 403–13.

79 Schulhofer and Nagel, "Plea Negotiations."

80 Linda Mills (2003) *Insult to Injury: Rethinking Our Responses to Intimate Abuse*, Princeton, N.J.: Princeton University Press.

81 Sherman, *Police Crackdowns*, p. 7.

82 Wright and Decker, *Armed Robbers in Action*, p. 15.

83 Fagan, *Do Criminal Sanctions Deter Drug Crimes?*, p. 201.

84 Aric Press (1988) "Piecing Together New York's Criminal Justice System: The Response to Crack," *The Record of the Association of the Bar of the City of New York*, 43 (5): 541–69.

85 Cook, Philip J. (1980) "Reducing Injury and Death Rates in Robbery," *Policy Analysis*, 6 (1): 21–45; p. 35.

6 The criminogenic implications of official practice

1 Frank E. Zimring and Gordon J. Hawkins (1973) *Deterrence: The Legal Threat in Crime Control*, Chicago, Ill.: University of Chicago Press, p. 158.

2 Frank E. Zimring, Gordon Hawkins, and Sam Kamin (2001) *Punishment and Democracy: Three Strikes and You're Out in California*, Oxford: Oxford University Press.

3 "Policy Statement on Deception" October 14, 1983, Federal Trade Commission, Washington, DC. Available online at http://www.ftc.gov/bcp/policystmt/ad-decept. htm (accessed 2003).

4 See http://www.nhtsa.dot.gov/people/outreach/SafeSobr/20qp/3d (accessed 2003).

5 See http://www.ncadd.com/tsra/abstracts/chronic.html (accessed 2003).

6 "Click it or ticket" pamphlet, Metropolitan Police Department/District Division of Transportation, no date.

7 Elaine Shannon (1999) "Have Gun, Will Travel," *Time Magazine*, August 16, p. 154.

8 The data are drawn from Bureau of Alcohol, Tobacco and Firearms, "The Illegal Youth Firearms Market in Richmond Virginia," The Youth Crime Gun Interdiction Initiative, Department of the Treasury, February 1999, p. 29, which the author helped prepare. These gun traces do not directly equate to individual

offenses: More than one gun could have been taken from one defendant, the underlying cases could involve firearms trafficking cases involving volumes of guns, some police departments submit guns removed for "safekeeping" at domestic violence calls, etc. However, most guns submitted for tracing with a possessors name attached are in fact recovered by police in association with possession offenses or other gun crimes. In addition, during the reporting period the Richmond Police Department submitted an additional 916 traces without possessor names attached. Experience with the tracing program showed that most such traces also represented possession and other gun crimes in which recordkeeping issues prevented the attachment of a name to the trace request. The 1,114 traces are therefore probably a lower bound for gun offenses known to the police during the reporting period.

9 See note 8.
10 Steven Raphael and Jens Ludwig (2003) "Prison Sentence Enhancements: The Case of Project Exile," in Jens Ludwig and Philip J. Cook (eds), *Evaluating Gun Policy: Effects on Crime and Violence*, Washington, DC: Brookings Institution Press, pp. 251–86.
11 Daniel Ostrovsky (2006) "No Magic Bullet for Gun-Crime Prosecutions," *Daily Record*, March 17.
12 John Klofas (2001) "Guns, Disputes, and Drug Sales: Focus Groups at Monroe Correctional Facility," Rochester SACSI Research Working Paper No. 12, Rochester Insitute of Technology, August 21, p. 6.
13 David Matza (1990) *Delinquency and Drift*, New Brunswick, N.J.: Transaction Publishers, p. 187.
14 Bruce Jacobs (1999) *Dealing Crack: The Social World of Streetcorner Selling*, Boston, Mass.: Northeastern University Press.
15 Jacobs, *Dealing Crack*, p. 48.
16 Bureau of Alcohol, Tobacco and Firearms (1992) *Protecting America: The Effectiveness of the Armed Career Criminal Statute*, Washington, DC: Bureau of Alcohol, Tobacco and Firearms, Department of the Treasury.
17 Zimring and Hawkins, *Deterrence*, p. 165.
18 Larry Cohen (1978) "Problems of Perception in Deterrence Research" in Charles Wellford (ed.), *Quantitative Studies in Criminology*, Beverly Hills, Calif.: Sage; cited in Julie Horney and Ineke Haen Marshall (1992) "Risk Perceptions Among Serious Offenders," *Criminology*, 30 (4): 575–94; p. 577.
19 Elijah Anderson (1999) *Code of the Street: Decency, Violence and the Moral Life of the Inner City*, New York: W.W. Norton & Company, Inc.
20 Klofas "Guns, Disputes, and Drug Sales," p. 13.
21 Lloyd Ohlin and Michael Tonry (1989) "Family Violence in Perspective," in Lloyd Ohlin and Michael Tonry (eds), *Crime and Justice: Family Violence*, Vol. II, pp. 1–18.
22 Philip J. Cook and Kristin A. Goss (1996) "A Selective Review of the Social-Contagion Literature," preliminary draft, July 24, p. 24.
23 See, for example, Tony Larry Whitehead, James Peterson, and Linda Kaljee (1994) "The 'Hustle': Socioeconomic Deprivation, Urban Drug Trafficking, and Low-Income, African-American Male Gender Identity," *Pediatrics*, 93 (6): Supplement, Part 2 of 2.
24 Wesley Skogan and Kathleen Frydl (eds) (2004) *Fairness and Effectiveness in Policing: The Evidence*, Washington, DC: National Research Council. For a review of this literature, see infra, Chapter 8.
25 P. Selznick (1969) *Law, Societies, and Industrial Justice*, New York: Russell Sage Foundation; cited in Skogan and Frydl, *Fairness and Effectiveness in Policing*, p. 303.
26 Jeff Grogger (1992) "Arrests, Persistent Youth Joblessness, and Black/White Employment Differentials," *Review of Economics and Statistics*, 74 (1): 100–6; p. 105.

27 Joel Waldfogel (1994) "The Effect of Criminal Conviction on Income and the Trust 'Reposed in the Workman,'" *Journal of Human Resources*, 29 (1): 62–81; p. 63.
28 Daniel Nagin and Joel Waldfogel (1995) "The Effects of Criminality and Conviction on the Labor Market Status of Young British Offenders," *International Review of Law and Economics*, 15 (1): 109–26; p. 121.
29 Richard Freeman (1991) "Crime and the Employement of Disadvantaged Youths," October 1, NBER Working Paper No. W3875. Available at http://ssrn. com/abstract = 226742. Emphasis in original.
30 Nagin and Waldfogel, "Effects of Criminality," p. 121.
31 S. Beth Atkin (1996) *Voices from the Streets: Young Former Gang Members Tell Their Stories*, Boston, Mass.: Little, Brown & Co., p. 27.
32 William Julius Wilson (1990) *The Truly Disadvantaged: the Inner City, the Underclass, and Public Policy*, Chicago, Ill.: University of Chicago Press.
33 Robert J. Bursik, Jr. (2002) "The Systemic Model of Gang Behavior: A Reconsideration," in C. Ronald Huff (ed.), *Gangs in America III*, Thousand Oaks, Calif.: Sage Publications, p. 76.
34 Todd Clear, Dina Rose, E. Waring, and Kristen Scully (2003) "Coercive Mobility and Crime: A Preliminary Examination of Concentrated Incarceration and Social Disorganization," *Justice Quarterly*, 20 (1): 33–64.
35 Clear *et al.*, "Coercive Mobility and Crime," p. 38.
36 David Simon and Edward Burns (1997) *The Corner*, New York: Broadway Books.
37 David M. Kennedy, Anthony A. Braga, and Anne M. Piehl (2001) "Developing and Implementing Operation Ceasefire," in *Reducing Gun Violence in Boston: The Boston Gun Project's Operation Ceasefire*, Washington, DC: National Institute of Justice, pp. 1–77.
38 Edward L. Glaeser, Bruce Sacerdote, and José A. Scheinkman (1996) "Crime and Social Interactions," *Quarterly Journal of Economics*, 111 (2): 507–48; p. 511.
39 Izabel Ricardo (1994) "Life Choices of African-American Youth Living in Public Housing: Perspectives on Drug Trafficking," *Pediatrics*, 93 (6): Supplement.
40 Bonita Stanton and Jennifer Galbraith (1994) "Drug Trafficking Among African-American Early Adolescents: Prevalence, Consequences, and Associated Behaviors and Beliefs," *Pediatrics*, 93 (6): 1039–43.
41 Anderson, *Code of the Street*, p. 317.
42 Anderson, *Code of the Street*, p. 30.
43 Anderson, *Code of the Street*, p. 94.
44 Anderson, *Code of the Street*, p. 103.
45 Anderson, *Code of the Street*, p. 112.
46 Xiaoming Li and Susan Feigelman (1994) "Recent and Intended Drug Trafficking Among Male and Female Urban African-American Early Adolescents," *Pediatrics*, 14: 491–508.
47 Loic Wacquant (2002) "Deadly Symbiosis," *Boston Review*, April/May, p. 23.
48 See, for example, Hubert Williams and Patrick V. Murphy (1990) "The Evolving Strategy of Policing: A Minority View," *Pespectives on Policing*, No. 13, Washington, DC: National Institute of Justice and Harvard University.
49 Whitehead *et al.*, "The 'Hustle.'"
50 Coramae Richey Mann (1997) "We Don't Need More Wars," *Valparaiso University Law Review*, 31 (2): 565–78.
51 The Infamous Pistol Pete (2003), untitled article, *Felon* (March/April).
52 *F.E.D.S.*, 3 (11), cover.
53 Robert Sampson, "Organized for What? Recasting Theories of Social (Dis)organization," in Elin Waring and David Weisburd (eds), *Crime and Social Organization*, New Brunswick, N.J.: Transaction Publishers, pp. 136–57.
54 The Infamous Pistol Pete, untitled.

55 Toni Makkai and John Braithwaite (1994) "The Dialectics of Corporate Deterrence," *Journal of Research in Crime and Delinquency*, 31: 347–73.
56 Makkai and Braithwaite, *Corporate Deterrence*, p. 363.
57 Makkai and Braithwaite, *Corporate Deterrence*, p. 364.
58 Makkai and Braithwaite, *Corporate Deterrence*, p. 365.
59 Makkai and Braithwaite, *Corporate Deterrence*, p. 364.
60 Jerome H. Skolnick, Theodore Correl, Elizabeth Navarro and Roger Rabb (1990) "The Social Structure of Street Drug Dealing," *American Journal of Police*, 9: 1–42.
61 Matthew Rabin (1998) "Psychology and Economics," *Journal of Economic Literature*, 36: 11–46.
62 Eric Rich (2005) "No-Show Witnesses Tossed in Jail," *Washington Post*, April 9, p. A1.
63 David Kocieniewski (2007) "Keeping Witnesses Off Stand to Keep Them Safe," *New York Times*, November 19, p. A1.
64 Donald Black (1983) "Crime As Social Control," *American Sociological Review*, 48 (February): 34–45.
65 Anderson, *Code of the Street*, pp. 199–203.
66 Bruce Jacobs (2000) *Robbing Drug Dealers: Violence Beyond the Law*, New York: Walter de Gruyter, Inc.
67 Jacobs, *Robbing Drug Dealers*, p. 38.
68 Jacobs, *Robbing Drug Dealers*, p. 39.
69 Black, "Crime As Social Control," p. 41.
70 Klofas "Guns, Disputes, and Drug Sales," p. 2.
71 Anderson, *Code of the Street*, p. 203.
72 Jacobs, *Robbing Drug Dealers*, p. 108.
73 It is also the case in many police departments that homicides are pursued vigorously no matter who the victim is; this has in fact been the author's usual experience in the many departments with which he has worked.
74 Black, "Crime as Social Control," p. 41.
75 K. Lindsey (1978) "When Battered Women Strike Back: Murder or Self-Defense?" *Viva*, 58/9: 66–74; cited in Irene Hanson Frieze and Angela Browne (1989) "Violence in Marriage," *Crime and Justice: Family Violence*, 11: 163–218; p. 205.
76 Anderson, *Code of the Street*, p. 34.
77 Barry Zuckerman (1994) "Effects on Parents and Children," in Douglas J. Besharov and Kristina W. Hanson (eds), *When Drug Addicts Have Children: Reorienting Child Welfare's Response*, Washington, DC: Child Welfare League of America/American Enterprise Institute, p. 53.
78 Jacobs, *Dealing Crack*, p. 5.
79 Mark A. R. Kleiman (1997) "Coerced Abstinence: A Neopaternalistic Drug Policy Initiative," in Lawrence M. Mead (ed.), *The New Paternalism: Supervisory Approaches to Poverty*, Washington, DC: The Brookings Institution, pp. 182–219.

7 Reflections II

1 Edwin H. Sutherland and Donald R. Cressey (1958) *Criminology*, Philadelphia, Pa.: J. B. Lippincott Company, p. 669.
2 George E. Capowich, Paul Mazarole, and Alex Piquero (2001) "General Strain Theory, Situational Anger, and Social Networks: an Assessment of Conditioning Influences," *Journal of Criminal Justice*, 29 (5): 445–61; p. 446.
3 Robert J. Sampson and Dawn Jeglum Bartusch (1998) "Legal Cynicism and (Subcultural?) Tolerance of Deviance: The Neighborhood Context of Racial Differences," *Law and Society Review*, 32 (4): 777–804; p. 782.
4 Sutherland and Cressey, *Criminology*, p. 101.

5 Albert J. Reiss and Michael Tonry (1993) "Organizational Crime," in Michael Tonry and Albert J. Reiss (eds), *Beyond the Law: Crime in Complex Organizations, Crime and Justice*, No. 18, Chicago, Ill.: University of Chicago Press, p. 1.

6 Albert J. Reiss, Jr (1988) "Co-Offending and Criminal Careers," in Michael Tonry and Norval Morris (eds), *Crime and Justice: A Review of Research*, Vol. X, Chicago, Ill.: Chicago University Press, pp. 117–70; p. 120.

7 Reiss, "Co-Offending and Criminal Careers," p. 126.

8 For discussion on these and related points, see Reiss, "Co-offending and Criminal Careers," and Franklin Zimring (1981) "Kids, Groups, and Crime: Some Implications of a Well-Known Secret," *Journal of Criminal Law and Criminology*, 27 (3): 867–85.

9 Joan McCord and Kevin P. Conway (2002) "Patterns of Juvenile Delinquency and Co-Offending," in Elin Waring and David Weisburd (eds), *Crime and Social Organization*, New Brunswick, N.J.: Transaction, pp. 15–30; p. 17.

10 Philip Cook (1980) "Reducing Injury and Death Rates in Robbery," *Political Analysis*, 6 (1): 21–45.

11 Reiss, "Co-Offending and Criminal Careers," p. 132.

12 Reiss, "Co-Offending and Criminal Careers," p. 128.

13 Mark Warr (1996) "Organization and Instigation in Delinquent Groups," *Criminology*, 34 (1): 11–37; p. 30.

14 Malcolm Klein and Cheryl Maxson (1989) "Street Gang Violence," in Neil Alan Weiner and Marvin E. Wolfgang (eds), *Violent Crime, Violent Criminals*, Newbury Park, Calif.: Sage Publications, pp. 203–9.

15 McCord and Conway, "Patterns of Juvenile Delinquency and Co-Offending," p. 19.

16 Klein and Maxson, "Street Gang Violence," p. 212.

17 Jerome H. Skolnick, Theodore Correl, Elizabeth Navarro, and Roger Rabb (1990) "The Social Structure of Street Drug Dealing," *American Journal of Police*, 9 (1): 1–41.

18 T. P. Thornberry and J. H. Burch (1997) "Gang Members and Delinquent Behavior," *Juvenile Justice Bulletin*, NCJ 165154, Washington, DC: US Department of Justice, cited in Finn-Aage Esbensen, Dana Peterson, Adrienne Freng, and Terrance J. Taylor (2002), "Initiation of Drug Use, Drug Sales, and Violent Offending Among a Sample of Gang and Non-Gang Youth," in R. Ronald Hugg (ed.), *Gangs in America*, 3rd edn, Thousand Oaks, Calif.: Sage Publications, p. 39.

19 Anthony A. Braga, David M. Kennedy, and George Tita (2002), "New Approaches to the Strategic Prevention of Gang and Group-Involved Violence," in C. Ronald Huff (ed.), *Gangs in America*, 3rd edn, Newbury Park, Calif.: Sage Publications; San Francisco analysis available from the author.

20 Robin Engel, S. Gregory Baker, Marie Skubak Tillyer, John Eck, and Jessica Dunham (2000) "Implementation of the Cincinnati Initiative to Reduce Violence (CIRV): Interim Report," issued by the University of Cincinnati Policing Institute, report update dated March 20, 2008.

21 Reiss, "Co-Offending and Criminal Careers," p. 128.

22 David M. Kennedy, Anne M. Piehl, and Anthony A. Braga (1996) "Youth Violence in Boston: Gun Markets, Serious Youth Offenders, and a Use-Reduction Strategy," *Law and Contemporary Problems*, 59 (1): 147–196.

23 Klein and Maxson, "Street Gang Violence," p. 219.

24 Peter Letkeman (1973) *Crime as Work*, Englewood Cliffs, N.J.:Prentice-Hall.

25 Neal Shover (1972) "Structures and Careers in Burglary," *Journal of Criminal Law, Criminology, and Police Science*, 63 (4): 540–9.

26 James A. Inciardi (1975) *Careers in Crime*, Chicago, Ill.: Rand McNally.

27 Bruce Jacobs (1999) *Dealing Crack: The Social World of Streetcorner Selling*, Boston, Mass.: Northeastern University Press.

28 Elin Waring (2002) "Co-Offending as a Network Form of Social Organization," in Elin Waring and David Weisburd (eds), *Crime and Social Organization*, New Brunswick, NJ: Transaction, pp. 31–48; p. 33.
29 Kennedy *et al.*, *Youth Violence in Boston;* David M. Kennedy, Anthony A. Braga, and Anne M. Piehl (1997) "The (Un)Known Universe: Mapping Gangs and Gang Violence in Boston," in D. Weisburd and J. T. McEwen (eds), *Crime Mapping and Crime Prevention* (Crime Prevention Studies, 8), Monsey, N.Y.: Criminal Justice Press, pp. 219–62.
30 Reiss, "Co-Offending and Criminal Careers," p. 147.
31 Carl B. Klockars (1974) *The Professional Fence*, New York: The Free Press.
32 Letkemann, *Crime As Work*, p. 29.
33 Raymond Paternoster and Sally Simpson (1996) "Sanction Threats and Appeals to Morality: Testing a Rational Choice Model of Corporate Crime," *Law and Society Review*, (30): 549–83.
34 Ralph H. Turner, Lewis M. Killian (1962) *Collective Behavior*, 4th edn, Englewood Cliffs, N.J.: Prentice-Hall.
35 William I. Thomas and Dorothy S. Thomas (1928) *The Child in America: Behavior Problems and Programs*, New York: Alfred A. Knopf, pp. 571–2.
36 David G. Myers and Helmut Lamm (1976) "The Group Polarization Phenomenon," *Psychological Bulletin*, 83 (4): 602–27; p. 603.
37 Myers and Lamm, "The Group Polarization Phenomenon," p. 608.
38 R. Glenn Hass (1981) "Effects of Source Characteristics on Cognitive Responses and Persuasion," in Richard E. Petty, Thomas M. Ostrom, and Timothy C. Brock (eds), *Cognitive Responses in Persuasion*, Hillsdale, N.J.: Lawrence Erlbaum Associates, pp. 141–71; p. 150.
39 Terry Connolly and Lars Aberg (1993) "Some Contagion Models of Speeding," *Accident Analysis and Prevention*, 25 (1): 57–66; p. 58.
40 McCord and Conway, "Patterns of Juvenile Delinquency and Co-Offending," p. 19.
41 Philip Cook (1980) "Research in Criminal Deterrence: Laying the Groundwork for the Second Decade," *Crime and Justice*, No. 2, pp. 211–68.
42 McCord and Conway, "Patterns of Juvenile Delinquency and Co-Offending," pp. 26, 19.
43 Letkemann, *Crime As Work*, 120.
44 Skolnick *et al.*, *The Social Structure of Street Drug Dealing*, p. 178.
45 Tom Mieczkowski (1992) "Crack Dealing on the Street: The Crew System and the Crack House," *Justice Quarterly*, 9 (1): 151–63.
46 Hass, "Effects of Source Characteristics," p. 146.
47 Frank E. Zimring and Gordon J. Hawkins (1973) *Deterrence: The Legal Threat in Crime Control*, Chicago, Ill.: University of Chicago Press.
48 Zimring and Hawkins, *Deterrence*, p. 88.
49 Letkemann, *Crime As Work*, p. 24.
50 Letkemann, *Crime As Work*, p. 26. For a dramatically contrasting view of a more contemporary setting, see Bourgois, *In Search of Respect*, pp. 205–12.
51 Jacobs, *Dealing Crack*, p. 39.
52 Skolnick *et al.*, *The Social Structure of Street Drug Dealing*, p. 182.
53 Bruce Johnson, Andrew Golub, and Eloise Dunlap (2000) "The Rise and Decline of Hard Drugs, Drug Markets, and Violence in Inner-City New York," in Alfred Blumstein and Joel Wallman (eds), *The Crime Drop in America*, New York: Cambridge University Press, pp. 164–206; p. 178.
54 Johnson *et al.*, "Rise and Decline," p. 186.
55 Philip J. Cook, Jens Ludwig, Sudhir A. Venkatesh, and Anthony Braga (2005) "Underground Gun Markets" Working Paper No. 11737, National Bureau of Economic Research, Cambridge, Mass., November 17.

56 Scott H. Decker and Janet L. Lauritsen (2002) "Leaving the Gang," in C. Ronald Huff (ed.), *Gangs in America*, 3rd edn, Thousand Oaks, Calif.: Sage Publications, pp. 103–22.

57 See, for example, the Knapp and Mollen reports.

58 Skolnick *et al.*, *The Social Structure of Street Drug Dealing*, p. 164.

59 Gresham Sykes and David Matza (1957) "Techniques of Neutralization: A Theory of Delinquency," *American Sociological Review*, 22: 664–70.

60 David Matza (1964) *Delinquency and Drift*, New York: John Wiley & Sons.

61 All these points are drawn from Matza, *Delinquency and Drift*.

62 Matza, *Delinquency and Drift*, p. 50.

63 Matza, *Delinquency and Drift*, p. 51.

64 Turner and Killian, *Collective Behavior*, p. 26.

65 Turner and Killian, *Collective Behavior*, p. 33.

66 Turner and Killian, *Collective Behavior*, p. 62.

67 Ladd Wheeler and Anthony R. Caggiula (1966) "The Contagion of Aggression," *Journal of Experimental Social Psychology*, 2: 1–10.

68 Pruitt, in Wheeler and Caggiula, "The Contagion of Aggression," p. 62.

69 Wheeler and Caggiula, "The Contagion of Aggression," p. 62.

70 Turner and Killian, *Collective Behavior*, p. 27.

71 Klein and Maxson, "Street Gang Violence," p. 211.

72 Gilbert Geis, *The Heavy Electrical Equipment Antitrust Cases of 1961*, p. 119.

73 Geis, *The Heavy Electrical Equipment Antitrust Cases of 1961*, p. 122.

74 Floyd H. Allport (1924) *Social Psychology*, Boston, Mass.: Houghton-Mifflin.

75 Matza, *Delinquency and Drift*, p. 52.

76 Matza, *Delinquency and Drift*, pp. 53, 56.

77 J. C. Turner (1982) "Toward a Cognitive Redefinition of the Social Group" in H. Tajfel (ed.), *Social Identity and Intergroup Relations*, Cambridge: Cambridge University Press, pp. 15–40; cited in David A. Levy and Paul R. Nail (1993) "Contagion: A Theoretical and Empirical Review and Reconceptualization," *Genetic, Social, and General Psychology Monographs*, 119 (2): 253–83; p. 263.

78 Turner, "Toward a Cognitive Redefinition."

79 S. D. Reicher (1984) "The St. Pauls' Riot: an Explanation of the Limits of Crowd Action in Terms of a Social Identity Model," *European Journal of of Social Psychology*, 14 (1): 1–21, cited in David A. Levy and Paul R. Nail (1993) "Contagion: A Theoretical and Empirical Review and Reconceptualization," *Genetic, Social, and General Psychology Monographs*, 119 (2): 253–83; p. 263.

80 L. Ross (1977) "The Intuitive Psychologist and His Shortcomings," in L. Berkowitz (ed.), *Advances in Experimental Social Psychology*, Vol. X, New York: Academic, pp. 173–220.

81 H. Wesley Perkins (2003) "The Emergence and Evolution of the Social Norms Approach to Substance Abuse Prevention," in H. Wesley Perkins (ed.), *The Social Norms Approach to Preventing School and College Age Substance Abuse*, San Francisco, Calif.: Jossey-Bass, pp. 7–8.

82 Perkins, "The Emergence and Evolution of the Social Norms Approach," pp. 7–8.

83 Perkins, "The Emergence and Evolution of the Social Norms Approach," pp. 7–8.

84 H. Wesley Perkins (2002) "Social Norms and the Prevention of Alcohol Misuse in Collegiate Contexts," *Journal of Studies on Alcohol*, Supplement No. 14: 164–72; p. 167.

85 Perkins, "The Emergence and Evolution of the Social Norms Approach," p. 9.

86 Perkins, "The Emergence and Evolution of the Social Norms Approach," p. 9.

87 Michael P. Haines and Gregory P. Barker (2003) "The Northern Illinois University Experiment: A Longitudinal Case Study of the Social Norms Approach," in H. Wesley Perkins (ed.), *The Social Norms Approach to Preventing School and College Age Substance Abuse*, San Francisco, Calif.: Jossey-Bass, p. 22.

88 Perkins, "The Emergence and Evolution of the Social Norms Approach," p. 9.
89 Matza, *Delinquency and Drift*, p. 157.
90 The Lifers Public Safety Steering Committee of the State Correctional Institution at Graterford, Pennsylvania (2004) "Ending the Culture of Street Crime," *The Prison Journal*, 84 (4, Supplement): 48–68, p. 58.
91 Lifers, "Ending the Culture of Street Crime," p. 57.
92 Lifers, "Ending the Culture of Street Crime," p. 58.
93 Lifers, "Ending the Culture of Street Crime," p. 58. The Lifers argue that those who can clearly see these wrong ideas, understand the way they play out on the street, and have the standing with offenders to challenge those ideas and intervene in those dynamics—people like themselves—can be the key to ending the culture. They are, at least to some extent, putting those ideas into practice. Lifers, "Ending the Culture of Street Crime," pp. 66 and following.
94 Mark Granovetter (1978) "Threshold Models of Collective Behavior," *American Journal of Sociology*, 83 (6): 1420–43; p. 1421.
95 William Bennett, John DiIulio, and John Walters (1999) *Body Count: Moral Poverty and How to Win America's War Against Crime and Drugs*, New York: Simon & Schuster, pp. 28, 29.
96 Joseph Sheley and James Wright (1995) *In the Line of Fire: Youth, Guns, and Violence in Urban America*, New York: Aldine de Gruyter.
97 Jeffrey Fagan and Deanna L. Wilkinson (1998) "Guns, Youth Violence, and Social Identity in Inner Cities," in Michael Tonry and Mark H. Moore (eds), *Youth Violence Crime and Justice: A Review of Research*, Chicago, Ill.: University of Chicago Press, pp. 105–88.
98 Fagan and Wilkinson, "Guns, Youth Violence, and Social Identity."
99 Geoffrey Canada (1995) *Fist Stick Knife Gun: A Personal History of Violence in America*, Boston, Mass.: Beacon Press.
100 Rob Garot (2006) "Inner-City Teens and Face-Work," in Leila Monaghan and Jane Goodman (eds), *A Cultural Approach to Interpersonal Communication: Essential Readings*, Oxford: Blackwell, pp. 77–105.
101 Mindy Thompson Fullilove, Gina Arias, Moises Nunez, Ericka Phillips, Peter McFarlane, Rodrick Wallace, and Robert E. Fullilove III (2003) "What Did Ian Tell God? School Violence in East New York," in Mark Harrison Moore, Carol V. Petrie, and Anthony A. Braga (eds), *Deadly Lessons*, Washington, DC: National Academies Press, pp. 198–246; p. 235.
102 David Weisburd (2002) "From Criminals to Criminal Contexts: Reorienting Crime Prevention Research and Policy," in Elin Waring and David Weisburd (eds), *Crime and Social Organization*, New Brunswick, N.J.: Transaction Publishers, pp. 204–5. For the basic frameworks of these more situational approaches, see Ronald V. Clarke (1980) "'Situational' Crime Prevention: Theory and Practice," *British Journal of Criminology*, 20 (2): 136–47; Ronald V. Clarke (1995) "Situational Crime Prevention," in Michael Tonry and David P. Farrington (eds), *Building a Safer Society: Strategic Approaches to Crime Prevention*, Chicago, Ill.: University of Chicago Press, pp. 91–150; Marcus Felson (1998) *Crime and Everyday Life*, Thousand Oaks, Calif.: Pine Forge Press.
103 David M. Kennedy (1994) "Can We Keep Guns Away From Kids?" *American Prospect*, 18: 74–80; Alfred Blumstein (1995) "Youth Violence, Guns, and the Illicit Drug Industry," *Journal of Criminal Law and Criminology*, 86 (1): 10–36; Kennedy *et al.*, *Youth Violence in Boston*.
104 Kennedy, "Can We Keep Guns Away From Kids?"; Kennedy *et al.*, *Youth Violence in Boston*.
105 Philip J. Cook, personal communication.

106 On the general lack of street crack markets in Detroit, see Mieczkowski, *Crack Dealing on the Street;* on the general elimination of street crack markets in Tampa, see David M. Kennedy (1993) *Closing the Market: Controlling the Drug Trade in Tampa, Florida,* National Institute of Justice Program Focus Series, Washington, DC: US Department of Justice.

107 David A. Levy and Paul R. Nail (1993) "Contagion: A Theoretical and Empirical Review and Reconceptualization," *Genetic, Social, and General Psychology Monographs,* 119 (2): 236. For a very useful review of the social contagion literature, see Philip Cook and Kristin A. Goss (1996) *A Selective Review of the Social Contagion Literature,* Terry Sandford Institute Working Paper, Duke University.

108 Turner and Killian, *Collective Behavior,* p. 136.

109 Robert T. Holden (1986) "The Contagiousness of Aircraft Hijacking," *American Journal of Sociology,* 91 (4): 874–904.

110 David P. Phillips and Lundie L. Carstensen (1986) "Clustering of Teenage Suicides After Television News Stories About Suicide," *New England Journal of Medicine,* 315 (11): 685–9.

111 David M. Kennedy (1999) "A LOOK AT...Reacting to Violence; But Boston Proves Something Can Be Done," *Washington Post,* May 23.

112 Mercer Sullivan and Rob T. Guerette (2003) "The Copycat Factor: Mental Illness, Guns, and the Shooting Incident at Heritage High School, Rockdale County, Georgia" in Mark Harrison Moore, Carol V. Petrie, and Anthony A. Braga (eds), *Deadly Lessons,* p. 25–69.

113 Colin Loftin (1986) "Assaultive Violence As a Contagious Social Process," *Bulletin of the New York Academy of Medicine,* 62 (5): 550–5.

114 Loftin, "Assaultive Violence," p. 554.

115 Richard Rosenfeld (2000) "Patterns in Adult Homicide: 1980–85," in Alfred Blumstein and Joel Wallman (eds), *The Crime Drop in America,* New York: Cambridge University Press, pp. 130–63.

116 Johnson *et al.,* "Rise and Decline."

117 Peter Reuter, Patricia Ebener, and Dan McCaffrey (1994) "Patterns of Drug Use," in Douglas Besharov and Kristina W. Hanson (eds), *When Drug Addicts Have Children,* Washington, DC: Child Welfare League of American, Inc., p. 13.

118 J. Boyle and A. F. Brunswick (1980) "What Happened in Harlem? Analysis of a Decline in Heroin Use Among a Generational Unit of Urban Black Youth," *Journal of Drug Issues,* 10 (1): 109–30.

119 Johnson *et al.,* "Rise and Decline."

120 Bobby Caina Calvan (2003) "Drug Problems Spread in Philippines," *Boston Globe,* August 31, p. A23.

121 See Johnson *et al.,* "Rise and Decline."

122 See, for example, James A. Fox (1996) "Trends in Youth Violence: A Report to the United States Attorney General on Current and Future Rates of Juvenile Offending," Northeastern University, Boston, Mass.

123 Letkemann, *Crime As Work,* p. 76.

124 Thomas Schelling (1978) *Micromotives and Macrobehavior,* New York: W. W. Norton & Co.; for an account of how tipping may have played out in New York City's crime reduction, see Malcolm Gladwell (2002) *The Tipping Point: How Little Things Can Make a Big Difference,* New York: Back Bay Books.

125 Rosenfeld, "Patterns in Adult Homicide," p. 133.

126 Thomas C. Schelling (1978) *Micromotives and Microbehavior,* New York: W. W. Norton.

127 Granovetter, "Threshold Models."

128 Granovetter, "Threshold Models," p. 1425.

129 Granovetter, "Threshold Models," p. 1428.

130 Granovetter, "Threshold Models," p. 1428.
131 Granovetter, "Threshold Models," p. 1429.
132 Connolly and Aberg, "Some Contagion Models of Speeding," p. 58.
133 Connolly and Aberg, "Some Contagion Models of Speeding," p. 59.
134 Connolly and Aberg, "Some Contagion Models of Speeding," p. 60.
135 Mark A. R. Kleiman (n.d.) "Getting Deterrence Right: Applying Tipping Models and Behavioral Economics to the Problems of Crime Control"; Mark A. R. Kleiman (1993) "Enforcement Swamping: A Positive-Feedback Mechanism in Rates of Illicit Activity," *Mathematical and Computer Modeling*, 17 (2): 65–75.
136 Kleiman, "Enforcement Swamping."
137 See, for example, "Strategies for Combatting the Criminal Receiver of Stolen Goods" Office of Regional Operations, Law Enforcement Assistance Administration, US Department of Justice, September (1976); Shover, "Structures and Careers in Burglary."
138 James D. Wright and Peter H. Rossi (1986) *Armed and Considered Dangerous: A Survey of Felons and Their Firearms*, New York: Aldine de Gruyter.
139 See, for example, Lawrence W. Sherman, Janell D. Schmidt, and Dennis P. Rogan (1992) *Policing Domestic Violence: Experiments and Dilemmas*, New York: Free Press.
140 James Q. Wilson and George Kelling (1982) "Broken Windows," *The Atlantic Monthly*, 249 (3): 29–38.
141 Wesley Skogan (1990) *Disorder and Decline: Crime and the Spiral of Decay in American Neighborhoods*, Berkeley, Calif.: University of California Press.
142 See, for example, Kennedy *et al.*, "The (Un)Known Universe"; Sampson and Bartusch, "Legal Cynicism," p. 784.
143 Deputy Superintendent William Johnston, Boston Police Department, personal communication.

8 Reframing deterrence

1 David M. Kennedy (1990) "Fighting the Drug Trade in Link Valley," John F. Kennedy School of Government Case Study C16-90-935.0, Cambridge, Mass.: Harvard University.
2 See, for example, Lawrence Sherman and Dennis Rogan (1995) "Effect of Gun Seizures on Gun Violence: 'Hot Spot' Patrol in Kansas City," *Justice Quarterly*, 12 (4): 673–93.
3 A "Terry stop" is a term of art in the US and refers to a search allowable under a well-known Supreme Court decision, *Terry* vs. *Ohio*.
4 Personal observation in San Francisco and Washington, DC.
5 See David M. Kennedy (1997) "Pulling Levers: Chronic Offenders, High-Crime Settings, and a Theory of Prevention," *Valparaiso University Law Review* 31(2): 449–484; Anthony A. Braga, David M. Kennedy, and George Tita (2002) "New Approaches to the Strategic Prevention of Gang and Group-Involved Violence," in C. Ronald Huff (eds), *Gangs in America*, 3rd edn, Newbury Park, Calif.: Sage Publications, pp. 271–86.
6 Lawrence W. Sherman (1990) "Police Crackdowns: Initial and Residual Deterrence," *Crime and Justice*, No. 12, Chicago, Ill.: University of Chicago Press, pp. 1–48.
7 Braga *et al.*, "New Approaches," p. 281.
8 For examples of jurisdictions pursuing such approaches, see David M. Kennedy, "Controlling Domestic Violence Offenders." Paper prepared for the Hewlett-Family Violence Prevention Fund (April 2002), available from the author.
9 The author has observed such practices in police departments in Baltimore and Rochester, New York.

10 Tim Byaum and Scott H. Decker, with John Klofas, Natalie Kroouand Hipple, Edmund F. McGarrell, and Jack McDevitt (2006) "Chronic Violent Offenders Lists: Case Study 4," Project Safe Neighborhoods Strategic Interventions, Office of Justice Programs, US Department of Justice, May.

11 See Kennedy, "Controlling Domestic Violence Offenders."

12 Anthony A. Braga, Jack McDevitt, and Glenn Piece (2006) "Understanding and Preventing Gang Violence: Problem Analysis and Response Development in Lowell, Massachusetts," *Police Quarterly*, 9 (1): 20–46.

13 See Thomas Mieczkowski (1990) "Crack Distribution in Detroit," *Journal of Contemporary Drug Problems*, 17: 9–30.

14 See Nancy E. Isaac, D. Cochran, M. E. Brown and S. L. Adams (1994) "Men Who Batter: Profile from a Restraining Order Database," *Archives of Family Medicine*, 3 (1): 50–4; Kennedy, "Controlling Domestic Violence Offenders."

15 For accounts of jurisdictions pursuing these approaches, see Kennedy, "Controlling Domestic Violence Offenders."

16 On the "Squash It" campaign, see http://www.hsph.harvard.edu/chc/squashit.html (accessed 2003).

17 On the narrow meaning that has come to be associated with "prevention," see David M. Kennedy (2002) "A Tale of One City: Reflections on the Boston Gun Project," in Gary S. Katzmann (ed.), *Securing Our Children's Future: New Approaches to Juvenile Justice and Youth Violence*, Washington, DC: Brookings Institution Press, pp. 229–61.

18 R. Glen Haas (1981) "Effects of Source Characteristics on Cognitive Responses and Persuasion," in Richard E. Petty, Thomas M. Ostrom, and Timothy C. Brock (eds), *Cognitive Responses in Persuasion*, Hillsdale, N.J.: Lawrence Erlbaum Associates, pp. 141–71.

19 "The Orange Hats of Fairlawn: A Washington, DC Neighborhood Battles Drugs" KSG Case C16-91-1034.0, 1991.

20 The author has discussed this possibility in Kennedy, "Controlling Domestic Violence Offenders."

21 Exactly this has recently been observed by the author in Rochester, New York.

22 See David M. Kennedy (1998) "Pulling Levers: Getting Deterrence Right," *National Institute of Justice Journal*, 236 (July): 2–8.

23 Fences do in fact distinguish between thieves who enter residences and those who do not. See Carl B. Klockards (1974) *The Professional Fence*, New York: Free Press.

24 See Albert J. Reiss, Jr. (1988) "Co-Offending and Criminal Careers," *Crime and Justice*, 10: 117–70.

25 See Klockars, *The Professional Fence*.

26 San Diego Police Department (1998) "Operation Hot Pipe, Smoky Haze, and Rehab," Submission to the Herman Goldstein Excellence in Problem-Oriented Policing Award.

27 See Braga *et al.*, "New Approaches"; Kennedy, "A Tale of One City."

28 See Jeffrey Fagan and Dean Wilkinson (1998) "Guns, Youth Violence, and Social Identity in Inner Cities," *Crime and Justice*, No. 24, Chicago, Ill.: University of Chicago Press, pp. 105–188; Elijah Anderson (1999) *Code of the Street: Decency, Violence, and the Moral Life of the Inner City*, New York: W. W. Norton & Company.

29 Klockars, *The Professional Fence*, p. 104.

30 See Stephen J. Schulhofer and Ilene H. Nagel (1997) "Plea Negotiations under the Federal Sentencing Guidelines: Guideline Circumvention and Its Dynamics in the Post-*Mistretta* Period," *Northwestern University Law Review*, 91: 1284–9.

31 See, for example, "Ashcroft Weighs an Order to Cut Back Plea Bargaining," *Wall Street Journal*, September 23, 2003.

32 Malcolm K. Sparrow (2000) *The Regulatory Craft: Controlling Risks, Solving Problems, and Managing Compliance*, Washington DC: The Brookings Institution, p. 178.
33 See David Simon and Edward Burns (1997) *The Corner: A Year in the Life of an Inner-City Neighborhood*, New York: Broadway Books.
34 David Matza (1999) *Delinquency and Drift*, New Brunswick, NJ: Transaction.
35 Richard T. Wright and Scott H. Decker (1997) *Armed Robbers in Action: Stickups and Street Culture*, Boston, Mass.: Northeastern University Press.
36 Philippe Bourgois (1996) *In Search of Respect*, Cambridge: Cambridge University Press.
37 David Moore (1993) "Shame, Forgiveness, and Juvenile Justice," *Criminal Justice Ethics*, 12 (winter/spring}: 3–25; p. 5.
38 Moore, "Shame, Forgiveness, and Juvenile Justice," p. 16.
39 John Braithwaite (1989) *Crime, Shame, and Reintegration*, Cambridge: Cambridge University Press.
40 Heather Strang and John Braithwaite (2002) *Restorative Justice and Family Violence*, Cambridge: Cambridge University Press; Linda G. Mills (2003) *Insult to Injury: Rethinking our Responses to Intimate Abuse*, Princeton, N.J.: Princeton University Press.
41 There is an enormous restorative justice literature, all of it very useful in informing a reframed deterrence approach. For one review, see John Braithwaite (1999) "Restorative Justice: Assessing Optimistic and Pessimistic Accounts," in Michael Tonry (ed.), *Crime and Justice: A Review of Research*, Vol. XXV, Chicago, Ill.: University of Chicago Press, pp. 1–127.
42 H. Wesley Perkins (1997) "College Student Misperceptions of Alcohol and Other Drug Norms among Peers: Exploring Causes, Consequences, and Implications for Prevention Programs," in *Designing Alcohol and Other Drug Prevention Programs in Higher Education*, Newton, Mass.: The Higher Education Center for Alcohol and Other Drug Prevention, US Department of Education, pp. 177–206.
43 Robert Garot (2007) "Inner-City Teens and Face-Work: Avoiding Violence and Maintaining Honor," in Leila F. Monaghan and Jane E. Goodman (eds), *A Cultural Approach to Interpersonal Communication: Essential Readings*, Oxford: Blackwell, pp. 294–317.
44 Sampson, Robert J. and Bartusch, Dawn J. (1998) "Legal Cynicism and (Subcultural) Tolerance of Deviance," *Law and Society Review*, 32 (4): 777–804.
45 Sampson and Bartusch, *Legal Cynicism and (Subcultural) Tolerance of Deviance*, p. 793.
46 Martha Minow (1998) *Between Vengeance and Forgiveness*, Boston, Mass.: Beacon Press.
47 Kleiman models such a process in Mark A. R. Kleiman (1999), "Getting Deterrence Right: Applying Tipping Models and Behavioral Economics to the Problems of Crime Control," Perspectives on Crime and Justice lecture series, National Institute of Justice, Washington, DC, pp. 1–27; p. 22.
48 See David M. Kennedy, Anthony Braga and Anne Piehl (2001) *Developing and Implementing Operation Ceasefire, Reducing Gun Violence*, Washington, DC: US Department of Justice, National Institute of Justice, pp. 1–49.
49 Scott Decker and Richard Rosenfeld (2004) "Reducing Gun Violence: The St. Louis Consent-to-Search Program," US Department of Justice, Office of Justice Programs, National Institute of Justice.
50 See Kennedy *et al.*, *Developing and Implementing Operation Ceasefire*.
51 Benson P. Shapiro and John Wyman, "New Ways to Reach Your Customers," in Benson P. Shapiro and John J. Sviokla (1993) *Seeking Customers*, Harvard Business Review Book Series, pp. 7–24; p. 8.

52 Braga *et al.*, "New Approaches," p. 275.
53 Shapiro and Wyman, "New Ways to Reach Your Customers," p. 9.
54 "Thoughts about the Future of Advertising: A White Paper," The Faculty, Department of Advertising, College of Communication, University of Texas at Austin December (1995).
55 See, for example, Paul J. Peter and Jerry C. Olson (2002) *Consumer Behavior and Marketing Strategy*, Boston, Mass.: Irwin McGraw-Hill.
56 Mullen, "Project Safe Neighborhoods."Available from author.

9 Applications I

1 Such a formal evaluation of the High Point and several related interventions is at this writing being conducted with National Institute of Justice support and under the direction of Dr. James Frabutt, formerly of the University of North Carolina, Greensboro, and now at Notre Dame, and with the participation of the author.
2 J. M. Frabutt, M. J. Gathings, E. J. Hunt, and T. J. Loggins (2004) *High Point West End Initiative: Project Description, Log, and Preliminary Impact Analysis*, Greensboro, NC: Center for Youth, Family, and Community Partnerships, University of North Carolina at Greensboro; J. M. Frabutt, M. J. Gathings, D. T. Jackson, and A. P. Buford (2006) *High Point Daniel Brooks Initiative: Project Description and Preliminary Impact Analysis*, Greensboro, NC: Center for Youth, Family, and Community Partnerships, University of North Carolina at Greensboro; Mark Shoofs (2006) "Novel Police Tactic Puts Drug Market Out of Business," *Wall Street Journal*, September 27, p. A1.
3 See, for example, Ric Curtis, Travis Wendel, and Barry Spunt (2002) "We Deliver: the Gentrification of Drug Markets on Manhattan's Lower East Side," Final Report, John Jay College of Criminal Justice.
4 Bruce A. Jacobs (1999) *Dealing Crack: The Social World of Streetcorner Selling*, Boston, Mass.: Northeastern University Press.
5 David Boyum and Peter Reuter (2005) *An Analytic Assessment of US Drug Policy*, Washington, DC: AEI Press.
6 Schoofs, "Novel Police Tactic Puts Drug Market Out of Business."
7 Schoofs, "Novel Police Tactic Puts Drug Market Out of Business."
8 Lynn K. Harvey (2005) "A Collaborative Approach to Closing an Open-Air Drug Market and a Blueprint for Other Communities: The New Hope Initiative," Center for Community Safety, Winston-Salem State University.
9 Amanda Milkovitz (2007) "Closing Crack Highway," *Providence Journal*, March 10; Amanda Milkovitz (2007) "Police Try a Different Way to Reduce Drug Dealers," *Providence Journal*, March 18; Amanda Milkovitz (2007) "'Lucky 7' Finally Get 2nd Chance," *Providence Journal*, March 25.
10 Amanda Milkovitz (2008) Calm Comes to Lockwood Neighborhood, *Providence Journal*, January 7.
11 Milkowitz, "Calm Comes to Lockwood Neighborhood."
12 This phenomenon was also seen in the Newburgh intervention.
13 Raleigh Police Department (2007) "The CHOICE Project Newsletter," 1 (3, November), p. 4.
14 Email of April 22, 2008 from Fran (last name withheld at sender's request).
15 The High Point drug strategy won a 2007 Innovations in Government Award from the Kennedy School of Government and is being expanded to ten new jurisdictions through the US Department of Justice Bureau of Justice Assistance's Drug Market Intervention Program.

10 Applications II

1 Interestingly, internet providers are beginning to offer such services. One, OnlineDetective.com, advertises,

> Let's face it, the world is a dangerous place. A misplaced credit-card receipt can, in the wrong hands, lead to thousands of dollars in unauthorized charges, or worse yet, make you the victim of identity theft, which is both costly and time-consuming to correct. And how do you really know that the guy you've started dating isn't actually a convicted wife-beater with several restraining orders on him, or that the new employee you're about to hire really has all the qualifications she says that she does? What if your new neighbor that's suddenly started playing with your kids after school is actually a convicted child molester? You need to know these things in order to protect yourself, your family, and your business. And now you can! Here is just a partial list of what you can find—and more stuff is being added all the time, so you never know what you might stumble across.

See http://www.spylogic.com/index.mp?szFileName = moreinfo.html (accessed 2003).

2 The National Center for Victims of Crime has advocated the creation of such a national database. Susan Herman, Pace University, former Director, National Center for Victims of Crime, personal communication.

3 See press release dated March 18, 2002, "Thirteen Individuals Indicted for False Statements and/or Domestic Violence Firearm Charges," United States Attorney, District of Maine, Portland, Maine.

4 Westminster Police Department (1998) "Improving Domestic Violence Prosecution Through Police Training and Multi-Agency Cooperation," Westminster Police Department, Westminster, California. This report does not examine absolute rates of successful prosecution, recidivism, or impact on domestic violence offending.

5 Gerald G. Hotaling, Murray A. Straus, and Alan J. Lincoln (1989) "Intrafamily Violence, and Crime and Violence Outside the Family" in Lloyd Ohlin and Michael C. Tonry (eds), *Family Violence, Crime and Justice*, Vol. II, Chicago, Ill.: University of Chicago Press, pp. 315–75; p. 321.

6 Hotaling *et al.*, "Intrafamily Violence," p. 322.

7 Hotaling *et al.*, "Intrafamily Violence," p. 323.

8 Hotaling *et al.*, "Intrafamily Violence," p. 365.

9 Hotaling *et al.*, "Intrafamily Violence," p. 357, Table 10.

10 Amy Solomon and Gillian Thomson (1997) "Serious Assaults in Lowell: Opportunities for a Collaborative Crime Control Effort," January 22. Policy Analysis Exercise, Kennedy School of Government, Harvard University, p. 21.

11 Nancy E. Jones, D. Cochran, M. E. Brown, and S. L. Adams (1994) "Men Who Batter: Profile from a Restraining Order Database," *Archives of Family Medicine*, 52: 350–4.

12 Victoria Frye, Susan Wilt, and David Schomburg (1999) "Female Homicide in New York City, 1990–97," New York Department of Public Health.

13 M. Benson, G. L. Fox, A. DeMaris, and J. Van Wyk (2003) "Neighborhood Disadvantage, Individual Economic Distress and Violence Against Women in Intimate Relationships," *Journal of Quantitative Criminology*, 9 (3): 207–34; R. Miles-Doan (1998) "Violence Between Spouses and Intimates: Does Neighborhood Context Matter?" *Social Forces*, 77 (2): 623–45.

14 Chitra Raghavan, Amy Mennerich, Ellen Sexton, and Susan E. James (2006) "Community Violence and its Direct, Indirect and Mediating Effects on Intimate Partner Violence," *Violence Against Women*, 12 (12): 1132–49; p. 1133.

15 Eve Buzawa and Carl Buzawa (1996) *Domestic Violence: The Criminal Justice Response*, Thousand Oaks, Calif.: Sage Publications, p. 88.
16 Jeffrey Fagan, D. Stewart, and K. Hanson (1983) "Violent Men or Violent Husbands? Background Factors and Situational Correlates of Domestic and Extra-Domestic Violence," in David Finkelhor, Richard J. Gelles, Gerald T. Hotaling, and Murray A. Straus (eds), *The Dark Side of Families*, Thousand Oaks, Calif.: Sage Publications, pp. 49–68.
17 Marianne Hinkle, Office of the US Attorney, Boston, Mass., personal communication, April 16, 2002.
18 Confidentiality questions regularly arise in this setting. They are dealt with in part by getting "civilian" participants formal access to criminal history information, in part by partitioning information (an advocate may inform the group that a particular offender is suddenly a particularly high risk without saying how she knows this is so), and in part by simply not sharing information within the group that the group would in fact like to share. Hinkle, personal communication.
19 Captain Deborah Friedl, personal communication, April 17, 2002.
20 Coerced abstinence from alcohol would likely pay huge dividends in violence prevention in this context. Monitoring for alcohol use is more troublesome than for other substances because of its rapid elimination from the body. However, it is not impossible; ankle monitors can test for alcohol consumption and report violations electronically.
21 Daniel G. Saunders and Richard Hamill (2001) "Offender Interventions to End Violence Against Women: A Research Synthesis for Practitioners," Document prepared for the National Institute of Justice, 27 July, p. 7.
22 Judith M. McFarlane, J. C. Campbell, S. Wilt, C. Sachs, Y., Ulrich, and X. Xu (1999) "Stalking and Intimate Partner Femicide" *Homicide Studies*, 3 (4): 300–16; p. 308.
23 Peggy Grauwiler, Nicole Pezold, and Linda G. Mills (2006) "Justice Is in the Design: Creating a Restorative Justice Treatment Model for Domestic Violence," in J. Hamel and T. Nicholls (eds), *Family Approaches to Domestic Violence: A Guide to Gender-Inclusive Research and Treatment*, New York: Springer Publishing, pp. 579–601, p. 589.
24 Donna Coker (2006) "Restorative Justice, Navajo Peacemaking, and Domestic Violence," *Theoretical Criminology*, 10 (1): 67–85; p. 75.
25 Grauwiler *et al.*, "Justice Is in the Design," p. 7.
26 Judy Villa (2006) "Victims' Perspectives Connect with Prisoners: Program Puts Face on Crime's Toll, Attempts to Repair Harm," *The Arizona Republic*, October 7, available at http://www.azcentral.com/news/articles/1007victims1007.html.
27 Lieutenant Gary French, personal communication.
28 Rhagavan *et al.*, "Community Violence," p. 1145.
29 Jeffrey Fagan and Deanna Wilkinson (1998) "Social Context and Functions of Adolescent Violence," in Delbert Elliot, Beatrix Hamburg, and Kirk Williams (eds), *Violence in American Schools: A New Perspective*, Cambridge: Cambridge University Press, pp. 55–93. Juanjo Medina (2002) "The Social Geography of Violence Against Women," draft paper prepared for the National Research Council, p. 8.
30 Shannon Reid and Caterina Roman, Urban Institute, Washington, DC: personal communication, November 20, 2007. These findings are an Urban Institute analysis of data collected by the Urban Institute and the author.
31 Philippe Bourgois (1996) *In Search of Respect*, New York: Cambridge University Press.
32 The social construction of violence and responses to violence is telling here; the author's experience is that enforcement authorities quite readily endorse the kinds of strategies described when the victims are other chronic offenders subjected to "street" violence, such as a gang dispute, or "innocent" victims hurt inadvertently,

but that authorities rarely endorse the idea of expanding these strategies to domestic and sexual assault, which they do not see as emerging from the same "street" dynamic.

33 All information about the Killingbeck intervention is drawn from Jalma Hanmer, Sue Griffiths, and David Jerwood (1999) "Arresting Evidence: Domestic Violence and Repeat Victimization," Police Research Series, Paper 104, Home Office; Policing and Reducing Crime Unit; Research and Statistics Directorate.

34 Hanmer *et al.*, "Arresting Evidence," p. 38.

35 Hanmer *et al.*, "Arresting Evidence," p. 37.

36 Hanmer *et al.*, "Arresting Evidence," p. 37.

11 Listening to Lysistrata

1 "Colombian Gangsters Face Sex Ban" BBC World News, September 13, 2006.

2 "Colombian Gangsters Face Sex Ban."

3 "Lose the Gun or Sleep on the Sofa" *CBS News*, September 14, 2006.

Index